Working the
Organizing Experience

Working the Organizing Experience:

Transforming Psychotic, Schizoid, and Autistic States

with a Foreword by James S. Grotstein and
a Case Illustration by Frances Tustin

Lawrence E. Hedges

JASON ARONSON INC.
Northvale, New Jersey
London

Production Editor: Judith D. Cohen

This book was set in 11 point Goudy by Lind Graphics of Upper Saddle River, New Jersey, and printed and bound by Haddon Craftsmen of Scranton, Pennsylvania.

Library of Congress Cataloging-in-Publication Data

Working the organizing experience : transforming psychotic, schizoid, and autistic states, with an introduction by Dr. James S. Grotstein and a case illustration by Frances Tustin / Lawrence E. Hedges.
    p. cm.
  Includes bibliographical references and index.
  ISBN 1-56821-255-0
  1. Schizoid personality – Treatment. 2. Intimacy (Psychology)
3. Remoteness (Personality trait) 4. Treatment.
5. Psychoses – Treatment. 6. Mother and infant. 7. Attachment
behavior. 8. Object relations (Psychoanalysis)
  [DNLM: 1. Psychotic Disorders – psychology. 2. Autism – psychology.
3. Psychoanalytic Theory. 4. Psychoanalytic Therapy. 5. Mother-
Child Relations.   WM 203 H453w 1994]
RC569.5.S35W67 1994
616.89'1 – dc20
DNLM/DLC
for Library of Congress   94-7821

Manufactured in the United States of America. Jason Aronson Inc. offers books and cassettes. For information and catalog write to Jason Aronson Inc., 230 Livingston Street, Northvale, New Jersey 07647.

This book is dedicated to
Gary Conway,
whose inconstancy
stimulated the reappearance of my psychotic mother
and whose constancy
made possible the definition and working through of
my organizing experience.

"Many people have pockets of what is called 'madness' or 'mental illness.' These may extend over large or small areas of someone's personality, causing a greater or lesser degree of disturbance in his life, his work and leisure, and his relationships."

— Margaret Little, *Psychotic Anxieties and Containment*

"It is, however, disagreeable if psychotic features make their appearance in the course of symptom transformation, but it would be mistaken to be excessively alarmed by them. I have seen cases in which there was no way to a final cure except through a temporary psychosis."

— Sandor Ferenczi, *Final Contributions to the Problems and Methods of Psycho-Analysis*

Contents

Part III
The Path to Organizing Experience

Special Contributors

Significant clinical contributions to this book
have been made by these colleagues:

Marilyn Boettiger
James S. Grotstein
Joyce Hulgus
Marc Kern
Alitta Kullman
Milton Olson
Dolly Platt
Linda Reed
Karyn Sandberg
Diana Seeb
Sean Stewart
Frances Tustin
Gayle Trenberth
Ruth Wimsatt

Foreword
James S. Grotstein

Hedges has set out on a bold exploratory journey, the goal of which is to reformulate an archaic stage of psychopathology and to extend or even modify our current concepts of psychoanalytic technique in order to address it. He employs the term *organizing* as the keystone for this stage and uses this adjective in a variety of ways, for example, "organizing themes," "organizing experiences," "organizing states," and so on. This term, which originated with Hedges (1983) and which he has considerably elaborated (Hedges 1992), has been used by Yorke (1986) and by Stolorow and Atwood (1992) to designate a state of psychological organization that takes place within the first four months of the infant's life—and which may have even earlier origins in the womb. In the organizing experience the infant fails significantly to organize fully and meaningfully around the ideally attuned presence of its mother and organizes instead in a reflex-like manner around aspects of itself (in terms of its sensorimotor schemata), inanimate objects, and so on. Thus, the infant becomes significantly aversive to the presence of, or contact with, the primary nurturing object, who herself had been *subjectively experienced* as having been critically unable to adequately and properly attune to and affirm her infant's budding personhood and affective/physiological needs.

Put another way, the infant who feels critically unable to *attach* to a mother who may have difficulties in *bonding* may experience him/herself to be at risk for annihilation and may therefore seek to preserve him/herself by *withdrawal into alienation*—from the mother and from the self. Bion (1962, 1963) calls this "infantile catastrophe," Winnicott (1952a, b) the "failure to go on being," Mahler (1952, 1958, 1968, 1972) "annihilation anxiety," and Tustin (1966, 1972, 1980, 1981a, b, 1984, 1986, 1987, 1988, 1989a, b, 1990a, b, c) and myself (Grotstein 1990a, b, 1991) as " 'black hole' anxiety." In other contributions I have referred to this phenomenon as a "precocious closure" of the personality, referring to an early massive dissociation in the personality, one that Balint (1968) referred to as the "basic fault" (Grotstein 1977a, b, 1981).

Classical analysts of yesteryear experienced great difficulty in formulating how trauma had impact on the infant in its earliest years because of their allegiance to the concept of primary narcissism, which disallowed the infant's experience of separateness from the object. The conceptualizations of Melanie Klein did allow for it because of her belief that the infant was separate from the very beginning and that its instincts were always object-seeking. Stern (1985), summarizing the findings from empirical research in infant development, agrees with Klein that the infant is indeed separate from its maternal object from the very beginning. But in opposition to Klein Stern believes that the infant has a reality orientation and is capable of *perception* from early on, but not capable of phantasy until the second year of life, when symbolization and verbalization capacities develop. More recently Subbotsky (1993) refutes this last opinion and states, on the basis of empirical evidence, that the infant *is* capable of employing phantasy from the beginning and that it occurs in parallel with reality testing. Thus, from the points of view of these two authors (collectively), *there is never a time when the infant cannot properly perceive and adaptively phantasize about all the events and traumata that occur to him/her.*

Further, Share (1994), in an exquisite study of dreams from

analytic patients, has been significantly successful in demonstrating that dreams do convey veridical memories of early infantile trauma — and even of fetal trauma — with confirmation in each of the cases she cites! Moreover, the infant development research studies of Bower (1974, and personal communication) confirm that, when children achieve the capacity for symbolization and verbalization, there seems to occur a *retrospective application of symbolic processing to emotional experiences that had occurred before this capacity was operant!* What Stern, Subbotsky, Share, and Bower are clearly explicating is that there may *never* be a time in the infant's life when experiences and perceptions are not encoded or encodable for mental representation and memory.

Returning now to Hedges's work, from the infant's failure to achieve significant success in attaching to its bonding mother, it prematurely organizes its failures into an amalgam, according to Hedges, and then seemingly undergoes an implosion into itself characterized by a reflexive return to its own sensorimotor self, where it establishes a pattern of an alternative relating to itself and only hesitantly to the needed mother or to others after her.

This sector of psychopathology has had earlier explorers. Winnicott's concepts of "transitional objects" (1951), the "holding environment" (1952a), and "illusion" (1971) were a landmark, as were the concepts of Bion [notably the "container and the contained" (1959, 1962), "beta elements" (1963), and "dream function alpha" (1962, 1963, 1965, 1970, 1992)], Bick (1968, 1986), Meltzer (1975), and Meltzer and colleagues (1975). Each of them, independently observing the patterns of autistic[1] children, found that they suffered from anxieties that formed earlier than even the persecutory anxieties posited by Klein (1940) when she postulated the paranoid-schizoid position. Bick and Meltzer believed that these children suffered from "adhesive identity" and molded tenaciously to mother's body in order to form a precarious

---

[1]The term *autistic* has been used by a good number of psychoanalysts in recent years, but a note of caution should be exercised in this regard. There probably is a significant difference between the actual constitutional (genetic) autism as described by Ritvo and colleagues (1969, 1989a, b, 1990) and that described by psychoanalysts since Mahler (1952, 1958, 1968, 1972). I myself prefer the term *schizoid* to *autistic* when the condition is ultimately or largely psychological in nature.

sense of identity. Mahler (1958, 1968) postulated the concept of "secondary autism" and of "symbiotic psychosis" in order to address her findings on the same kind of children studied by Bick and Meltzer. Anzieu (1989, 1990), in the same vein, postulated the primary importance of skin and formulated the ideas of the "skin ego" and "skin envelope," discerning archaic psychopathology to be understandable in these terms. Tustin psychoanalytically treated autistic children for over thirty years and made a significant contribution to our understanding of their unique ways of relating and not relating to objects. Her enumerations of the "black hole" phenomenon, autistic objects, encapsulation, entanglement, autistic shapes, the "rhythm of safety," and so on, have greatly enriched our knowledge of this archaic stage of development.

Apposite to this line of approach by Hedges in this present work, Meltzer and Tustin independently found that the autistic children whom they had studied employed the technique of *dismantling*, in which the terrified infant or child (terrified of the separation from the mother) encounters a cataclysmic "me/not me" interface from which he or she massively withdraws but at the same time dismantles (in phantasy) the needed part-object features of the maternal object, disidentifies them from the mother, and appropriates them for oneself by re-identifying them with one's own body parts, sense organs, mouth, and so on. Thus, one's own body parts now stand for the object, but not in a transitional way, where the connection with the object would continue to be acknowledged. Tustin calls this phenomenon "autistic autosensuality."[2] For an elaboration of Tustin's work with many neo-Kleinian innovations, one should also read Mitrani (1993).

Marcelli (1983) formulated the concept of the "autistic position" in an attempt to bring all these diverse ideas together into a single metapsychological construct. Ogden (1989) independently formulated the concept of the "autistic contiguous position," which describes how the infant obtains its sense of identity from its contiguous contact with

---

[2]My own concepts of the "skin boundary frontier organization" and the "background presence of primary identification" were also attempts to address this stage of development (Grotstein 1980, 1990c, d).

mother's skin and then differentiates when there is enough satisfactory experience with it. Kristeva (1982), extending the semiotic concepts of Lacan into the earliest stages of the infant's life (the "pre-mirror stage") formulates the concept of the "abject," by which she means that the infant is uncoordinated and normally unorganized and unintegrated but gradually becomes integrated and organized as it learns to communicate with its mother in the preverbal sensual language of "*le sémiotique*." Mother's failure to "speak" this language or the infant's failure to engage in it with her results in a cataclysmic plunge back into the abject.

More than just mere mention must be accorded, however, to the pivotal work of Bowlby (1958, 1969, 1973, 1980) and his followers, Ainsworth, Main, Klaus, and others. The concept of bonding and attachment has been more appreciated and applied in infant development and empirical psychiatry than it has in psychoanalytic theory, where I believe that it needs to be accepted and applied. Taking off from Hedges's formulations, I wonder if he would join me in hypothesizing that *all* emotional illnesses spring from failures or disorders of bonding and/or attachment in some measure—and that the task of psychoanalysis and/or psychoanalytic psychotherapy is to help establish anew or to restore the conduit of attachment and bonding!

An outgrowth and extension of Bowlby's psychological concept of bonding and attachment are the psychosomatic studies of Hofer (1978, 1981, 1982, 1983a,b, 1984, 1987), Krystal (1988), Taylor (1977, 1984, 1987, 1993), and McDougall (1974, 1978, 1980, 1982, 1985, 1989). Somatization disorders, which may loosely include behavioral stereotypies, eccentric mannerisms, and so on, can be considered in this regard. The patients that Hedges describes seem to have assigned their pain as infants and the sensorimotor inscriptions of it to various aspects of their body, including hypochondriacal anxieties, mannerisms, eccentricities, and enactments generally. A common thread that runs through all these authors' works is the importance of the skin as a part-object organ and of the touch modality that contacts it. The infant's senses in general, and perhaps that of touch in particular, seem to be the conduit of earliest contact with the object.

A word is in order about the contributions of Melanie Klein in regard to "organizing experiences." Dr. Hedges emphasizes that one of

the factors that distinguishes "organizers" from the borderline syndrome is that the latter, springing as it does from failed symbiosis, is
clinically characterized by *abandonment anxiety* and its consequences,
whereas "organizers" are characterized by an intense fear of *contact*
because the condition carries with it the unconscious (and presymbolic) memories of failed contacts in the archaic past. In her psychoanalytic technique, Klein deals with both anxieties, the abandonment
anxieties of absence (and the persecutory objects that fill the emptiness) and the anxiety of presence. In regard to the latter she posited
that the infant inherently experiences the feeling of *envy* in the
presence of the good breast and, as a defensive consequence, mitigates
(in phantasy) the importance and goodness of the breast, thereby
spoiling its function for the infant. Further, she emphasized the
importance of unconscious phantasy and the omnipotence of thought
and the concreteness of perception with which infants imbue it.

Perhaps the analysts whose work most approximates this area of
organization are Balint (1968), with his concept of the "basic fault,"
and particularly Fairbairn (1952), who, complementarily to Klein's
concept of projective identification, emphasized schizoid isolation and
detachment and the psychopathology that resulted from introjective
identification. Most importantly, he brought the schizoid person's
dilemma to our attention, a situation that emerges when the infant's
love (not hate) is treated as if it were bad and in which the infant is not
treated as a person in his own right! To my mind, Fairbairn's concept
of the basic schizoid nature of man comes the closest to Hedges's
depiction of the organizing experience, and I believe that it anticipated
and transcended Winnicott's (1960) concept of the "true and false
selves."

Hedges is careful to distinguish this archaic stage of organizing
experience from the symbiotic abandonment anxiety of borderlines
and the symbolic anxieties of neurotics, as well as from Winnicott's
(1960) distinction between the "true and false selves." He also takes
considerable pains to allow this form of pathology, considered by
many as functional psychoses, to be understood instead as organizing
experiences, a term that conveys the simultaneity of their idiosyncratic nature existing side by side with their thwarted attempts at
contact.

In E. M. Forster's *Howards End*, the protagonist exclaims, "Only connect!" This is the underlying theme of the novel and of this book, too. Hedges, who speaks from the newer relational perspective, defines all psychopathology in general as disorders of relationships, but he singles out organizing experiences as being the ultimate in this regard. There are at least two different ways in which this concept can be applied. First, Hedges seeks to establish the credibility of this archaic state as an entity in its own right, one that has specific psychopathology that is implicitly idiosyncratic to it and for the treatment of which certain psychoanalytic considerations must be rethought. Second, he cites the infant development researchers Tronick and Cohn (1988) as demonstrating that even in normal situations, infants establish meaningful contact with their mothers only thirty percent of the time.

The ramifications of this finding pose, according to Hedges, a significant problem for our therapeutic consideration. The ultimate conclusion from this second idea is that all human beings suffer from cryptic organizing experiences, but they remain unnoticed thanks to the effective screening of the normal personality. From this awesome statement I would consequently advocate the following: psychopathology has hitherto been considered as based on the neurotic model, which presupposes one or another form or degree of object relatedness. Thus, the dialectic of mental illness was that between neurosis and psychosis. Since the rise of interest in narcissism and borderline disorders, a newer dialectic emerged between the narcissistic or self disorders and object-related disorders.

Perhaps we could now formulate that there exists a dialectic, not only between "narcissism and socialism," as Bion (1992) intriguingly calls it, but also between the two of them on one hand and ontological insecurity on the other, where in the latter case the individual suffers both from no object relationships and from no narcissism. The concept of ontological insecurity, which has been put forward by only a few analysts in the classical-Kleinian disciplines, addresses the concept of a lack of a sense of self as a continuing entity. Though Kohut and his followers attempt to deal with it in their own conceptions of the "enfeebled self," I believe the nature of the disarray of the self in ontological insecurity is more profound than their theories address. R. D. Laing (1960) attempted to address this issue with his ideas of the defenses against it, petrification, engulfment, and implosion. These ontological anxieties have haunted the works of Dostoyevsky, Hesse, Camus, Sartre, and so many others. One is also reminded of Michelangelo's haunting "prisoners" or "unborns" who failed to escape from the marble of their origin. More recently studies in personality disorders have uncovered a syndromic collection of symptomatologies that seem to converge into the concept of an avoidant personality that is associated with social phobia and sometimes with agoraphobia and other state disorders such as obsessive-compulsive disorders.

These patients are inhibited, socially avoidant, immature, and are characterized by a propensity toward compliance rather than spontaneity and adjustment. Furthermore, they seem to be pathologically self-conscious (or "self-reflective") insofar as they seldom experience themselves wholly participating in an event with which they may be involved; instead, they, as disembodied observers, observe themselves participating in the event. In other words, they do not play or have sex, for example—they *watch themselves* playing or having sex! I believe that these are the existential vagabonds whom Hedges is discussing.

Hedges seeks to raise our consciousness about this formidable entity by alerting us to how it subtly manifests itself in the developmental and clinical situation. He tells us that the organizational period he is describing extends from prior to birth through the first four months of life and is presymbolic. Therefore, according to him, memories from that period are not encoded symbolically for working through in traditional analysis. The memories become stored in permanent rituals of sensorimotor enactment schemata, that is, patterns of relating, seeking contact, and then avoiding it when the desired contact seems immanent. One is reminded here, on the one hand, of Isaac's (1952) idea of the "principle of genetic continuity," and, on the other hand, of the recently proposed notion from chaos and complexity theory (sensitive dependence on initial conditions) that psychoanalysis has until now privileged regression over fixation (because of its allegiance to the concept of primary narcissism) and has consequently failed to recognize the importance of the impact of real trauma and neglect—and their perseverating consequences—in the earliest months of life.

Lacan (1966) adds yet another dimension to the concepts addressed by Hedges. In his formulations about the "registers" of the "imaginary," the "symbolic," and the "real" he states that the "register of the real," which he differentiates from our more traditionally modern (as opposed to postmodern) conception, designates those experiences that are outside imagination and symbolization, that is, are beyond them and impervious to them. His "real" corresponds to Bion's (1963) "beta elements." A similar idea would be that of the pure traumatic moment before imagination, phantasy, or memory steps in. It is, in Bion's words (personal communication), the "thing in itself!"

Most importantly, Hedges believes that this organizing entity is characterized clinically by an enactment replay in the transference in which the "speaker" first seeks contact with the "listener" and then, at the moment when this contact becomes experienced or activated, a sudden, massive withdrawal occurs, often accompanied by a negative therapeutic reaction. What is being relived is the desire for contact and it is being superseded by a sudden wave of terror in regard to the dreaded return of the unconscious "psychotic mother" (a phantasmal construct of the image of the original mother with the memory of her deficits and impingements and the exaggerated "editorial" processing of this image by the patient) and the terror that always waits at the threshold of traumatic memory, which has grown in intensity in the meanwhile since it has not been mediated by effective and curative interaction with the object.

The unique "spin" that Hedges places on the treatment of this disorder, however, is perhaps the most challenging of all. He believes, and courageously so, I think, that the analytic frame must be mercifully and empathically relaxed a bit in order to accommodate the unique idiosyncrasies of these patients.[3] He believes, in short, that the "listener" (the author's term for the analyst) must be highly empathically attuned to the moment of the "speaker's" (his term for the patient) approach for contact and then for the moment following this

---

[3]One is reminded here of a similar plea from Ehrenberg (1992) and her ideas about the flexible application of relational concepts to psychoanalytic technique.

where there is the characteristic rupture of contact. The author recommends that, at this juncture, the listener must persuade the speaker to remain in contact, not to withdraw, to bear the pain of the return of the "psychotic mother" imago and the feelings attendant upon this. Further, he recommends that often, if not generally, it is of consummate importance for the listener to be prepared to initiate or to provide some actual physical contact (such as an extended hand to be held) as a remedial gesture in order to support the encouragement. These injunctions certainly sound like the techniques of hypnosis and smack of extra-analytic parameters. Notwithstanding this, however, the author attempts to base his suggestions firmly on the concept that the traumata implicit in the organizing experience occur very early, long before the advent of the attainment of the capacity for symbolism and verbalization and therefore are never subjected to symbolized mental processing. They consequently do not follow the pathways of symbolized-verbalized thoughts and feelings. The memories remain in the body schemata and at this time are only retrievable through activation of the body schemata, notably the eyes and skin, in transference experiencing.

Hedges has embarked on a unique journey of exploration and of advocacy, both in terms of psychoanalytic theory and of technique as well. What differentiates his work from some of his less fortunate innovative forebears in this regard, such as Ferenczi, Wilhelm Reich, Alexander, Sechehaye, and others, is his methodology and protocol. The conclusions he has arrived at are part of an ongoing group research program and are subject to many kinds of monitoring and checking. Furthermore, he recommends caution in the pursuit of any physical parameter, such as having a third party supervisor or a third party case monitor of the procedure.

This is a truly cutting-edge work. It challenges psychoanalysts and psychotherapists to reexamine their ideas about infant development and its impact upon our current psychoanalytic theories and practice styles and technical strictures. One could argue with Hedges, especially in terms of his advocacy of discrete, limited, and well-timed physical interpretive touching, that psychoanalysis does not need to employ physical contact, no matter how limited, to constitute a very "touching" experience in its own right—and perhaps all the more so because of the protection of the sacred drama that especially allows both therapist and patient to become "touched" by the presentations of the unconscious that disciplined frame protection offers. I am especially reminded of the contribution of Bion (1992) in this regard in which he proffers that the container-reverie capacity of the mother and the analyst lies in their capacity for "dream work alpha," that is, the analyst must dream (daydream) the patient, allow him/her into one's inner dream space! This is more intimate that physical touching, in my experience.

Despite my caveats, the reader has much to look forward to in this revolutionary work.

REFERENCES

Anzieu, D. (1989). *The Skin Ego.* (Translated by Chris Turner.) New Haven and London: Yale University Press.

_____ (1990). Formal signifiers and the ego-skin. In: *Psychic Envelopes,* trans. D. Briggs, pp. 1–26. London: Karnac Books.

Balint, M. (1968). *The Basic Fault: Therapeutic Aspects of Regression.* London: Tavistock.

Bick, E. (1968). The experience of the skin in early object relations. *International Journal of Psycho-Analysis* 49:484–486.

_____ (1986). Further considerations on the function of the skin in early object relations. *British Journal of Psychotherapy* 2:292–299.

Bion, W. R. (1959). Attacks on linking. In *Second Thoughts,* pp. 93–109. London: Heinemann, 1967.

_____ (1962). *Learning From Experience.* London: Heinemann.

_____ (1963). *Elements of Psycho-analysis.* London: Heinemann.

_____ (1965). *Transformations.* London: Heinemann.

_____ (1970). *Attention and Interpretation.* London: Tavistock.

_____ (1992). *Cogitations.* London: Karnac.

Bower, T. G. R. (1974). *Development in Infancy.* San Francisco: W. H. Freeman.

Bowlby, J. (1958). The nature of the child's tie to his mother. *International Journal of Psycho-Analysis* 39:350–373.

_____ (1969). *Attachment and Loss. Vol. 1: Attachment.* New York: Basic Books.

_____ (1973). *Attachment and Loss. Vol. 2: Separation: Anxiety and Anger.* New York: Basic Books.

_____ (1980). *Attachment and Loss. Vol. 3: Loss: Sadness and Depression.* New York: Basic Books.

Ehrenberg, D. B. (1992). *The Intimate Edge: Extending the Reach of Psychoanalytic Reaction.* New York and London: W. W. Norton.

Fairbairn, W. R. D. (1952). *Psychoanalytic Studies of the Personality.* London, Henley, and Boston: Routledge and Kegan Paul.

Grotstein, J. S. (1977a). The psychoanalytic concept of schizophrenia: I. The dilemma. *International Journal of Psycho-Analysis* 58: 403–425.

_____ (1977b). The psychoanalytic concept of schizophrenia: II. Reconciliation. *International Journal of Psycho-Analysis* 58:427–452.

_____ (1980). A proposed revision of the psychoanalytic concept of primitive mental states: I. An introduction to a newer psychoanalytic metapsychology. *Contemporary Psychoanalysis* 16(4):479–546.

_____ (1981). *Splitting and Projective Identification.* New York: Jason Aronson.

_____ (1990a). Nothingness, meaninglessness, chaos, and the "black hole": I. The importance of nothingness, meaninglessness, and chaos in psychoanalysis. *Contemporary Psychoanalysis* 26(2): 257–290.

_____ (1990b). Nothingness, meaninglessness, chaos, and the "black hole": II. The black hole. *Contemporary Psychoanalysis* 26(3): 377–407.

_____ (1990c). The mirror and the frame. *Bulletin of the Society for Psychoanalytic Psychotherapy* 5(3):21–34.

_____ (1990d). The contribution of attachment theory and self-regulation theory to the therapeutic alliance. *Modern Psychoanalysis* 15(2):169–184.

_____ (1991). Nothingness, meaninglessness, chaos, and the "black hole": III. Self regulation and the background presence of primary identification. *Contemporary Psychoanalysis* 27(1):1–33.

Hedges, L. E. (1983). *Listening Perspectives in Psychotherapy.* New York: Jason Aronson.

_____ (1992). *Interpreting the Countertransference.* New York: Jason Aronson.

Hofer, M. A. (1978). Hidden regulatory processes in early social relationships. In *Perspectives in Ethology*, vol. 3, eds. P. P. G. Bateson, and P. H. Klopfer, pp. 135–163. New York: Plenum Press.

_____ (1981). Toward a developmental basis for disease predisposition: the effects of early maternal separation on brain, behavior, and cardiovascular system. In *Brain, Behavior, and Bodily Disease*, eds. H. Weiner, M. A. Hofer, and A. J. Stunkard, pp. 209–228. New York: Raven Press.

_____ (1982). Seeing is believing: a personal perspective on research strategy in developmental psychobiology. *Developmental Psychobiology* 15:339–408.

_____ (1983a). On the relationship between attachment and separation processes in infancy. In *Emotion: Theory, Research, and Experience. Vol. 2: Early Development*, ed. R. Plutchik, pp. 199–219. New York: Academic Press.

_____ (1983b). The mother-infant interaction as a regulator of infant physiology and behavior. In *Symbiosis in Parent-Offspring Interactions*, eds. L. Rosenblum, and H. Moltz, pp. 61–74. New York: Plenum Press.

_____ (1984). Relationships as regulators: a psychobiologic perspective on bereavement. *Psychosomatic Medicine* 46:183–197.

_____ (1987). Early social relationships: a psychobiologist's view. *Journal of Child Development* 58:633–647.

Isaacs, S. (1952). The nature and function of phantasy. In *Developments in Psycho-Analysis*, ed. J. Riviere, pp. 67–121. London: Hogarth and the Institute of Psycho-Analysis.

Klein, M. (1940). Mourning and its relation to manic-depressive states. In *Contributions to Psycho-Analysis, 1921–1945*, pp. 311–338. London: Hogarth Press and the Institute of Psychoanalysis, 1950.

Kristeva, J. (1982). *Powers of Horror: An Essay on Abjection*, trans. L. S. Roudiez. New York: Columbia University Press.

Krystal, H. (1988). *Integration and Self-Healing: Affect, Trauma, Alexithymia*. Hillsdale, NJ: Analytic Press.

Lacan, J. (1966). *Ecrits*. Paris: Seuil.

Laing, R. D. (1960). *The Divided Self*. London: Tavistock.

Mahler, M. S. (1952). On child psychosis and schizophrenia. *Psycho-*

analytic Study of the Child 7:286–305. New York: International
Universities Press.

———— (1958). Autism and symbiosis: two extreme disturbances of
identity. *International Journal of Psycho-Analysis* 39:77–83.

———— (1968). *On Human Symbiosis and the Vicissitudes of Individuation.*
New York: International Universities Press.

———— (1972). On the first three subphases of the separation-
individuation process. *International Journal of Psycho-Analysis*
53:333–338.

Marcelli, D. (1983). La position autistique. Hypothèses psychopatho-
logiques et ontogénétiques. *Psychiatrie Enfant* 24(1):5–55.

McDougall, J. (1974). The psychosoma and the psychoanalytic process. *International Review of Psycho-Analysis* 1:437–459.

———— (1978). *Plea For a Measure of Abnormality.* New York: International Universities Press, 1980.

———— (1980). A child is being eaten. I: Psychosomatic states, anxiety
neurosis, and hysteria—a theoretical approach. II: The abysmal
mother and the cork child—a clinical illustration. *Contemporary
Psychoanalysis* 16:416–459.

———— (1982). Alexithymia: a psychoanalytic viewpoint. *Psychotherapy
and Psychosomatics* 38:81–90.

———— (1985). *Theaters of the Mind: Illusion and Truth on the Psychoanalytic Stage.* New York: Basic Books.

———— (1989). *Theaters of the Body: A Psychoanalytic Approach to Psychosomatic Illness.* New York and London: Norton.

Meltzer, D. W. (1975). Adhesive identification. *Contemporary Psycho-
analysis* 11:289–310.

Meltzer, D. W. Bremner, J., Hoxter, S., et al. (1975). *Explorations in
Autism.* Strath Tay, Perthshire, Scotland: Clunie Press.

Mitrani, J. (1993). On the survival function of autistic maneuvers in
adult patients. *International Journal of Psycho-Analysis* 73(3):
549–560.

Ogden, T. (1989). On the concept of an autistic-contiguous position.
International Journal of Psycho-Analysis 70(1):127–140.

Ritvo, E. Ornitz, E., Eviatar, A., et al. (1969). Decreased postrotatory
nystagmus in early infantile autism. *Neurology* 19:653–658.

Ritvo, E., Freeman, B., Pingree, C., Mason-Brothers, A., et al. (1989a).

The UCLA-University of Utah epidemiologic survey of autism: prevalence. *American Journal of Psychiatry* 146(2):194–199.

Ritvo, E., Jorde, L., Mason-Brothers, A., Freeman, B., et al. (1989b). The UCLA-University of Utah epidemiologic survey of autism: recurrence risk estimates and genetic counseling. *American Journal of Psychiatry* 146(8):1032–1036.

Ritvo, E., Mason-Brothers, A., Freeman, B., Pingree, C., et al. (1990). The UCLA-University of Utah epidemiologic survey of autism: the etiologic role of rare diseases. *American Journal of Psychiatry* 147(12):1614–1621.

Share, L. (1994). *Birth and Infant Trauma Is Reconstructed from Dreams and Lived Out in Character.* Hillsdale, NJ: Analytic Press.

Stern, D. (1985). *The Interpersonal World of the Infant.* New York: Basic Books.

Stolorow, R., and Atwood, G. (1982). Psychoanalytic phenomenology of the dream. *Annals of Psychoanalysis* 10:205–220.

_____ (1992). *Contexts of Being: The Intersubjective Foundations of Psychological Life.* Hillsdale, NJ: Analytic Press.

Subbotsky, E. V. (1993). *Foundations of the Mind: Children's Understanding of Reality.* Cambridge, MA: Harvard University Press.

Taylor, G. J. (1977). Alexithymia and countertransference. *Psychotherapy and Psychosomatics* 28:141–147.

_____ (1984). Alexithymia: concept, measurement and implications for treatment. *American Journal of Psychiatry* 141(6):725–732.

_____ (1987). Alexithymia: history and validation of the concept. *Transcultural Psychiatric Research Review* 85–95.

_____ (1993). Clinical application of a dysregulation model of illness and disease: a case of spasmodic torticollis. *International Journal of Psycho-Analysis* 74(3):581–596.

Tronick, E., and Cohn, J. (1988). Infant–mother face-to-face communicative interaction: age and gender differences in coordination and the occurrence of miscoordination. *Child Development* 60:85–92.

Tustin, F. (1966). A significant element in the development of autism. *Journal of Child Psychological Psychiatry* 7:53–67.

_____ (1972). *Autism and Childhood Psychosis.* London: Hogarth.

_____ (1980). Autistic objects. *International Review of Psycho-Analysis* 7:27–39.

_____ (1981a). Psychological birth and psychological catastrophe. In *Do I Dare Disturb the Universe: A Memorial to Wilfred R. Bion*, ed. J. Grotstein, pp. 181–196. Beverly Hills: Caesura.

_____ (1981b). *Autistic States In Children*. London: Routledge and Kegan Paul.

_____ (1984). Autistic shapes. *International Review of Psychoanalysis* 11:279–290.

_____ (1986). *Autistic Barriers in Neurotic Patients*. New Haven and London: Yale University Press.

_____ (1987). The rhythm of safety. In *Winnicott Studies: The Journal of the Squiggle Foundation* 2:19–31.

_____ (1988). To be or not to be: a study of autism. In *Winnicott Studies: The Journal of the Squiggle Foundation. A Celebration of the Life and Work of Marion Milner*, pp. 15–31. London: The Squiggle Foundation.

_____ (1989a). What autism is and what autism is not. *Melanie Klein and Object Relations* 7(1):12–18.

_____ (1989b). The black hole—a significant element in autism. *Free Associations* 11:36–50.

_____ (1990a). Autistic encapsulation in neurotic patients. In *Master Clinicians: On Treating the Regressed Patient*, eds. L. B. Boyer, and P. Giovacchini, pp. 117–138. Northvale, NJ and London: Jason Aronson.

_____ (1990b). A revised scheme for understanding autistic pathology. *Psychoanalytic Inquiry*. Accepted for publication.

_____ (1990c). *The Protective Shell in Children and Adults*. London and New York: Karnac Books.

Winnicott, D. W. (1951). Transitional objects and transitional phenomena. In *Collected Papers: Through Paediatrics to Psycho-Analysis*, pp. 229–242. New York: Basic Books, 1958.

_____ (1952a). Anxiety associated with insecurity. In *Collected Papers: Through Paediatrics To Psycho-Analysis*, pp. 97–100. New York: Basic Books, 1958.

_____ (1952b). Psychoses and child care. In *Collected Papers: Through Paediatrics to Psycho-analysis*, pp. 219–228. New York: Basic Books, 1958.

_____ (1960). Ego distortion in terms of true and false self. In *The Maturational Processes and the Facilitating Environment*, pp. 140–152. New York: International Universities Press, 1965.

_____ (1971). *Playing and Reality*. London: Tavistock.

Yorke, C. (1986). Reflections on the problem of psychic trauma. *Psychoanalytic Study of the Child* 41:221–238. New Haven, CT: Yale University Press.

Acknowledgments

Ideas like the ones presented in this book necessarily spring from a community of minds working to solve a series of common problems. In my previous two books it was possible to credit in great detail those writers and colleagues who have contributed most to my personal development. However, in the middle of preparing this book I experienced a devastating robbery in my home and twenty years of research materials into the problems of psychosis were stolen along with two computers containing additional research materials. It would have been impossible both to replace twenty years of research materials and to continue working on the book. I chose to continue. The good news is a refreshingly unencumbered text. The bad news is a severe lack of backup of ideas from other writers and a most regrettable inability to quote and to properly credit antecedent work in each area. In Grotstein's foreword the deficit has been made good and my ideas are effectively contextualized within the field of psychoanalytic research. Here is a list of the major contributors, and I regret that it is not possible to give proper credit in the text: Fred Bailey, Bruno

Bettelheim, Wilfred Bion, Marilyn Boettiger, Hedda Bolgar, Christopher Bollas, Bryce Boyer, Tony Brailow, Suzanne Buchanan, Janet Chasseguet-Smirgel, Bill Cone, Carolyn Crawford, Jolyn Davidson, Kim Dhanes, Cecile Dillon, Leslie Drozd, Michael Eigen, David Eisenman, Rudolf Ekstein, Robert Emde, Kathryn Fields, Beatrice Foster, Anna Freud, Seymour Friedman, Frieda Fromm-Reichmann, Dee Fryling, Tim Gergen, Jacquelyn Gillespie, Peter Giovacchini, Andre Green, James Grotstein, Heinz Hartmann, Lyda Hill, Robert Hilton, Virginia Wink Hilton, Ron Hirz, Denise Ibsen, Jane Jackson, Edith Jacobson, Sandra Jorgensen, Marc Kern, Otto Kernberg, M. Masud R. Khan, Kim Khazeni, Melanie Klein, Sydney Klein, Michael Kogutek, Heinz Kohut, Alitta Kullman, Marlene Laping, Steve Lawrence, Margaret Little, Alexander Lowen, Timothy Maas, Margaret Mahler, Vallory Medlroy, Marion Milner, Thomas Ogden, Milton Olson, Dolly Platt, Jack Platt, Karen K. Redding, Linda Reed, Jeanna Riley, Margot Robinson, Howard Rogers, Herbert Rosenfeld, J. Michael Russell, Sandra Russell, Sabrina Salayz, Karyn Sandburg, Andrew Schwartz, Harold Searles, Diana Seeb, Jackie Singer, Daniel Stern, Sean Stewart, Robert Stolorow, Harry Stack Sullivan, Mariana Thomas, Gayle Trenberth, Frances Tustin, Robert Van Sweden, Mary E. Walker, Patti Wallace, William White, Ruth Wimsatt, Donald Winnicott, Itamar Yahalom, and Marina Young.

My editors at Jason Aronson Inc. (David Kaplan, copy editor and Judy Cohen, production editor) have been sources of expertise and creativity and have enhanced the text greatly through their work.

Many of the ideas that appear in this book were conceived and thought out in collaboration with Joyce Hulgus. In discussing individual cases together we arrived at a number of conclusions that appear throughout this text, especially in Part IV. I am deeply indebted to her and appreciative of her time and her significant contribution to this text.

PART I

THE ORGANIZING EXPERIENCE AND ITS CONTEXT IN PERSONALITY

1

A Shattered Self[1]

Darryl seeks therapy for an exorcism. "What exactly is it that you want exorcised?" Suzanne inquires. "My attraction to Laura," he replies, his face wincing with pain even as he speaks her name. Darryl is a good-looking, 45-year-old man who has been married fifteen years. He and his wife have no children. Over the years his wife has had several affairs. Their marriage is characterized by little or no interpersonal contact and no sexual interaction. He stays with his wife out of a sense of duty, since he has made a life commitment to her.

Darryl knows Laura through his job where he first asked her out to lunch to discuss some business matters. They related well and begin exchanging books and ideas. He felt understood by Laura and very attracted to her. Over time anxiety due to his attraction to her had begun to develop and then to escalate to the point that he knew he must do away with the attraction altogether but could not. He wants Suzanne to find a way of exorcising the attraction. Of course, she

[1] I am grateful to Gayle Trenberth for providing this clinical illustration.

cannot promise anything and thinks an exorcism is unwise, but invites him to talk about himself.

Darryl soon begins speaking in images, giving her pictures about himself. He has no words to express whatever feelings might accompany his experiences. Trained as an analyst in bioenergetics, Suzanne views him as having a schizoid body type (Lowen 1975), meaning his body is thin, elongated, and undeveloped, lacking energy flow in his limbs and face. His bioenergy is perceived by her to be drawn into his torso giving the impression of great frozenness in the central portion of the body.[2] Darryl tries to discern what Suzanne wants from him, what he can provide her with. In the world he does not know how to be, so he looks around to figure out a way to be human by imitating others. He often becomes frustrated when he wants to say something but does not know how to. He repeatedly says, "I want to make you happy."

Three months into therapy he produces the first image that is accompanied by strong affect. He says the image is like a memory. Somehow it is him and it isn't him. The image is of a little boy in the backyard of his mother's house. He is making a clay figure of a knight. It has to be perfect and after much effort it is. He becomes excited by its perfection. He picks it up and starts toward the house carrying the knight to his mother but either his legs do not support him or he trips and falls. The figure shatters. Darryl, in the telling of the story, begins sobbing deeply, gasping, "He's never been able to put it back together. He's never been able to recapture that wonderful, excited time. He's never been able to rebuild that perfection."

Suzanne attempts to explore the image of the shattered knight with him in terms of a possible desire to give something to his mother, a need to show off for his mother, the wish for perfection, his desire for contact with mother when he feels clumsy, inept, careless, or simply does not know how to reach her, or the possibility of a need for

---

[2]Based in psychoanalytic understanding, bioenergetics analysis is a psychotherapy that has devoted itself to understanding the ways in which early psychological concerns remain embedded in body tissue. Because of the essentially somatic nature of the organizing experience I have found that bioenergetics has much to teach the psychoanalyst about the early muscular constrictions that continue to bear witness in the person's life to the nature of early trauma.

negative attention related to shattering of the sense of self. None of these leads helps Darryl elaborate his image. Instead, he speaks of the complete impossibility of ever having contact with his mother at all. His memories of mother are of nothingness.

Suzanne's psychotherapy consultant points toward Darryl's overlearned or internalized inability to ever achieve meaningful emotional contact with mother, and therefore with all subsequent people as well. Just at the moment of presenting an excited, perfect self—mother's knight in shining armor, as it were—a weakness or inability in his legs takes over and he falls, shattering forever the perfect self he wishes to connect to mother. The image appears to describe a cycle that is endlessly repeated in his life. The image implicitly contains primary guilt, the kind Searles (1979) speaks of. It is as though Darryl is saying, "The reason my mother couldn't be a better mother was because I couldn't present her with a perfect, excited, desiring self that would enable her to function as an adequate mother. In order to be a whole mother she needed more than I was able to supply for her. I wanted to help her but it didn't work, it feels somehow my fault. I failed her, and in so doing shattered my perfect self and my possibility of ever knowing how to connect to another human being."

Suzanne's consultant points out that the organizing (or psychotic) transference invariably operates in this way. That is, there is always some kind of searching, reaching, or yearning for human contact. But exactly at the moment of potential contact something happens to prevent it. That moment of contact failure reproduces in an uncanny way the original contact trauma. At a critical point of contact between mother and infant—whether in utero or in the earliest months of life—a primordial trauma was experienced. The contact moment (not simply a single moment in time but an event learned over time) might have served to promote a bonding dance, a mutually cued scenario, an internalized symbiotic structure of some sort. But instead, the moment of potential contact was experienced by the infant as over- or understimulating—as so overly intrusive or overly distant that satisfying human contact could not be made or sustained. In the organizing transference the cycle leading to contact failure is faithfully repeated on a paraverbal, interactive, affective plane. The person living out an organizing experience regularly, in some way or another, orients and approaches as if to put desiring lips around a warm and full nipple held out in readiness. But no sooner than the nurturing other is within smelling or tasting distance there is an internal disruption or an external interruption that destroys the potential contact moment. The nurturance, the potential love, the longed-for bond, the enlivenment of a human soul—in an instant becomes impossible. Unrealistic formations of one sort or another (often seen as psychotic symptoms) then appear to register the aborted contact attempt.

Darryl has succeeded in establishing with his wife (and no doubt with many others) the moment of shattered contact wherein he dutifully approaches but is unable to give or take anything from her. Continuous reliving of what Darryl metaphorically expresses as the weak, collapsed, and shattered moment insures a measure of psychic safety—he never has to experience the excruciatingly painful excitement of that lost moment of perfection that can only be attained in striving for, achieving, and sustaining perfect union with mother. Perhaps not having friends or children serves to maintain the same safety zone. But now Darryl has a real problem. He feels his new woman friend "understands" him. She attracts and excites him. But he has gone a step too close to her and he is once again experiencing that primordial terror of excited desire that, given the internalized cycle of trauma, can only culminate in a repetition of the anticipated, overwhelming pain. He must have his attraction exorcised. He dare not desire human contact.

Three months into therapy Suzanne reports to her consultant, "It's now become like we've entered some kind of mystical trance-like world together. Like when you walk into a room full of people meditating, with all of the silent energy present. It is weird." The next image is more like something that happened to him. Suzanne: "Darryl reported one of the few meaningful things that has happened in his life. He was camping and went wandering out into the desert by himself. He saw the sky in deep sepia red tones. He came across some bones—animal bones—and started to cry. He was sobbing for all of the dead things that die without anybody ever knowing they lived or that they died. And he started crying in my office. People often look two dimensional to him. When he sits in a restaurant and looks at people they look flat and two dimensional. In his images he sees a lot of cartoon characters. Once he saw himself as a baby. His head blew up in a grotesque cartoon kind of way and then floated off like a balloon. He saw it as an ugly thing and said, 'That's me.' Once he saw cartoon characters falling out of his eye sockets. He likened himself to a car beside the freeway. All the other cars are rushing past. They all have motors and they all know how to run. His car looks okay on the outside, but there's nothing on the inside. It can't run."

Traditional psychoanalysis has espoused a doctrine of total abstinence from physical contact between doctor and patient. Bioenergetics analysis involves an explicit study of muscular constrictions related to or containing psychological inhibitions. Accordingly, bioenergetics employs a controlled series of exercises and maneuvers to promote conscious focus on somatic life (see Lowen 1975). A number of these necessitate actual physical contact between psychotherapist and client, which is carried out systematically and with informed consent. The bioenergetics purpose in touching is to promote conscious awareness of psychic conflict that resides in somatic constrictions and symptoms. In Chapter 12 (Transformation Through Connection) I discuss how limited and token physical touch may be required in the treatment of organizing experiences for the purpose of concretizing the *interpretation* of the delusional need to rupture interpersonal contact once it is sensed as near or has been experienced. Appendix A provides a sample informed consent form for use by the therapist who believes physical contact of any kind may have a legitimate place in psychotherapy.

Being a trained bioenergetics analyst Suzanne understands how isolated Darryl's head is from his body and with his consent on occasion has attempted gentle contact with his head, from behind, on top, and with light touch to his forehead. He responds that there is a part of him that opens to her touch and a part of him that closes. Suzanne: "The part of him that opens says things like, 'I don't want to ever leave this office.' The part of him that closes says he's not really feeling my touch at all, 'there's nothing to it.'"

Darryl begins looking forward to his time with Suzanne when he can be more himself, when he does not have to be a robot, an automaton taking care of other people. But he becomes easily frustrated, "I can't focus on anything. . . .I can't say something that will make you happy. . . .Maybe our time together is useless and our attempts to understand me are futile."

Suzanne describes the development of an interesting thread of relatedness that begins to form between the two of them. Amidst all the chatter and despair they begin exchanging small items. He brings her Steinbeck's *Tortilla Flat* to read. He wants to live there. She brings him Kafka's *Metamorphosis*, suggesting this is where he actually lives! He brings a tape of music by Harry Chapin that is important to him. Suzanne: "One especially important track is called 'Sniper.' It's about the guy in the tower at the University of Texas who killed thirty-seven people. The question in the music is, 'Do I exist? The way I know I exist is by having an impact on people, by my touching them and them touching me.' Only in this case it is, 'I kill them and they kill me.' The lyrics continue something like, 'Mom I wanted you to nurse me, I wanted you to hold me.' I asked Darryl, 'Did you relate to that part of the song?' He said, 'Well I'll say yes, but I don't know why.' The song goes on something like, 'I'll never forgive you for your blindness.' And then, 'I hate you, Mom.' This is all while this guy is shooting thirty-seven people and then getting killed himself.

"The other track on the tape he relates to is called, 'Burning Herself.' I wasn't sure whether the person burning herself with the cigarette was himself, his wife, his mother, or me, so I posed a general question and it turned out it's himself. The painful, burning feeling on the outside serves to represent what it really feels like on the inside. He likens it to the day when he took all the books and papers in his office that represented anything personal about himself and threw them away. Another day he threw away all of his old photographs. There's nothing personal on the inside, why should there be on the outside? I was worried for a while and explored the possibility of suicide. He was not actively suicidal, but he has no ordinary will to live."

Through discussion of a sequence of images and exchanges of reading and listening material, Darryl and Suzanne are able to achieve the preliminaries of relating. That is, they get together regularly, they find ways to speak about personal things, and they experience a limited reaching out toward each other. But she senses him withdraw from her offer of touch and from every opportunity for interpersonal contact.

One day Darryl reports, "I had a dream within a dream. I was dreaming that I was asleep having a dream. In the dream within the dream I went to work only because they were producing an opera. A co-worker was introducing her sister. I kept avoiding them. I was backing away, feeling like I was retreating into a fish trap. You know, one of those round, spiral fish baskets. I was retreating into the corner where the fish can't get out. Finally I was cornered and the co-worker said, 'This is my sister, Amelia.' I didn't know what to do and woke up to the first level of the dream. I was lying in a bed, not my own, looking toward an open door. I woke to the sound of a harsh woman's voice coming through the door. I thought, that's my wife's voice—or is that my mother with my wife's voice? Then I woke up."

Darryl spoke of opera as the most useless waste of time and how much opera was like going to work and having a useless experience. Only today, he had finished a project and was wandering around the office repeating to himself, "It's all meaningless. It's all meaningless." He came to his therapy appointment but before he got there he went to have dinner. Suzanne: "He said that in front of the restaurant there was a homeless person sitting on a bedroll asking for change. Darryl gave him some change and he invited him to dinner. The homeless man said, 'No, I've had breakfast.' Darryl asked him to dinner again and he said, 'No, I've had breakfast.' Darryl started to cry at this point in the session. He said, 'That's too bad. I think he might have known something.' He was crying over something that this homeless man might have known—what he might have told him about being alive, about the meaning of life. With touching affect he said, 'I wanted to be him. I wanted to be the homeless person.' Then suddenly the session got choppy, jumpy, and Darryl couldn't stay with anything. He began developing tension and kept bouncing around to different things. Frustrated, he complained, 'I can't focus on anything. I can't come up with anything.' I had the impression of a baby in a tension state, one of those extreme, frustrated tension states."

Suzanne's consultant noted that in this session Darryl had achieved a certain sense of connection with her while telling her about being trapped in meaninglessness so profound it would be better to be homeless, but to at least know something about the meaning of life. His sobbing connected him momentarily to her but he could not tolerate sustaining the connection with her and immediately lost his focus. He began to jump around with frustrated, rising tension, complaining of not knowing what to say to her. The transference trauma had been manifest in the session through his move toward connection and the disruption that occurred at the point he and Suzanne were beginning to connect.

Suzanne: "He resembled an infant with perhaps some kind of intestinal distress—with the baby crying and there's nothing you can do to soothe him. So I asked if I could sit next to him and place my hand very lightly on his shoulder. Then he said, 'I feel like a pressure cooker.' We did a little dialogue about my being the steam and he the overloaded container. I doubt the content mattered much at this point—the touch and talk was for soothing him and attempting to regain the contact. While attempting to hold him in contact with me, I spoke about his becoming frustrated with himself again in session. Then I said I felt like I was holding a baby who was looking at everything else in the room but my eyes. I said, 'I am trying to entice you to look into my eyes, to get you to take comfort in being in contact with me, but I can tell you are not able to do that right now. But I'm not going away. Somehow we will find a way to make contact that is useful to you, contact that feels good.' I feel like there is this autism to him when he retreats into a shell like that. He is terrified of relating to me as a person. For a while there I'm sure I was just a robot to him."

The consultant reflected Suzanne's attempt to maintain contact with Darryl in concrete ways, in this instance by asking if she could sit next to him and lightly touch his shoulder. The emotional contact he felt earlier in the hour stimulated terror—like the terror expressed in the double-layered image of being a fish caught in a trap and a harsh woman's voice coming through an open door (the seduction of a black hole of relatedness, which is experienced by him as a dangerous trap? (Tustin 1981). It is not his bed he is lying in (not a situation of his own making?). A co-worker approaches to introduce him to Amelia (a *me* lia—his passive, feminine side that appears without a *me*, when he is approached—without identity?). The dream portrays the sense of trapped terror he feels (no doubt in relation to his therapist as well as to all people in his life), along with the meaninglessness of it all. The tearful moment of contact as he wishes to trade places with the homeless person, who at least knows something of the meaning of life, is interrupted by the emergence of transferential confusion and a retreat to a somatic tension state from which there is no being comforted, no capacity for receiving soothing, and no ability to experience his personality as being grounded in another. (He is encapsulated as a pressure cooker.) Unlike the so-called borderline or symbiotic states in which abandonment is the central fear, a person living an organizing state cannot readily use the other for containment or interpersonal grounding, because it has been learned that human contact itself is dangerous, terrifying, overstimulating, or understimulating.

Suzanne intuitively understands that Darryl is not yet able to be in full emotional contact with the human environment and that he can ultimately only be brought there by experiencing being reached out to and touched by another human being. Darryl experiences himself as an automobile without a motor, as a robot, as an automaton, as a cartoon character, as dead animal bones in the desert, as a bloated balloon head floating away, as a fish caught in a trap, as a pressure cooker, and as a clay knight errant, shattered while reaching toward mother. These images that Darryl brings to Suzanne, like most emanating from the organizing experience, are nonhuman. The importance of nonhuman imagery in organizing states is discussed at length in Chapter 11. The question that Darryl poses for Suzanne is the central question to be considered in this book: *How can the enlivenment of human touch reach a person living basically in a world experienced as nonhuman?* Darryl requests that his desire for human contact be exorcised because (as organizing transference) it threatens so much pain. Can Suzanne gradually coax him toward experiencing human desire that is safe, comforting, and growth enhancing? If so, how will she proceed from this beginning? And what do the Darryls of the world have to teach us about human nature and about the hidden organizing aspects of ourselves?

THE ORGANIZING THEMES TO BE CONSIDERED IN THIS BOOK

Suzanne's report of her experience with Darryl moves us immediately to the heart of working the organizing experience. Some of the basic theoretical and technical understandings that will be elaborated later have already been suggested. Clinicians are seeing more individuals like Darryl in their consulting rooms today than ever before. The more understanding we gain about Darryl's experience, the more sensitized we become to the earliest layerings of psychic structure in all people. This book maintains that organizing experiences like Darryl's are, in one form or another, common to all human experience. As the book unfolds the reader will find a series of themes that recur in studying the organizing experience. These themes will be briefly introduced now.

Private Madness Is Universal

Throughout all time and in all cultures people have developed a variety of ideas and prejudices about madness. The general tendency, which is echoed in our own culture, has been to see madness as separate from ourselves and mad people as fundamentally different from ourselves. The human tendency has been to externalize and then to persecute our own sense of fear and uncertainty—our own private madness—which is basic to the foundations of psyche.

As psychological sophistication increases, we are better able to discern the nature of the basic organizing processes and to perceive blocked off channels for interpersonal relating as they occur in all people. What has heretofore been referred to as a universal core or kernel of psychosis I will discuss as *enclaves, pockets,* or *layerings of organizing experience* as they necessarily exist in all people by virtue of the conditions of early child rearing. With optimal experiences in early life, the ordinary parental failures to attune with the needed supply in a timely fashion are generally overshadowed by favorable experience so that only small areas of potential functioning may be closed off. However, many individuals experienced their earliest yearnings for human contact as so traumatizing that they have massively withdrawn in a variety of ways from the world of social consensus, from the world of ordinary interpersonal-relatedness possibilities. Their organizing experience is pervasive and governs all aspects of daily life. We might think of a spectrum based upon the degree of pervasiveness, intensity, and the urgency with which people's lives are colored by aspects of their early organizing experience.

Terror of Contact Is Central to the Organizing Experience

Unlike the so-called borderline states where the theme of abandonment is central, in organizing (and psychotic) states the fear of interpersonal (affective) contact is central. At the beginning of an analytic experience it is not at all clear why a given individual failed to bond, failed to enter into a reciprocal symbiotic dance with some parental figure. But for reasons that emerge in the course of analytic transference relating, the person living in an organizing state must avoid interpersonal contact at all cost. Contact is traumatic either because it is over- or understimulating, and so-called psychotic symptoms clearly serve to ward off interpersonal contact, which is feared as unsafe.

The Organizing Transference Functions to Prevent Bonding

Transference in organizing states exists as a memory of the way the infant (for whatever reason) became frightened of connection to the primary nurturing other, usually the biological mother. Conceptualizing the organizing or psychotic transference as "the moment of emergence of the (internalized) psychotic mother" helps to identify the *intrapsychic* experience that compels a breaking off of contact. That is, in terms of the infant's urgent need systems, the inference is that it was not possible for the responsiveness of the mothering person to be sufficiently attuned to his or her immediate reality. This says nothing about the objectively viewed capacities of the real mother that may have been "average and expectable" in every regard. But from the infant's subjective perspective the mothering process was crazy or psychotic, and is retained in memory as such. The clarifying notion is that developmentally, for whatever reason, the other who might have been turned to for providing nurturance, contact, stimulation, comfort, and an ordering of experience that would permit the evolution of personal spontaneity and creative potential within an interpersonal context, was somehow experienced as traumatizing due to over- or understimulation, or to a failure to organize the infant's experience into smooth and efficient relatedness patterns. The "psychotic mother" is here used as a theoretical construct and is not seen as necessarily related to any real person as objectively perceived, but is the internalized representation of the other who was experienced as traumatizing to connecting possibilities. For example, even the best parenting cannot provide perfect attunement and responsiveness to a child in pain due to some birth defect, childhood anomaly, or disease. The technical problem is how to grasp, from the infant's point of view, the fault with the mothering processes without faulting the real mother. By speaking of "the appearance of the psychotic mother" I point to the internal representation of the other that appears at moments of potential human contact as psychotic or an organizing transference that can be secured for analysis.

Resistance Is to the Emergence of the Psychotic Mother Transference

The resistance in the psychoanalysis of organizing states is to making or sustaining certain forms of contact that are bound by virtue of internalized experience to be traumatic. To attempt to sustain personal contact is to raise the threat of the reappearance in transference memory of the traumatizing other, who is so internalized and integral to experiencing that terror and pain accompany any possibility of subsequent emotional linking. Resistance to the organizing transference appears in many forms to ward off human contact experiences that threaten a reexperiencing of transference terror.

Interpretation of the Organizing Transference Is Concrete and Paraverbal

The organizing experience is related to some primary blocking of experience during earliest infancy. Contact with organizing states is necessarily paraverbal and concrete in nature. Interpretation of the appearance of the psychotic mother transference is almost invariably accomplished by some form of physical (concrete) touching. Touch, which serves to interpret inhibiting organizing structures, like all interpretation, is very specific in nature and timing. Concrete interpretive touch is accomplished and timed in such a way as to communicate paraverbally to the person in analysis, "You have achieved contact with me right now and we both feel it. I know that you believe you now must flee, break contact, withdraw emotionally because contact in your history is dreaded. But you are no longer an infant and you have the ability as an adult to stay in contact with me. You can maintain contact. The pain and fear you now feel is left over from infancy. We can find ways for you to hold on to me safely. You do not have to break away. We can experience your traumatic history together. We can share your fear and pain and come to understand its nature. We can grow together." The touching advocated in this technique is solely aimed at these purposes and offered in such a way and at such a time that the person feels safe and willing to receive these messages or it will be intrusive, wrong, and potentially overwhelming and dangerous. There is no place in psychoanalytically informed psychotherapy for physical touching that is for the purpose of comfort, reassurances or containment. The touch advocated here is of a token nature and provides a concrete interpretation of preverbal organizing ruptures in interpersonal contact.

Countertransference Brings Its Own Madness

There are several kinds of countertransference to organizing states that can be expected by listeners[3] working the organizing experience.

1. Denial of Human Potential

The most common form of countertransference has seen organizing personalities as witches, evildoers, hopelessly psychotic, and in

---

[3]In this text the social role designations of doctor–patient, analyst–analysand, counselor–client have been abandoned in favor of the more functional designations of listener and speaker.

other ways not quite human. In this attitude is a denial of human
potential and a denial of the possibility of being able to stimulate
desire in such a way as to reawaken it and to analyze blocks to human
relating. We hear: "I can't reach you, you are too sick. You are
untreatable so we will lock you up or give you drugs to sedate or pacify
you."

2. Fear of Primitive Energy

When an analytic listener invites the organizing experience into
a transference relationship, he or she is asking that the full impact of
primitive aggressive and sexual energies of the analytic speaker be
directed squarely at the person of the listener and at the process of
therapy. Listeners fear the power of this experience because it can be
quite disorienting to both people involved and, if not carefully as-
sessed and monitored, potentially dangerous. But fear of basic human
affectivity is irrational and we now have at our disposal many rational
ways of inviting and managing the organizing level affects and energies. The key technical consideration is not whether the person on the
basis of *a priori* criteria is "treatable," but whether the listener has
sufficient holding and supportive resource available to him or her on
a practical basis to make the pursuit of treatment practical and safe for
all concerned.

3. Encountering Our Own Organizing Experiences

When we as listeners invest ourselves emotionally in reaching
out again and again to an analytic speaker only to be repeatedly
abandoned or refused, it stimulates our own most primitive experiences of reaching out to our own mothers during our organizing
developmental period, hoping for a response and feeling traumatized
when the desired response was not forthcoming. Our own "psychotic
mother" transference can reappear projected onto the analytic speaker
as we attempt to provide systematic and sustained connection for
people living organizing states. How each of us as an individual
practitioner develops staying power is the crucial question. Our own

therapy is essential as is consultation with colleagues during difficult phases of this work. Attempting to work the organizing experience without adequate resource and backup support is like a single mother trying to manage a difficult or sick baby while holding down a job to support herself, caring for several other children, and trying to live some life of her own. We need support to do this very taxing kind of work. We further need support in monitoring and containing in a safe manner both the organizing level transference and the organizing level countertransference.

4. Empathy Leading to Breaks in Contact

After the preliminary phases are well under way, that is, after comfortable and safe working rhythms have been established, and after the listener has been able to discern and bring up for discussion the specific ways in which the speaker engages in and searches for contact and then cuts off contact, we notice the speaker begins excitedly to see in outside contacts as well as in the analytic hour how the breaking of contact is being regularly accomplished. Speakers in analysis are often excited by the therapeutic process at this point because for the first time in their lives something is finally making sense about themselves. They begin a valiant struggle to maintain contact nearly everywhere they go, especially with the listener. Then we notice a tendency on the part of the analytic listener to begin withdrawing into inattentiveness, preoccupation, or even drowsiness. This type of countertransference activity, which tends to occur well into the treatment process, represents the listener's empathy for the terror that contact provides for the speaker. That is, the speaker for the first time in his or her life feels that he or she is hot on the trail of something that promises human satisfaction—sustained contact. But in the person's enthusiasm to achieve as much contact as possible as fast as possible, it is the listener who senses the internalized danger and in some way is deliberately (unconsciously) slowing things down a bit. This countertransference reaction can be pointed out to the speaker so that the listener and the speaker may gain a fuller appreciation of the joys and dangers of human contact.

All Organizing States are Transformable

Psychotherapy research over the last decade suggests that all functional (as opposed to organic) states that are due to traumatically interrupted channelings in infancy are, in principle, transformable. I know of no reason that, given the proper containing conditions, organizing experience cannot be brought into an analytic relationship for analysis so that channels once closed off can be analyzed, thereby opening them to human contact and further development.

In practice, however, the question of whether or not a given person can be worked with revolves around the actual resources required for physical and psychological containment during the analytic process. For example, a person with psychotic, homicidal rage cannot safely be treated once or twice a week in a private practice outpatient setting. Likewise, a person whose channels have left him or her with severe limitations in learning capacity may require parallel tutoring or other support along the way. A person whose organizing experience pervades his or her entire existence may require almost daily contact over long periods of time in order to fully engage in the transformational process. A person who was repeatedly assaulted (physically or sexually) in infancy will develop a persecutory psychotic transference and the therapist practicing without auxiliary help in case management may be in for a malpractice suit (that may be avoided if the psychotic transference is managed effectively). The emergence of a psychotic transference is, after all, what is being promoted in this kind of work in order to analyze the organizing experience. This means that at the moment a person is subjectively experiencing the psychotic or organizing transference, the therapist is perceived as the internalized psychotic mother imago and an ordinary sense of reality testing is not fully present.

Part of the ongoing assessment procedure with organizing states is to begin imagining what the experience of the internalized psychotic mother imago will look like to each person and to be sure the actual practical dimensions of the treatment setting can tolerate the emergence of such a powerful primitive transference. There are many psychotic transferences that clearly are not safe for the therapist in unmonitored independent practice to take on. Risky psychotic transferences should be treated in public or private nonprofit clinics or residential settings where there is wider support for the work and lower risk of legal consequences to the therapist or treatment team when the psychotic transference emerges. Many psychotic transferences may require a secured residential facility and the availability of medication and/or physical restraint.

The Backdrop of Sustained Contact

The basic rule of free association was developed by Freud to promote the analysis of neurotic states. Over time, following the command to "say everything that comes to mind" has come to be thought of as neither desirable nor possible, in principle. But the notion or ideal of feeling completely free in the presence of an analytic listener to let one's mind ramble uninhibitedly still serves as a valuable backdrop against which to perceive whatever actually does happen. Suddenly one's thoughts are interrupted by something, or one's mind goes blank, or one forgets a thought in the middle of a sentence. The analytic investigator is interested in each event. Why at that moment was free association interrupted? The ideal of free association points a direction, sets a pace, defines a ground for a psychic figure (of transference or resistance) to be seen against.

Likewise, in working the organizing experience, the ideal of sustained interpersonal contact serves as a backdrop against which to see the ways in which an analytic speaker approaches contact, reaches for it, momentarily lights up with affect, and then just as quickly darts away—sometimes obviously, sometimes not so perceptibly. In this book the ideal of sustained human contact in working the organizing experience is analogous to the ideal of free association in the analysis of neurosis—both serve as backdrops against which transference experiences can appear and be secured by the listener and the speaker for psychoanalytic transformation.

SUMMARY

Darryl and Suzanne's experience brings immediately before us a number of aspects of the organizing experience and poses a series of questions. As this book unfolds the reader will encounter a number of different kinds of organizing experiences from very different kinds of people. I hope to show that what has been shunned for ages as madness can now be understood as a universal human experience traceable to the earliest psychic experience of becoming disorganized or traumatized in face of failed contact.

The hallmark of the organizing transference is a terror or horror of interpersonal affective linking or contact. The dread of contact relates to one's personal history of reaching out affectively as an infant and being received in such a way as to have been traumatized to the point of refusing to reach out that way ever again. The organizing transference is conceptualized here as a memory formation of the experience of the traumatizing other, whom I have chosen to label the "psychotic mother," an internalized representation of the experienced failure of environmental responsiveness to be fully attuned to the infant's real and immediate need states. Whether the real mother or other nurturing persons could have done more than they did is an altogether different question. Resistance is to reexperiencing the transferential trauma that results from opening the long-closed channels of potential experience. Interpretation is necessarily paraverbal and concrete—usually simply a timely being with, or interpretive touch that communicates the analytic listener's awareness of the present contact and the urge to flee—along with the coaxing to stay, to remain open to experiencing contact, and the invitation to share together the sense of trauma and physical pain that necessarily accompanies the opening of blocked channels. Countertransference may deny the person's basic humanity or raise a fear in the analytic listener of the opening up of primitive energies that are bound to be directed at the person of the listener. Working the organizing experience is bound to stir up the analytic listener's own terrifying organizing experiences, or manifest itself as some form of withdrawing, seen as empathy with the speaker's terror of contact.

I have taken the position that only practical considerations regarding the available resources for appropriate containment need limit working with organizing states, not the nature of the experience itself. The overlearned or internalized tendency to repeatedly break off contact according to a style once experienced in the primordial past (and often seen as psychotic symptoms in the present) can best be perceived against a background that promotes sustained contact between analytic speaker and listener. While it might seem that learning to sustain contact is the primary aim of this kind of work, that cannot be true. If it were, we would need only good teachers or re-parenting specialists, not analysts. The goal is to analyze, to break down, the primordial organizing structures that still manifest themselves as the psychotic transference accompanied by powerful resistance. Promoting interpersonal emotional contact is the frame through which the organizing level transferences and resistances to contact can be secured for analysis.

Organizing structures can be brought into the light of day and relinquished by a dedicated speaker who is determined over time to learn not to retreat from developing contact with the analytic listener, even in the face of terror and pain. The analytic listener who has developed staying power through his or her own analytic work and who can be sustained by ongoing support from colleagues is in a position to coax the contact and, in the process, to frame for analysis the structures that emerge to block affective experience and exchange and result in some form of (symptomatic) flight.

CONCLUSION

Before moving to a discussion of the features that are likely to be encountered along the organizing path, it is important to place the context of this study in historical perspective. Chapter 2 will review the Freudian legacy and the historical development of three paradigms for psychoanalytic thought. The third and prevailing paradigm, the relatedness paradigm, is a psychology based upon establishing an appreciation of a person's developing experiences of self in contrast to experiences of others.

Chapter 3 will demonstrate how the paradigm shift in psycho-analysis opens the way to conceptualizing psychoanalytic experience with early developing aspects of personality. The crucial dimensions of the paradigm shift will be briefly defined along with the four distinctly different listening perspectives that have evolved in psychoanalysis in the last three decades. The reader will see how the kind of work proposed in this book is very different from other kinds of psychoan-alytic work, but why it still belongs under the ever-broadening canopy of psychoanalysis.

The chapters in Part II address issues that arise as we envision a series of potential developments along the path to psychic organization.

2

The Backdrop for the Organizing Experience

THE ORGANIZING EXPERIENCE DELINEATED

From its beginning the human zygote has the task of organizing channels to its environment that bring required nutrients and evacuate unneeded metabolic by-products. Through predominantly biochemical and electrical means the fetus extends its domain from the immediate intrauterine environment into virtually all parts of its mother's body and in some respects even to her physical and social surround. At birth the infant's means of continuing to expand its purview shift predominantly to the construction of psychological channels. Utilizing all sensorimotor modalities and a wide range of inborn affective potentials, the baby's extensory signals assume the presence of a human nurturing environment with which it can establish further emotional/psychological channels.

The subject of this book is the ways in which the construction of biological and psychological channelings to the human environment are attempted, the reasons attempted channelings may fail to become organized, and the subjective nature of attempted and failed experience as it is laid down in memory and transferred into later interpersonal-relatedness experience. This study will illustrate many of the potential consequences of failed psychological connections. It will point to some of the kinds of psychic structures that may develop in lieu of the possibility of establishing smooth and efficient channelings to the human milieu. Furthermore, through extension of existing theory and through case examples, some of the ways in which these structures can be identified, analyzed, and thereby transformed in later life will be specified and illustrated.

A central thesis of this book is that no baby achieves perfectly harmonious two-way psychological channeling of all of its instinctual needs with the human caretaking environment. As a result, all people are left with potential channels for spontaneous and creative activity that have been systematically cut off or blocked at rudimentary levels. Basically adequate physical and psychological caretaking [cf. Winnicott's (1965) "good-enough" mothering] leaves only small pockets or enclaves of early organizational experiencing that are blocked from further creative development. More massive failure of the infant to connect psychologically with the human psychological environment results in larger portions of the personality continuing to live in subsequent life various aspects of early organizational striving. No matter how well these people may learn to imitate human behavior and interaction, or to develop apparently normal or even superior intelligence and thereby to "pass" as ordinary people, they will be the first to acknowledge that they perceive themselves as somehow different from other people, that something is missing, which seems to make them in some regard "somewhat less than, or not quite human."

Specific kinds of warpings or convolutions of basic organizational strivings produce clinical pictures commonly referred to as psychotic—schizophrenic, manic-depressive, schizo-affective, schizoid, and autistic. [For specific formulations that distinguish the various genetic possibilities for the formation of thought disorders, mood disorders, and schizoid and autistic states, and the basic picture of organizational aspects of personality see Hedges (1983, Chapter 12).]

The present study takes the position that, in principle, all functional (as opposed to organic) organizing states are potentially transformable. Identifiable psychological structures exist at the organizing level of human psyche, which can be isolated, defined, analyzed, and subsequently transformed into more complex and flexible psychic states. The practical question regarding what conditions may be required for the transformation of severely warped or convoluted organizing states is a related but separate issue that will also be addressed as issues in case management. (See Hedgers 1994b, which illustrates how a group of therapists have successfully met the challenge of responding to limited as well as pervasive organizing states.)

THE FREUDIAN LEGACY

Freud's (1895) earliest understanding of the origins of psychic functioning specifies in quasi-neurological terms exactly what occurs when organizing psychic extensions into the environment meet painful reception. The potential channel is blocked off with a memory trace that essentially reads, "never go there again." Freud's presumption is that this basic blocking of potential channels due to painful encounters with the environment is a universal human experience warranting the term *primary repression*. But Freud himself chose not to develop these thoughts further, preferring to follow instead a lead that emerged over the next two years in his own self-analysis. As a result his subsequent life's work defines and elaborates the developmentally much later but highly critical (3 to 7 years of age) oedipal era in which the child attempts to assimilate fully the human symbolic system. Despite Freud's basic move away from considering the earliest organizational aspects of human existence, his subsequent theorizing always includes a consideration of the biological aspects of human nature.

Freud was painfully aware of the absence of physiological and psychological tools, which severely limited research into the origins of human life during his lifetime. It seems not wholly by accident that Freud's pen dropped when he himself had come full circle and once again considered the earliest origins of psychic inhibitions in his final and unfinished paper, "The Splitting of the Ego in the Process of Defence" (1940).

Freud formulates that psyche's first task is that of organizing reliable pathways linking the organism's instinctual demands to available environmental possibilities (1895). He specifies three broad classes of neuronal activity that are involved in early psychic functioning: (1) the organization of sensory and motor channels linking psyche directly to the external environment, (2) the organization of internal channels linking psyche to biological systems, and (3) the organization of a monitoring system with channels informing psyche of the nature (quality) of information being received and transmitted to and from the external as well as the internal environments.

Bettelheim (1983) states that Freud deliberately chooses to speak of "psyche" (soul) rather than "mind" or "mental apparatus" in order to accent by way of allusion to ancient mythology the humanistic, if not the spiritualistic, nature of his chosen subject matter. *Psychoanalysis*, Freud's term for his method of study, is metaphorically derived from nineteenth century chemistry. To "analyze" meant to understand by taking apart or breaking down a complex compound in order to reveal its component elements. Whatever else psychoanalysis has come to mean through the years, it always includes the arrangement of an interpersonal situation in which complex psychic structures come to be understood in terms of their constituent parts (especially transference and resistance) as they make themselves known in the course of the analytic relationship. As the scope of psychoanalytic studies has broadened, analysts have learned to identify a variety of structures that begin developing from the commencement of psychic life. To analyze or break down structures, a notion once applied only to advanced neurotic structure, now takes on a variety of meanings and encompasses a variety of technical procedures. [For a detailed discussion of the expansion of psychoanalytic theory and technique to preoedipal psychic structures see Hedges (1983, 1992).]

In 1896 to 1897 Freud conducted a self-analysis using his own dreams, slips of the tongue, humor, and sexuality (Freud 1954). Based upon his self-analysis Freud becomes interested in the psychological complex that he named after Sophocles's hero, Oedipus. Freud comes to believe that the mythic triangular-relatedness themes in *Oedipus*

Rex, which are echoed forcefully in *Hamlet*, pervade human language and culture. In describing what he takes to be the universal aspects of the Oedipus complex, Freud specifies a variety of ways in which a young child (aged 3 to 7) might come to organize his or her three-party or triadic emotional-relatedness experiences—the so-called Oedipal triangle or family romance. The ground-breaking importance of Freud's delineation of the Oedipus complex is not so much the reorganization of ancient mythic themes as his insight that human mentality itself is drastically altered by the presence of third-party relating. The father symbolizes the structuring effects of language and culture.

By 1900 Freud formulates his doctrine of symbolically repressed mental activity as it relates to the oedipal-aged child's decisions not to feel, think about, or even to "know" consciously about his or her intense sexual and aggressive, loving, and hateful impulses, fantasies, and strivings. Freud comes to believe that the causative factors in neurosis are the overlearned or "internalized" inhibitory relatedness patterns derived from repressions accomplished during the oedipal developmental period. The oedipal child feels forced to repress various aspects of his or her inner impulse life in order to insure harmonious familial and social relations. These repressed emotional-relatedness patternings, Freud says, continue to operate subtly and silently in interpersonal life but, because they are disavowed, are not noticed by the developing individual. This spelling out in consciousness at the symbolic level of the socially forbidden aspects of instinctual life and deliberately renouncing them has become referred to as *secondary repression* or simply *repression* and contrasts sharply with Freud's (1895) notion of *primary repression*, a blocking of organizing pathways that occurs at a quasi-neuronal level of activity. Freud's first paradigm to guide thought and study is thus founded on a metaphor of mental *topography*—that is, a study of which aspects of mental life are perennially available for conscious scrutiny and which are repressed (i.e., the biological drives) but nevertheless continue to operate systematically and unconsciously or preconsciously (1900).

The popular press has recently attributed to Freud and to psychoanalysis the notion that people can be subjected to externally based trauma in early childhood and then repress it for many years, only to recover the memory in videocassette accuracy while under-going psychotherapy with hypnosis and sodium pentothal. Freud never said any such thing nor is this a psychoanalytic doctrine; rather, this notion is a Hollywood invention to create horror and suspense. Freud's doctrine of repression only includes stimulation of an instinc-tual nature arising from *within* the body that is unacceptable to the child's developing social sense (i.e., the superego). Freud's notion of repression is widely misunderstood as operating to make things some-how magically vanish. This idea is misleading. Rather, the Freudian doctrine of repression holds that a child elects not to spell out certain urges in consciousness any more because they conflict with his or her social sense. While the ideas may not enter into conscious thought they certainly do not disappear, but are always present in dreams, slips of the tongue, psychological activities or symptoms, and sexuality. I have elaborated extensively these and related ideas on what psycho-analysis has to say about recovered memories in *Remembering, Repeat-ing, and Working Through Childhood Trauma* (Hedges 1994a).

In 1923 Freud elaborates a second thought paradigm for psycho-analytic research. He creates a vision of psyche that contrasts the sense of personal agency (the "I" or ego) with the psychic aspects of organic destiny (the "it" or id). These agencies or structures are likewise contrasted with a third agency that evolves as the "I" becomes system-atically modified by social pressure. In the formation of the Oedipus complex Freud held that social convention becomes assimilated as a part of the "I," referred to by Freud as the "over-I" (or superego). Distinct in its vision from the earlier topographic point of view, this later tripartite paradigm has become known as the *structural* point of view.

Freud's psychoanalysis and the many schools of psychotherapy that it has spawned are all derived from the basic assumptions of the topographical and structural points of view with additional genetic, economic, dynamic, and adaptive considerations. [For a detailed analysis of Freud's general and specific metapsychology refer to Hedges (1983, Chapter 5).] According to these points of view, the central assumptions of the psychoanalytic and psychotherapeutic enterprise aim at understanding (by breaking down, analyzing) the Oedipus complex, the family romance, or the child's various relations with early familial figures that stand as the presumed cause of neurosis in otherwise well-developed personalities. Neurotic relatedness patterns represent overlearned and often repeated emotional response patterns that develop as the well-developed 3- to 7-year-old child negotiates the demands of instinctual life within the contexts of family and social restriction. These early response patterns are thought to become crystallized or structured in the psyche as internalized relatedness patterns that persistently influence a person's experience of and response within subsequent social relationships.

Freud formulates that when an emotional response pattern is retained from the oedipal period and transferred into a current adult relationship the result is "neurotic." Freud's psychoanalytic technique rests upon studying in the psychoanalytic situation this transference phenomenon and the accompanying resistance to its emergence into the full light of consciousness (which is also understood as further manifestation of inhibitory emotional transfer from early childhood). A person is thought not to resist the analyst or the analysis per se, but the emergence into consciousness of previously repressed emotional-relatedness issues.

SELF AND OTHER PSYCHOLOGY: THE THIRD PARADIGM OF PSYCHOANALYSIS

Heinz Hartmann (1950) conceptually distinguishes the "self" as the evolving and integrating subjective center of the personality from Freud's "I" or "ego," which has come to be studied as a set of regulating functions. Edith Jacobson (1954, 1964) reports psychoanalytic case studies of persons who, because of less than optimal developmental experience during the preoedipal period, have not developed their personalities in ways so that either of Freud's major thought paradigms or approaches to studying neurosis can be consistently and fruitfully employed. That is, neither Freud's doctrine of the repressed unconscious nor his tripartite division of psychic agency provides useful ways of considering these people's (preoedipal, preneurotic) psychic functioning or of analyzing (breaking down) whatever inhibiting or limiting psychic formations may have evolved to influence or dominate their personalities.

Jacobson (1964) introduces the third and presently prevailing thought paradigm, which fosters a systematic study of the ways in which a person organizes experiences of self in contrast to experiences of others. Like most paradigm shifts, retrospectively the "self and other" paradigm seems so obvious and compelling one wonders why it was not thought of earlier (Kuhn 1962). That is, it now seems perfectly self-evident that the basic subjective tasks of infancy and toddlerhood are to formulate various ideas and attitudes about "who I am and can be in relation to various others who appear and reappear in my environment. Long before I can possibly be fully cognizant of the demands of a complex and triadically organized social environment, I have necessarily learned a variety of ways of bringing what I need for personal development from others toward myself." Self and other psychological studies serve to throw light on what kinds of emotional-relatedness experience preceded and/or foreclosed the development of the Oedipus complex.

Patternings of self and other emotional relatedness developed during the preoedipal period have been spoken of as the "pre-reflective unconscious" (Stolorow and Lachman 1980), the "unreflective consciousness" (Russell 1978, 1981, 1992; Sartre 1956), "tacit knowing" (Polonyi 1969), and "the unthought known" (Bollas 1987) and have become the focus of much systematic psychoanalytic study over the past few decades. Internalized or overlearned patternings of self and other relatedness that evolve before the oedipal period are generally not the subject of conscious thought. Nor have they been systematically excluded from consciousness as have the subjects of oedipal-level repression. Recent psychoanalytic study demonstrates, however, that various representations of preoedipal self and other experience are manifest and available for systematic study and transformation within the context of the interpersonal situation of psychoanalysis. This book studies the earliest manifestations of self and other experience and demonstrates the ways through which these primary structures for experiencing interpersonal reality may be secured or framed for study, thus becoming the object of systematic psychoanalytic investigation, intervention, and transformation.

Like other major paradigm shifts, the later formulated "self and other" relatedness paradigm is capable of taking under its more encompassing canopy the basic findings that have previously emerged in the field. Oedipal neurosis as conceptualized by Freud and studied by traditional psychoanalysis is now understood as a specific instance within a much broader self and other relatedness spectrum. (For a fuller account of the historical shift to the relatedness paradigm see Hedges [1983, Chapter 1] and Hedges [1992, Chapters 2 and 3]. For a more detailed analysis of paradigm shifts in general and how this line of thought applies to psychoanalysis see Hedges [1992, Chapter 4].)

But far more than simply a neat shift in how the psychoanalytic enterprise is thought about, the self and other relatedness paradigm brings into question, by way of requiring expansion, every major consideration regarding the theory and practice of psychoanalysis that has gone before. Further, it makes possible a move from nineteenth century investigative modes prevalent in psychoanalysis to approaches that are more in keeping with those of contemporary thinkers who have been influenced by relativity and the astounding findings of quantum physics and chaos studies. [For a detailed analysis of how self and other psychology dovetails with modern scientific thought see Hedges (1992, Chapters 4, 5, and 6).] With the emergence of the relatedness paradigm psychoanalysis comes of age. But its offspring—the many schools of psychotherapy, a large movement of groups, family systems studies, counseling techniques, and insights into couples dynamics—all lag seriously behind.

This book seeks to illuminate one of the many areas of personality study opened up by the emergence of the new relatedness paradigm. This study brings psychoanalytic thinking full circle back to Freud's original 1895 notions about the earliest organizational strivings of psyche. It elaborates from a standpoint within self and other psychology Freud's formulation that the earliest tasks of psyche are to organize safe and efficient channels from the instinctual core of the organism to available environmental supplies and to develop the capacity to monitor the quality of these channels—to close off unproductive or painful channels and to open fruitful and pleasurable ones for further creative development.

This book develops the thesis that at the root of all personality functioning lie closed-off enclaves of potential creativity and pockets of organizing experience that continue to limit each person's ability to cultivate and endure interpersonal connectedness and to function freely with maximal creativity in the world. The psychoanalytic research to be reported here holds forth the prospect that whether organizational experience comprises only small pockets of an individual's overall personality or whether the personality is heavily influenced or dominated by organizing experience, the meaningful identification, elaboration, and transformation of this experience are possible.

The technique advocated here for working the organizing experience aims at creating a sense of safety and comfort within the psychoanalytic situation so that the desire for interpersonal relatedness can be coaxed, stimulated, and then systematically studied. By studying the ebb and flow of moments of potential affective connectedness between analytic speaker and listener, it is possible to bring into bold relief and to secure for analysis (breakdown) those inhibitory structures developed in the earliest months of psychic life that have served to block off organizing channels and to limit the ways in which a person is free to reach out and to achieve comfort and growth in communicating emotionally with other human beings.

3

Listening to Relatedness Experience

NEW FREEDOMS AFFORDED BY THE SHIFT TO THE THIRD PARADIGM

The innovative approaches to understanding the human experience of private madness being put forward in this book have been made possible by a major shift in psychoanalytic thought. Freud's seminal contribution was the discovery of a way for humans to obtain a fresh view of themselves, a view based on more than mere conscious reflection. Although throughout his career Freud sought to tie his studies to biology and to the ways in which drives very early in life place a demand on the human psyche for work, it was Freud's lot to investigate the journey of individuals toward full assimilation of the culturally symbolic. It was the hold that the symbolic has on psyche that determined, in his own self-analysis and in the classical analytic work that followed, the structure and the neurotic symptoms of the Oedipus complex that he was destined to explore. To be sure, Freud and many others attempted to generalize his heuristic concepts to psychic structuring, which was predominantly preoedipal (cf. Freud's cases of Schreber [1911] and the Wolf Man [1918]), but without equivalent psychoanalytic result. It has only been with the advent of the thought shift to the relatedness dimension that preoedipal structuring has been effectively and transformationally studied psychoanalytically. What are some of the new freedoms being enjoyed within the thought shift to the relatedness paradigm?

From Healing to Consciousness Raising

Consciousness raising or consciousness expansion becomes the aim of work with preoedipal structures rather than the medically based notion of curing the symptom that served Freud well in the study of focal neurotic symptoms. Preoedipal patterns of self and other relatedness do not produce clear symbolic psychological symptoms subject to being conceptualized in a cure motif as in neurosis, but rather affect the way a person experiences and relates to his or her immediate interpersonal environment and to the world at large. What the analytic practitioner must now grasp are the various kinds of self and other experience that are possible and expectable at various levels of psychic integration. The analytic listener can now be prepared to listen (in the broadest sense) and to interact with the speaker's experience as it is actually brought to and lived out within the context of the analytic situation.

Because preoedipal experiences are, by definition, those that precede the full assimilation by the body self of the complex symbolic ordering of human culture, the psychological structures to be analyzed are not integrated into the verbal-symbolic system and are not subject to the "talking cure" as are oedipal (neurotic) experiences. Affective attunement or resonance (for studying narcissistic transferences), affective interaction or reverberation (for studying symbiotic transferences), and affective contact with somatic experience (for studying organizing transferences) will be the expectable modes of psychoanalytic action for the three main preoedipal modes identified to date

(Hedges 1983). It is consciousness raising (sometimes referred to as personality growth or expansion of consciousness) rather than curing (neurotic) symptoms that governs the psychoanalytic way of working with preoedipal relatedness structures.

From Scientific Objectivity to Systematic Subjectivity

Systematic subjectivity replaces in the psychoanalytic study of preoedipal relatedness patterns Freud's attitude of scientific objectivity, which served well for studying the nature of the symbolically determined neurotic symptoms. With a psychological symptom that results from symbolic repression, the analytic listener is best advised to sit back and remain neutral and objective since, given time and a receptive ambiance, it is the analytic speaker who produces all of the symbolic verbalizations required for the analysis of the neurotic symptom. However, the attempt to understand preoedipal relatedness patterns requires that those relatedness patterns be allowed to actually develop in some form within the analytic situation. Thus the contributions of the analyst to the interactions and to the mutually evolving understanding of those interactions require greater subjective involvement on the part of the analyst and come to center stage for psychoanalytic investigation.

From Historical Truth to Narrative Truth

To understand how a symbolically determined psychological (neurotic) symptom is formed, the analytic listener must be prepared to encourage the speaker to search his or her memory for the symbolic origin of the symptom in the past. Because much of the instinctual life of the genetic past has undergone repression, the analyst who wishes to grasp something of the historical truth of the neurotic symptom begins the painstaking task of reconstruction through inference from how the neurotic transference and resistance emerge symbolically in the analytic relationship. However, with preoedipal self and other relatedness patterns there is no historical moment in which symbolic

repression laid the groundwork for the emergence of symbolic symptoms and therefore no analogous urgency to search for historical
truth. Rather, the self and other relatedness patterns retained from
the past that are preventing the speaker from developing more differentiated and flexible modes of experiencing life and of interacting with
others, operate fully in the relational present and can be brought to
light through narrational and narrative interactional means. That is,
the truths required for consciousness raising are living truths that
slowly unfold in the actual here-and-now interaction between analytic
speaker and listener.

If the listener is aware of the general kinds of possible and
expectable self and other relatedness modes and how to secure
through the affective interaction of the analytic situation these self
and other patternings, he or she is in a position to encourage and to
collaborate in the construction of an ongoing and ever-expanding web
of narrational truth that is replete with stories, images, pictures,
metaphors, archetypes, and somatic experience (Schafer 1976, Spence
1982). It is the ongoing collaborative construction of narration about
how we relate to one another that serves to bring what Bollas (1987)
has termed the "unthought known" onto the plane of conscious
reflection. The very meaning of "consciousness" is derived from ancient Greek—"knowing together." The most fundamental of human
truths, of knowing together, have always been secured through narrational means—stories, images, metaphors, archetypes, and body
sensations. The exact details of one's historical past are only required
if one is seeking to establish the origin of a specific, symbolically
determined repression that is producing a neurotic symptom.

From Relativity to Quantum Realities

Contemporary thinkers from the fields of physics, chemistry,
biology, and, now with the advent of chaos theory, from numerous
other fields of systematic investigation as well have long since transcended the model of scientific investigation initiated by Newton. The
universe is no longer viewed as a giant clockwork set in motion by the

hand of God, which it is our task to study so that we may know how things work. The classical laws of physics have been subsumed as specific instances of broader principles of relativity. The astounding discoveries of quantum physics and chaos theory now leave no room for doubt that the universe is not at all what we have always imagined it to be. We now know that our knowledge of the nature of things is not only finite but, in principle, forever incomplete. Responsible investigators no longer seek to know the true nature of things but rather seek to define positions or stances from which to make observations of things that interest them for various reasons.

In psychoanalysis, if we are to remain on respectable investigative ground, our search for the true nature of psyche must likewise be relinquished. Was it not, after all, Freud who shattered the Cartesian certainty shibboleth, "I think, therefore I am," with his dictum that it is in our moments of greatest uncertainty—dreams, slips, jokes, symptoms and sexuality—that psyche makes her presence felt ever so fleetingly? If the study of neurosis comforts itself with a search for historical certainty, this same certainty need not be claimed for the study of preneurotic relatedness structures, which require fresh metaphors, stories, and images for defining and understanding every new human relationship we engage in! To make room in psychoanalysis for an infinity of possibilities, we can stop pretending that we now know or can ever know the true nature of psyche, and find ways of defining stances, positions, points of view, and listening perspectives from which to receive and interact with an ever-expanding and evanescent human psyche.

From Mythical Beasts to Listening Perspectives

The notion of scientific objectivity that emerged from the seventeenth century was one that sought to define and categorize everything in God's creation. If something could be defined, then, in principle, it had qualities that would lend themselves to classification and systematic study. In psychiatry this trend has led to the definition of an endless array of mythical beasts that have been carefully described and classified in that Noah's Ark of mythical beasts, the *DSM-IV*! If the attitude of classifying has served well in the psychoanalytic study of neurosis, it may be because there are specific, culturally identifiable ways in which people seem to assimilate body and soul into the symbolic system. These neurotic styles of dealing with the problem of the symbol can certainly be associated with different types of symbolic symptoms, and may well be useful in the study of neurosis.

The same matching of personality styles with descriptive symptomatology has been tirelessly attempted in the study of preneurotic self and other relatedness patterns with less convincing results. Perhaps this is because of the infinite variety in the ways people experience their evolving selves in relation to others and the relative paucity or absence of reliably present focal symptoms across individuals. Further, the proliferation of definitions of preoedipal beasts seems to offer little that is consistent or compelling in terms of systematic transformational possibilities.[1] Lastly, the identification and classification of the beasts of the universe so that we might once and for all know their true nature was an endeavor begun in the seventeenth century and abandoned by responsible investigators in other fields by the mid–twentieth century as a major avenue to reliable knowledge in

---

[1] Some people are disturbed by my dim view of descriptive diagnosis currently in vogue. While descriptive diagnosis may serve many statistical, administrative, and sociopolitical-economic purposes, even the new *DSM-IV* is several decades behind our knowledge. Further, its definitions arise from legal, political, and economic compromise so it cannot possibly be considered a responsible way to think about psychotherapy or psychoanalysis. I am reminded of the place that particle physics moved to as the politics of discovery reached its zenith. Particles of all sorts were predicted based upon working equations that held paradoxes. Each time an equation could be shown to "predict" a particle, investigators would set up experiments that "observed" the existence of the particle. Physicists were left with the uneasy situation of noting that if you could think up the existence of a particle then you could find some means of observing it. The mythical beasts of descriptive psychiatry seem to have originated from the same ground as the mythical beasts of physics, rich and creative human imagination. The fact that one has learned to think according to a certain set of assumptions and biases and that one has come to appreciate that they make a certain kind of sense doesn't at all mean that this way of considering the world is efficient or even appropriate. It means that a person is continuing to uncritically accept a system of assumptions and biases much like one accepts religious principles, on faith or because of a tradition.

an age of relativity, quantum leaps, and chaotic happenings. The contemporary scientific attitude is to define clearly and systematically our subjective frames for observation and what we note from these vantage points—not the true nature of the beasts themselves. In psychoanalysis and psychotherapy this means our search for mythical (diagnostic) beasts must be relinquished in favor of developing viable frames of reference—listening perspectives—from which to listen and from which to be responsive to the relatedness experiences that people bring to our consulting rooms.

From Frame Technique to Variable Responsiveness

The final consideration regarding the new freedoms implicit in the self and other relatedness paradigm is an expansion from the classical psychoanalytic notion of "frame" technique. In the study of neurotic constellations that are governed by symbolically determined symptoms, the features of neurotic transference have been thought to be optimally securable for analysis within an atmosphere character-ized by analytic neutrality, abstinence, privacy, relational continuity, regressive relaxation, rigidly defined boundary maintenance, evenly hovering attention, and an attitude of general objectivity with the analyst serving as an opaque mirror for the elements of a symbolically based transference to be projected upon.

In studying the preneurotic, preoedipal self and other relatedness patternings, a fixed frame approach with arbitrary, *a priori* definitions of boundaries and relationships, is inimical to establishing within the analytic relationship the relatedness dimensions required for this kind of analytic work. That is, preoedipal relatedness patterns—unlike those governed by symbols, which when properly deciphered permit a return of what was repressed during the oedipal period—can only be secured for analysis when they are actually lived out or experienced by two in some manner in the here-and-now analytic relatedness situa-tion. The notion of the well doctor with stable personal boundaries and the capacity for consistent, reliable, and appropriate relationships in contrast to the sick, merged, unstable patient who cannot relate sensibly is no longer a viable investigative attitude. [For a detailed consideration of these aspects, which are involved in the paradigm shift and the many contributors to the shift, see Hedges (1992, Chapters 4 and 5).]

Because there is infinite variety in preoedipal relatedness pattern-ings, how might a psychoanalytic investigator sensibly go about developing perspectives from which to discern the kinds of interper-sonal relatedness being brought by each individual for analysis? And what modes of interaction and interpretation might be required for the analysis of patterns that are not now, and never were, embedded in the cultural system of words and symbols?

The listening perspectives that have emerged in the field during the past few decades and that I have defined along an axis of self and other relatedness (Hedges 1983) might be compared with a compass on a ship. The compass does not tell the captain where to go. Nor does it map out how to get there. The compass merely serves to orient the mind of the captain to the general terrain he or she is traversing. How he is to navigate, what adventures are to befall him, and how he makes note of them in the ship's log and in his own memory are all choices to be made—choices that can be more effectively made with a compass in hand. How might listening perspectives be defined to be maximally helpful in raising consciousness, developing systematic subjectivity, creating narrational truths, living in a quantum universe, avoiding limiting mythical beasts, and in transcending the limitations of a fixed frame?

LISTENING PERSPECTIVES: MODES OF PSYCHOANALYTIC INQUIRY

In a relativistic universe there is no limit to the number or variety of perspectives one might define in order to make observations from different vantage points with different purposes in mind. On a prac-tical basis one selects certain perspectives based upon what is of interest to the investigator. Current thinking in psychoanalysis sug-gests that as an infant becomes initiated into human society, what is of importance to that infant is how it comes to experience, distinguish, and develop his or her own sense of personal agency in relation to other forms of agency. The question this book considers is, Along what path might a developing human infant be thought to differentiate his or her own volitional capabilities from the volitional aspects assigned to others who eventually come to be experienced as separate centers of initiative?

A somewhat arbitrary schema has evolved in the collective thinking of psychoanalysts, which borrows metaphors from observations in child development in order to abstract an ideal developmental line of self and other relatedness experience. It is along this ideal axis that various defined points can be established from which to gather observations and from which to better understand each idiosyncratically developing human being. The four listening perspectives to be summarized here have emerged from the psychoanalytic literature, possess a certain inherent logic, are reasonably distinguishable from one another, are few enough in number so as to be readily kept in mind at all times by an analytic listener, and have the power to generate an infinity of questions for research. Table 3-1 summarizes the salient features of each of the four perspectives.

I. The Personality in Organization:
The Search for Relatedness

This listening perspective is used when the relatedness issues to be studied fall within the traditional diagnostic categories of functional psychosis, schizoid personality, and autism, as well as within the more recently spoken of categories of asymptomatic psychosis, organizing personality, and the more regressed aspects of multiple personality, as well as some forms of eating disorders and addictions. The source of many flashback-style recovered memories and the psychological foundations of experiences of alien abductions and other science fiction and unreal kinds of experience seem to come from this level of psychic experience. The developmental metaphor upon which this perspective is defined is that of an infant in utero or in the first few

TABLE 3-1
Listening Perspectives: Modes of Psychoanalytic Inquiry

I. **The personality in organization: the search for relatedness**
   Traditional diagnosis: Organizing personality/ psychosis
   Developmental metaphor: + or − 4 months−focused attention vs. affective withdrawal
   Affects: Connecting or disconnecting, but often appearing inconsistent or chaotic to an observer
   Transference: Connection vs. rupture, discontinuity, and disjunction
   Resistance: To connections and consistent bonds
   Listening mode: Connecting, intercepting, linking
   Therapeutic modality: Focus on withdrawal/destruction of links− connecting as a result of mutual focus
   Countertransference: Fear of intensity of psychotic anxieties in both self and other

II. **Symbiosis and separation: mutually dependent relatedness**
   Traditional diagnosis: Borderline personality organization
   Developmental metaphor: 4−24 months−symbiosis and separation
   Affects: Split "all good" and "all bad"−ambitendent
   Transference: Replicated dyadic interactions
   Resistance: To assume responsibility for differentiating
   Listening mode: Interaction in replicated scenarios
   Therapeutic modality: Replication and differentiation−reverberation
   Countertransference: Reciprocal mother and infant positions−a "royal road to understanding merger relatedness"

III. **The emergent self: unilaterally dependent relatedness**
   Traditional diagnosis: Narcissistic personality organization
   Developmental metaphor: 24−36 months−rapprochement
   Affects: Dependent upon empathy of selfother
   Transference: Selfothers (grandiose, twin, idealized)
   Resistance: Shame and embarrassment over narcissism
   Listening mode: Engagement with ebb and flow of self experiences
   Therapeutic modality: Empathic attunement to self experiences−resonance
   Countertransference: Boredom, drowsiness, irritation−facilitating

IV. **Self and other constancy: independent relatedness**
   Traditional diagnosis: Neurotic personality organization
   Developmental metaphor: 36 + months−(Oedipal) triangulation
   Affects: Ambivalence; overstimulating affects repressed
   Transference: Constant, ambivalently held self and others
   Resistance: To the return of the repressed
   Listening mode: Evenly hovering attention/free association
   Therapeutic modality: Verbal−symbolic interpretation−reflection
   Countertransference: Overstimulating−an impediment

This table is revised from Hedges 1992.

months of life (plus or minus four months from birth) who is alternatingly focusing attention on reaching into the environment for the purpose of extracting nutrients and information, and then lapsing into apparent affective withdrawal, presumably for rest or for internal-processing time. The inborn affect potentials provide a primary mode for communication as the infant appears to reach out for contact with others and then to pull back into a more mediative state.

When these issues appear in the psychoanalytic situation as transference and resistance manifestations, they can be tracked by the observer in terms of *the search for* some sort of affective connection and *the movement away* from that connection, usually seen as a frightened retreat or withdrawal from interpersonal relatedness. When resistance to an ongoing psychoanalytic investigation is observed, the motive seems to be to avoid achieving or maintaining affective connections, presumably because in that person's developmental history affective links and interpersonal connections were in some way traumatic— that is, over- or understimulating or disorienting.

The mode for listening to organizing issues begins with fostering or coaxing the person toward affective personal connection and interaction so that the disconnecting transference can emerge for study. The therapeutic or interpretive modality is to find concrete ways of focusing on the moments of withdrawal, of blocked, broken, or ruptured connection, by finding acceptable concrete (and usually physical) ways to encourage maintenance of the here-and-now affective connection.

Expectable countertransference reactions to working the organizing experience include (1) an attempt to deny the speaker's fundamental humanity by believing that he or she is untransformable, (2) a fear of inviting primitive sexual and aggressive energies into the analytic situation, (3) the stimulation of the listener's own primitive organizing experiences as a result of the speaker's persistent failure to respond to the listener's personal affective cuing, and (4) in advanced stages of the analytic relationship the listener empathically withdrawing at moments when the speaker seems threatened with a primordial terror of connecting.

This is the listening perspective to be elaborated in this book. The other three perspectives for studying more differentiated self and other patternings are summarized in order to contrast their analytic focus and technique.

II. Symbiosis and Separation:
Mutually Dependent Relatedness

This listening perspective is used when the issues being brought for analytic understanding appear to stem from the symbiotic or characterological level of human development (at ages 4 to 24 months). The traditional diagnostic categories include borderline personality organization, as well as most character disorders, addictions, perversions, and many eating disorders, which all generally contain mutually dependent relatedness issues. The affective life of the individual is often perceived by the observer to be "split" or "ambitendent," meaning that from situation to situation there is a tendency to view self and/or other as "all good" or "all bad" at the moment, based upon whether or not that other person is presently conforming to the mutually dependent or mutually engaged relatedness demand.

The replicated transference in the psychoanalytic situation manifests itself in replicated "scenarios" (Hedges 1983) or replicated affective engagements, which are defined and presumed to be derived from the symbiotic, character, or "mommy and me" level of self and other relatedness development. These replicated emotional engagements or scenarios may appear in a passive form (with the analytic speaker in the infant position vis-à-vis the listener experienced as parent) or in an active mastery form (with the speaker taking the parental role vis-à-vis the listener as infant). Resistance is to the full emotional experiencing of the replicated dyadic interaction derived from the symbiotic level engagement with familial figures. Resistance to transformation often takes on the subjective sense of "I can't do it by myself."[2]

The therapeutic or interpretive modality is for the analytic

---

[2]This insight into the nature of resistance to the establishment and relinquishing of the symbiotic transference experience I have credited to Mariah Hood (Hedges 1984).

listener to permit, as fully as his or her personal and professional boundaries are able under the circumstances, an affective replication of the symbiotic engagement in both passive and active forms. Once the replication is alive within the analytic relationship, the listener and the speaker can discern its qualities and, within the context of the interaction, the analytic listener is then in a position to stand against the scenario or to refuse to engage further in it. Likewise the analytic speaker, having once seen and experienced in the context of the analytic relationship his or her internal demands for a certain quality, style, or mode of dyadic relatedness, is in a position to relinquish or to renounce exclusive or excessive reliance on overlearned symbiotic modes of mutually dependent relatedness in favor of more diverse and flexible self and other relatedness possibilities.

In the countertransference the listener feels thrust into both parent and infant roles vis-à-vis the analytic speaker. The affective qualities of both roles are preverbal and have heretofore only existed in the self and other affective and interactive demands of the speaker's nonconscious life—Bollas's (1987) "unthought known." It is the analytic listener who must initiate speaking and therefore interpreting the nature of these passively experienced interactive roles known through the countertransference (or projective identification or reciprocal scripting) so that they can become known to the speaker and more accurately elaborated by him or her in full consciousness.

III. The Emergent Self: Unilaterally Dependent Relatedness

This listening perspective has been devised for listening to self and other relatedness issues that a growing child (prototypically aged 24 to 36 months) experiences as he or she ventures away from the parent out into the world on various exploits and adventures, and then quickly rushes back to feel affirmed, confirmed, or inspired by parental support. These issues are paramount in the traditional diagnostic categories of (secondary) narcissism and disorders of the self in which analytic speakers are seen as needing confirmation of various aspects of self for the purposes of developing more reliable self cohesion and enhancing self-esteem. The affective life and development of concomitant self skills and talents are seen to be dependent upon the admiration, confirmation, and inspiration provided by the empathic support of the selfother (the "selfobject" as Heinz Kohut [1971, 1977, 1984] has termed this unilaterally dependent partner, or the "selfobject function," which the partner performs.

There exists at this developmental level a basic awareness of the separateness of self and other; but the other is regularly depended upon or used for the purposes of confirming the self, of providing a sense of cohesive, coherent self functioning, which the person has not yet learned to reliably attain on his or her own. Transference, as specified by Kohut, may include (1) a demand for the sense of the grandiose self to be mirrored, (2) an insistence that the other be experienced as a psychological twin, and (3) an urgency to experience the selfother as an ideal other whose inspiration is required for self-esteem and self cohesiveness. Resistance, according to Kohut, is to experiencing culturally induced shame and humiliation over the (natural, developmentally based) narcissistic wish to be the subjective center of the universe.

The listening mode is attending to the ebb and flow of empathic attunement as the sense of self feels more and then less consolidated by the empathic support of the analytic listener. The therapeutic modality consists of the listener tuning in to the ebb and flow of self-esteem as related to a greater or lesser sense of self cohesion. When self-esteem falters, the listener engages the speaker in a search for how the listener's empathic attunement failed so that self experience took a dive. Over time, the speaker learns the function of empathy from experiencing it from the listener and begins to be more tuned into, more empathic with, his or her own self needs, so that more differentiated and flexible self and other relatedness modes are permitted to evolve. Kohut (1971) specifies drowsiness, inattentiveness, boredom, and irritation as expectable countertransference responses on the part of an analytic listener who is required, often for protracted periods of time, to set aside his or her self needs in deference to performing a confirming, affirming, or inspiring function for the analytic speaker.

IV. Self and Other Constancy:
Independent Relatedness

This is the listening perspective devised by Freud for listening to the internal conflicts that accompany the formation of neurotic symptoms. Neurotic personality organization is assumed to evolve in the (3- to 7-year-old) child who has been able to differentiate him- or herself more or less adequately from the primary symbiotic love relationship and who has had reasonably satisfactory experiences of self consolidation. He or she is then ready to experience the subjective joys and dangers of independence within fully triangular relationships and society at large. The affects are more clearly ambivalent rather than the earlier split or ambitendent. That is, both loving and hating attitudes can be held simultaneously (whether consciously or repressed) rather than alternating.

The transference to the analytic listener consists of a highly condensed, displaced, and symbolized series of cognitive and affectively held attitudes from relationships with ambivalently held familial figures established during the oedipal period. Those intensely instinctual cognitive and affective attitudes, which were prohibited by internalized versions of social pressure, have undergone repression. The resistance is to the return to consciousness of those dreaded, forbidden, repressed transferential attitudes. The reflective listening mode is one of neutrality with an attitude of evenly hovering attention that is equidistant from the internalized personal agencies of id, ego, and superego conflicts being presented for analysis. The therapeutic modality is verbal-symbolic interpretation—as it was originally through the condensing and displacing power of word and symbol that the oedipal child accomplished his or her repressions. Countertransference reactions in this listening perspective are generally considered a distraction or an impediment to the listener's task of assisting in the gradual unfolding of the speaker's symbolically repressed life.

SUMMARY

This chapter has condensed drastically a plethora of considerations regarding the newly found freedoms and flexibility that psycho analysts now enjoy as a result of the paradigm shift for considering the self and other relatedness dimension. The sketchy remarks about the four listening perspectives serve to provide an overall context for study of the organizing experience. The reader interested in pursuing various aspects of the overall context is encouraged not only to consult two of Hedges's texts (1983, 1992), but on the basis of references there, to branch out to the numerous and rich primary resources authored by many contributors from psychoanalysis and other fields of study.

PART II

THE ORGANIZING EXPERIENCE AND TRANSFERENCE PSYCHOSIS

4

Listening to
Organizing Experience

THE STORYLINE:
MOTHER AND CHILD CONNECTING

Organizing experience is a concept developed in order to consider the most rudimentary of human activities. A human zygote may be considered as organizing channels to the intrauterine environment that allow for incoming nutrients and outgoing wastes. A human infant organizes idiosyncratic physical as well as psychological channels to the human environment that allow for incoming stimuli and outgoing responses. The exact ways in which a fetus or neonate organizes his or her connections to the physical and psychological environment depend, of course, upon his or her own unique, inborn nature as well as the particular and peculiar features available in the nurturing environment. The personal modes, patterns, and styles that an infant develops in the process of organizing its earliest experiences in relation to its environment are conceptualized as forming the foundations of its subsequent psychic life. That is, the individual's earliest exchanges with the human psychological environment are thought to form basic personality or character templates that all subsequent experience tends to be built upon, molded around, or filtered through. Psychological studies consider the cognitive, affective, and conative aspects of each person's unique ways of orienting and organizing personal connections to the human environment.

Earliest organizing experiences may be constructed in an open and flexible manner so that the person can freely adapt his or her rudimentary orienting responses to a wide range of subsequent environmental circumstances. Or a person's basic ways of organizing experience may become constructed so as to limit systematically, to close off, or to warp his or her fundamental ways of orienting to stimuli and producing responses.

The personalities of the infant's caregivers necessarily influence how each infant organizes psychological connections to them. How then, might we consider the nature of that influence? If we were to imagine a relatively unformed infant to be born with a thousand invisible tendrils for establishing channels to the human environment, then we might also imagine any average expectable parent to have evolved a highly individualized or differentiated personality structure with, say, three hundred ways of being potentially available to that infant. Considered in this way, even in an environment rich with human potential there are bound to be many ways in which an infant will seek and yearn for connections that cannot possibly be made. The infant's first psychological task is to map out the personality contours (conscious and unconscious) of its caregivers. Those ways of expressing or reaching out that work to bring satisfying and stimulating environmental response will thereby be reinforced and tend to persist, while those tendrils of infant psyche that have not been met or have been actively thwarted tend to wither or to become withdrawn from environmental involvement.

Following this metaphoric way of thinking about an infant's formative connecting experiences, first with mother's body and later with her mind and the minds of other available mothering persons, we can conclude that all humans possess potentials for spontaneous and creative relating to others that have been systematically limited, closed off, or warped in fundamental ways. All caregivers have personalities that are more or less responsive to various kinds of expressions from each individual infant in different ways and at different times. So that not only are genetic and constitutional variables of the infant involved in influencing the ways in which an infant orients to the environment, but the personality responsiveness (conscious and unconscious) of each of its caregivers also determines the ways in which it is possible to connect to the environment for nurturance, comfort, safety, and stimulation. Thus all people's relatedness potentials are systematically sculpted and limited in highly individualized ways. Universally experienced areas of individually developed constricted personality functioning are conceptualized here as "enclaves" or "pockets" of organizing experience that are accompanied by inevitable psychic and somatic consequences.

The metaphor of enclaves or pockets of blocked, limited, and/or undeveloped areas of organizing experience as universal implies that in the average expectable development infants are able to create enough sustaining channels to nurturing others so that a psychological bonding experience can occur, even though certain areas of potential engagement with others have remained untapped, unstimulated, and/or undeveloped.

Professional listening experiences have demonstrated that there is no way to know in advance exactly what a person's undeveloped potential might look like in daily living or in psychoanalysis because it is, after all, highly idiosyncratic and, as potential, remains largely or wholly dormant, undeveloped, or unexpressed. But a century of psychiatric study has produced a wealth of descriptive data regarding what various types of organizing (psychotic) experience look like when they become active or pervasive features in an individual's personality functioning or when some life trauma brings them into focus, as in wartime psychoses or sensory deprivation experiments.

CONTACT EXPERIENCES AS PREREQUISITE TO SYMBIOTIC BONDING

The key word that orients our thinking about the organizing experience is "contact." The mutual cuing processes that characterize human bonding experience give rise to internalized symbiotic relatedness patterns and expectations. Thus the establishment of an internalized symbiotic relationship depends upon two people being able to achieve a mutual sense of personal contact or connection with one another.

Human contact differs significantly from mere physical or animal contact in that human contact is organized around complex signs and signals that are part of a much larger cultural/linguistic system handed down through the generations. A human infant is received into an environment rich with expectations and demands. A whole set of general notions about the nature of babies, their motivations and needs, as well as a set of notions about who this particular baby is and what he or she is to become necessarily color the welcome mat. There is not only a general set of cultural and subcultural verbal-symbolic interpretive possibilities, but each caregiver comes to the infant with a different ability and willingness to comprehend, assimilate, and put into action various child-rearing practices.

There are vast differences in the ways in which mothers approach, handle, and establish communication with each of their babies. Each mother relates to each of her babies in her own way. She brings to her relatedness with the child a certain creative intelligence about the way human beings are, might be, can be, and ought to be. This "relatedness intelligence" that each mother brings into the relationship with her baby no doubt stems partly from her own upbringing experiences, partly from prior experience in relating to infants, and partly from many other sources widely called "maternal instinct." Of crucial importance is the mother's personal system of emotional and cognitive responsiveness gleaned from a lifetime of relating experiences and how her responsiveness system is functioning in the current context of her life and her infant.

The more research that is directed toward understanding human embryos and neonates, the more astoundingly revealed are the immense possibilities and capacities with which the human neonate is endowed to greet the world. By now it is clear that even with the finest "good enough" mother who brings rich relatedness intelligence and responsiveness to her interactions with her baby, the baby's potentials for creative counterresponse far outstrip what any particular mother is prepared for or would know how to interact with, given her own finite experiences.

The emotional availability of the mother and other immediate

family members and auxiliary caregivers in these first few months of
life is so crucial in determining the direction of organizing experience
that serious thought needs to be given as to how maximum availability
of parents can be provided, given the other demands of family,
personal, and work life. The current trend toward "family leave" from
the workplace during these early months reflects our growing knowledge of how critical parent availability is during this period of life. But
the amount of work leave commonly allowed seems sadly insufficient.
Given the parents' personalities, their experience in empathic connections, their other prior commitments, and the availability of auxiliary
resources, we may still surmise that many of baby's early extensions of
potential expressiveness will go essentially unmet. The crucial question for our study is, What happens to unmet potentials? What
happens to baby when an extension that might potentially give rise to
individual creative expression is not noticed, not understood, or not
greeted enthusiastically or empathically? No parent can be one hundred percent responsive even if present. But if absent, vital opportunity for the infant to develop potentials is lost. So how do we think
about what happens when baby's extensions of potentials are systematically not noticed, not attended to, ignored, discouraged, or even
negatively responded to?[1]

What exactly is baby doing with all these looks, noises, movements, and expressions? Parents and others certainly have a variety of
ways of projecting into baby a wide array of adultopomorphic understandings and motivations, most of which are such sophisticated
notions that they cannot possibly be true. And although the baby
may have few ways of contradicting high-level interpretive projections, it has a robust sense of what is right and wrong for "me" right
now! A fetus or a neonate generally arrives in this world well endowed, animated, active, and assertive in terms of activities aimed
toward personal survival and growth, and these activities gradually
lead toward the establishment of reliable channels of nurturance and
connection with available sources of supply, comfort, safety, and
stimulation in the environment according to what is available and the
style with which responsiveness is offered and/or refused.

---

[1]A comprehensive study of these essential potentials has recently been completed by Sandra Jorgensen (1993).

A LISTENING PERSPECTIVE FOR
ORGANIZING EXPERIENCE

This book considers in the broadest strokes the various human experiences that might conceivably arise from the earliest stirrings of psyche to the point that an infant has established reliable psychological channels, which are requisite for the establishment of the mutual cuing process that gives rise to the intrapsychic experience of symbiosis. The goal is the formation of a perspective from which to listen (in the broadest sense) to each person's fundamental ways of orienting to the environment, and to permit systematic psychoanalytically informed study of the ways in which each person has closed off, limited, or warped private experience so that it remains unconnected to the human world. Every human being passes through such primary learning experiences. Imprinted on each of us is a series of overlearned modes for seeking and establishing physical and psychological safety, comfort, and stimulation wherever we go. Each of us is alert to and avoidant of dangers in our own way. When we enter a new place, join a new group of people, or begin a new relationship, our fundamental orienting modes are operative, although perhaps not readily visible due to a lifetime of superimposed learning experience.

What listening perspective can be developed to aid us in understanding the ways in which we continue to live — according to the ways we first learned to orient and to organize our experiences with the environment? What kinds of listening dimensions can be developed to help us define and then to analyze (break down for understanding) the enduring structures once built to wall out or systematically limit aspects of ourselves from spontaneous, creative, and rewarding contact with others?

The universality of the organizing experience thus acknowledged, new questions arise. The most obvious question revolves around what is really happening somewhere inside baby's mind. But this line of questioning must be relinquished not only because babies cannot tell us everything they know but also because our new thought paradigm no longer permits us to ask questions about the true or objective nature of things. Infant researchers are indeed discovering ways to ask babies interesting questions and are getting fascinating answers; but we can never get inside baby's head. Psychoanalytic researchers studying children and adults may also wish to know "how it really was way back then." But our new thought paradigm calls on us to give up the search for historical truths in analysis in favor of continuing to generate rich, overlapping, and perhaps at times even contradictory narratives that have a subjective, heuristic, and hermeneutic ring of usable truth that has been brought forward in the analytic relationship as a series of transference and resistance memories.

Resisting the strong urge to speak about the true nature of organizing experience in a positivistic way, we can, however, develop the "mother and child connecting" metaphor for the purposes of defining and elaborating a series of possible issues that may arise in the course of listening (with all our senses) and responding to organizing experiences articulated in word and deed by people every day. Part III of this book leads us on the path to organizing experiences so that we can imagine what kinds of issues are likely to arise in the psychoanalytic experience. But several more questions have to be addressed before embarking on that path.

WHY MIGHT AN INFANT FAIL TO ORGANIZE?

I have a very simple response: because he or she cannot find Mother. "If I cannot find Mother, I cannot psychologically organize myself, at least not in a reasonable or healthy way. I may organize a world devoid of humans, a world of imaginary relations, a world that is not real, or a world full of fragmentation and madness."

Why can an infant not find Mother? The following is a list of types of mothers who cannot be found:[2]

1. A mother who is preoccupied. She is absorbed in her affairs, her schedule, her activities, her work, her duties, her marriage, her

---

[2]I am indebted to Dr. Joyce Hulgus for this list.

other children, her world. Mother is not emotionally available for the infant to find.

2. A mother who may have a negative response to her child. Perhaps she did not want to be pregnant. Perhaps she did not want to have a child at this time. Perhaps she did not want a baby of this sex. Whatever the negativity, there is resistance to being emotionally available for this particular infant at this particular time.

3. A mother who might have to be separated from the infant for an extended period of time, perhaps because of illness, either her own or the infant's. Hospitals and nursing personnel are becoming more aware of the importance of nurturing the mother–child connection in whatever ways possible. Parents, family, and friends are now being encouraged to become a part of the process of bridging the gap when there is a strain on the early mother–child connection for whatever reason. Perhaps holding, touching, massaging, rocking, playing with, and singing to the baby are in order. Providing the baby with an audio recording of mother's voice and heartbeat, perhaps a garment with her smell, soft and fluffy musical toys, or whatever else may engage and stimulate the child toward the eventuality of organizing his or her experience around mother's body.

4. A mother who has negative experiences in pregnancy or complicating factors. Alcohol or drugs may be involved. Genetic or constitutional features may be operating such as an Rh factor, congenital deafness, or arteriosclerosis of the umbilicus (preventing adequate nutrition). Many factors may impinge on the mother–infant prenatal connection. There are many possible toxic and deficiency effects that might cause a child to tighten and struggle or to go limp— giving up long before birth.

5. A fragmented mother who is not organized herself. This type of mother does not have what is necessary emotionally to give her infant. Or at best, she may be sporadic in her maternal effectiveness or in her own demands on her baby. There may be abusive or molestive intrusions from the mother or from others at this time.

6. A mother whose lack of knowledge may cause her to attempt to regulate the infant too early or too late, thereby creating a trauma. Winnicott (1949) suggests that a mother should be completely adaptable to an infant's needs until the infant is able to react with frustration and anger, rather than permitting the baby to collapse in the face

of a failed attempt. He posits that trauma results from breaking the sense of continuity with the line of personal existence. If the mother remains optimally responsive until the infant can express desire and anger, it will not be so traumatic when the mother moves towards regulating the infant.

7. A mother who may be in the midst of a serious emotional reaction herself at the time of the birth of her infant. For example, she may be grieving the loss of a loved one or be coping with some major life trauma or illness. Tustin (1986), in working with functionally autistic children has reported informally that many of the mothers of autistic children with whom she has worked were deeply depressed at the time of the child's birth — through no fault of their own. Often they were not even fully aware of the extent of their own depression at the time. Any serious emotional preoccupation, especially depression, tends to limit a person's potential emotional responsiveness — and a mother's response to her newborn is no exception.

8. Self-absorbed mothers who want to take the infant into their own emotional life for reasons of their own. This total absorption does not encourage the infant to reach out and create or find a stimulating and growth-producing connection for him- or herself to organize around. Such babies may not be allowed to be frustrated sufficiently so that they can learn the function of their assertiveness and anger.

9. A mother who may not be able to tolerate the psychical impact of her infant, experiencing the infant as part of herself. Tustin (1986) suggests that there seems to be a period, immediately after birth, in which the infant reacts to the outside world in terms of his or her own body and its inbuilt sensations and dispositions. This establishes the body image as a basis for personal identity. This early time is a stage when body-centered sensation objects are treated as if they were a part of his or her own body. Such experiences are thought to prepare the infant for later relationships with not-self objects, experienced as separate from the body, to which he or she has to learn to adjust. In the early phase, mother must be able to tolerate simply being a sensation-providing, comforting object, and for a while must relinquish her private claim on separate personhood.

10. A mother who has limited responsiveness to the baby's potentials for creative encounters. This type of mother may unwittingly discourage psychic organization. Babies have a myriad of ways

to engage or to encounter, and the mother is not always going to be attuned to all of those invitations and explorations. This is one reason why all of us have pockets of organizing experience. A mother who is chronically passive or unresponsive may create an infant who is either passive or who clamors endlessly to be taken care of.

11. A mother who does not provide the needed emotional supplies due to her own defenses against intolerable anxiety that arises in interpersonal connectedness. Winnicott (1971) assures us that the mother does need to be "good enough" in her ability to be present, to provide what is required, and to be optimally responsive to the infant's needs, strivings, and spontaneous gestures.

As another possible factor, some infants are simply unable to use the nurturing that is available; whether there are genetic, constitutional, or congenital disturbances, or whether the mother–infant personality match up was faulty, the child simply cannot use what is physically and emotionally available from the mother and others.

Infants organize psychological channels around the forms of responsiveness that are available in their immediate human environment. The strongest responsiveness available usually comes directly from the mother's body and personality, thus providing a special sense of continuity between intrauterine and postnatal life. Considering the mother and child connecting metaphor provides the basis for forming a psychoanalytic listening perspective for organizing experience.

5

Defining the Organizing Experience

WHY "ORGANIZING EXPERIENCE" RATHER THAN "PSYCHOSIS"

In keeping with the overall paradigm shift that psychoanalysis has experienced in the past few decades, I have sought to keep my definitions and theory within the context of forming a listening perspective for experiences that have heretofore been conceptualized as objective studies on the nature of psychosis. The hallmark of psychosis, whether when talked about in its more overt and florid forms or in its more subtle, latent, incipient, or borderline forms, is the failure of the individual at the time to appraise, to appreciate, to test out adequately realities as defined by social consensus. This means that a person is not at that moment connecting with the interpersonal human environment in such a way that a two-way channel of recip-rocal and meaningful exchange can occur. Psychiatric diagnosis has succeeded in defining a series of "symptom pictures" that categorize the varieties of psychosis along the lines of mythic themes, according to the ways in which different people fail in their ongoing appraisal or appreciation of socially defined realities.

The present approach to studying the organizing experience lets the objectively defined term *psychosis* slip quietly into the background of our thinking for several reasons. First, *madness, insanity, lunacy,* and *psychosis* are terms with significant social stigma and are laden with overtones of evil, witchcraft, devil worship, darkness, and disarrangement of bizarre and sinister proportions. The present view is that the differences between the private madness experienced by each human being and the more colorful forms portrayed in literature, drama, and psychiatry are largely a matter of style, degree, and intensity. To stigmatize people in such a crippling way for having had less fortunate growing-up experiences than ourselves seems somehow wrong and unnecessary.

The second reason for preferring the term *organizing* over *psychotic* is that the mythical beast approach to categorizing the psychoses is accomplished primarily on the basis of descriptive content or mythical themes that characterize the personality style, the so-called symptoms, and, in the present psychotherapy context, has little to do with anything that is of more than just historical importance. No viable, reliable, or widely hailed transformational treatment approach has ever been derived from such categories. Even the current successful application of chemotherapy, which has contributed so much to alleviating the suffering of many of these people, readily crosses over the fine lines of differential diagnosis so that psychiatry has become more of an art than a science in which doctors practice mixing and matching drugs in a rainbow of colors and dosages until the desired relief from symptomatic distress is obtained.

The third reason for conceptualizing in terms of *organizing* instead of *psychotic* is that clinical studies in the last decade conducted within the context of the self and other conceptual framework suggest that there are many more persons than had been previously believed, who live pervasively in organizing experiences on a daily basis and who function fundamentally outside of consensual reality to a significant degree, but who are able to mimic and adapt to those around them well and who display none of the expectable symptoms of psychosis. It has only recently been learned how to define and to isolate the basic organizing experience for purposes of psychoanalytic study.

Observer bias appears to be the main cause of this delayed recognition. A bright, well-adjusted person with a workable family life and a relatively stable-appearing social life and employment history presents a very different look than a person actively reporting hallucinations, or racing madly about in manic abandon, or slumped in a stuporous depression. In short, organizing experiences are now seen as universal in one form or another. Objectifying or projecting a universal experience into a series of mythical beasts not only serves to stigmatize people but fails to put the basic issues into a "self and other" representation framework that can enhance listening possibilities and therefore transformational possibilities. The term *organizing* as I use it denotes an early personality fixation on a way of approaching the world, a way of attempting to organize channels or connections to other people. Overt psychotic manifestations have been retained modes of blocking or limiting the establishment of reliable channels. Psychotic "symptoms" may appear to an observer as the sudden onset of an illness. But more careful observation reveals these more bizarre manifestations of self and other relatedness to be but visible forms of a life-long personality structuring that have become manifest under some developmental, social, personal, or organic crisis. (See Hedges 1983, Chapter 12, for more elaborate formulations regarding psychotic symptomatology.)

PERSONALITY IN ORGANIZATION DISTINGUISHED FROM BORDERLINE PERSONALITY ORGANIZATION

While a person's various levels of ego functioning may suggest borderline personality organization to the average diagnostician, careful scrutiny of the basic modes of relatedness may point toward various forms of presymbiotic, contact-avoiding organizing patterns. Throughout this book an attempt is made to distinguish borderline, symbiotic relatedness modes from organizing relatedness modes. The following features may obscure observation of a person's living significant organizing experience on a daily basis:

1. *Intact intelligence* with the possibility of a very high IQ and/or a rich-appearing verbal, symbolic, or creative life.
2. *Social competence* or professional expertise in delineated or limited areas of functioning (possible by a mimical self).
3. *Adaptive conformity* to social convention or requirement (Winnicott's "false self").
4. *Self-destructive patterns* that are not, in fact, motivated patterns and do not stem from organized self-directed aggression or self-abusive borderline scenarios, but represent an uninformed searching, stumbling, or blundering, or an attempt at guessing oneself through the labyrinthine social world—indications of a struggle to maintain organized behavior in an object-related world that is incompletely or faultily comprehended.
5. *Lack of psychotic symptoms:* For every person presenting indications of the kind traditionally considered psychotic, it is rapidly becoming apparent that there are many more organizing personalities who are functioning with similar self and other representational systems, but without strange or bizarre modes of relatedness (i.e., so-called psychotic symptoms.)

The central characteristic that becomes differentially distinguishing between persons whose self and other relatedness potential may be considered arrested in the early organizational process and persons who can be considered as having achieved a symbiotic or borderline personality organization relates to whether and to what extent the personality and behavior can be said to bear the earmarks of some definite pattern of early symbiotic molding. That is, the mutual cuing process of every mother–child combination is unique and, in its own idiosyncratic way, subtle. But each symbiosis takes on particular styles based on the child's ways of relating to *the (m)other's idiom of caregiving,* which are retained in the personality as highly idiosyncratic modes of relatedness that are characteristic and reliable in their appearance. As peculiar as many of the borderline patterns may appear to the observer, there is nonetheless a definite *pattern of relatedness*, a definite, purposeful expectation of what the other may, must, or cannot provide. One might say there is "method in the madness." There are indications of definable fears and reaction patterns to momentary, as well as to sustained, loss of contact (abandonment) with the persons, groups, or cultural ideals that are experienced as symbiotically sustaining. It may be helpful to think in terms of "reciprocal scripting." Each person may be said to have developed a "life script," a way of being and relating. But symbiotic level scripting also includes the kinds of emotional responses that the other must reciprocate with for the person to feel safe and/or comfortable. These interactive scenarios contain the symbiotic replicated transference.

In contrast, people living organizing experience may display characteristic *behavior* patterns, but such patterns do not represent a stylized mode of relatedness. The self and other organizing pattern is one of incessant searching, orienting maneuvers attempting to organize sensorimotor and/or cognitive-affective experience toward the human environment. But the person has left behind a trail of broken or fragmented relationships, frequently (but by no means always) marked by affective or delusional attempts to reconstitute or to provide a reliable internal patterning when the capability for interpersonal cuing is defective, failing, or lost in some way. What is lacking is a reliable style of interpersonal relatedness. What can be observed is a series of often isolated, disconnected, or even bizarre attempts to derive some sort of meaning from fragments of experience of part-selves and part-others. This searching may be obscured from view so that the person can "pass" in social situations because of his or her capacity to mimic convention and to conform to social demands (i.e., the mimical and false self formations).

THE MYTHIC THEMES OF PSYCHOSIS

Hedges (1983) has formulated that psychotic pictures result when, for whatever reason, there is a failure or deficiency in interpersonal bonding during the earliest months of life. The reasons for the failure to develop mutual cuing scenarios, which are referred to as "symbiotic," range from genetic and constitutional to environmental. Psychotic pictures that are defined as "functional" presumably result from the failure of "match" between the needs of the child and the provision of environmental caregivers.

Depending on what the actual circumstances are in a baby's life during this searching and orienting period, he or she might develop many different reactions. The more common reactions to early contact failure have by now been well studied as the themes of psychosis. The more common mythic themes in traditional psychotic diagnostic categories are the following:

Depression: A biological or psychological understimulation leading to an apparent depletion of energy and motivation and a failure of the symbiotic provision to arouse and stimulate the affects and to regulate the level of energy and activity.

Mania: A biological or psychological overstimulation of the affective life and a failure of the symbiotic provision to contain perennially unregulated, elevated affects and activity.

Schizophrenia: Inconstant and erratic overstimulation or understimulation that was, for whatever reason, experienced as traumatic, deficient, erratic, or intrusive so that no reliable, satisfying picture of the interpersonal world was possible to construct. As a result of the failure to experience ordinary and reliable relatedness possibilities, the infant attempts alternative constructions and explanations for the way the world operates. These depend on intellectualization, mimicry, compulsive behaviors, rituals, and the predefenses—fight, flight, and freeze. These maneuvers all arise in an effort to construct a viable world where the ordinary interpersonal world that might have been offered by reliable and trustworthy object relations was not experienced as available or failed in its ability to contain, to soothe, to stimulate moderately, and to modulate effectively. The thought system that develops is idiosyncratic and based upon what experiences were available.

Paranoia: Resulting from a failure of infant-to-environment contact (for whatever reason), which might be reassuring and stimulate satisfaction, feelings of safety, and basic trust. Instead, the infant experienced repeated traumatic intrusiveness felt as aggression, molest, sadism, invasion, conspiracy, or a general failure of the world to provide a stimulating, satisfying, and safe place in which to live.

Autism: A withdrawing from unsatisfying and/or disruptive stimulation in the interpersonal world into a world filled with auto-sensuous experiences, where the motive power is manipulating the sensorium when contact with the world of object relations is frightening, painful, or grossly over- or understimulating.

Schizoid: A withdrawal into extreme shyness and unrelatedness likely due to a traumatizing or depriving interpersonal world. However, the withdrawn adjustment may not be merely to escape the real world of relationships, but also represents a particular style or mode of relatedness in a symbiotic structure so that the person is not dealing with organizing issues primarily but symbiotic relatedness patterns of a specific withdrawing sort. This last point is true for each of these mythic organizing themes but perhaps most frequently encountered in the withdrawing schizoid form. That is, each of these themes may be encountered in more differentiated self and other relatedness patterns as well. What distinguishes them here as organizing is their pervasive use as ways of not relating to interpersonal stimulation, of avoiding mutually stimulating contact, and of rupturing interpersonal connectedness.

Dissociation: In the face of overwhelming stimulation the person dis-associates his or her thinking and feeling self from the immediately stimulating relatedness situation. The person may then be quite clear on what is required in the relatedness situation but be completely cut off from personal experiencing of the interaction. Milder forms of dissociation are thought to be present in sleepwalking, sleeptalking, amnesia, and fugue. The more extreme forms of dissociation, such as those observed in multiple personality, tap into organizing issues.

Quite beyond these well-known basic mythic themes thought to characterize various forms of psychosis, there are any number of other symptom constellations or character disorders that are likely to have their roots in organizing issues such as the eating disorders, addictions, perversions, and psychosomatic illnesses.

The foregoing sketches of traditionally defined themes of the organizing period tend to be developed by persons who are organically impaired or under extreme forms of stress as well as by those whose environmental opportunities were limited or skewed for some reason. The same themes might appear as ways of relating if they are taken into the relatedness habit system of symbiotic bonding, into selfother resonance modes, or into triangular (oedipal) relationships. The causal hypothesis is simply that when, for whatever reason, the structuring effects of a symbiotic relationship have failed, the person remains perpetually caught in a searching, orienting attitude, perennially tending to experience any of a variety of types of organizing themes and issues. It is not uncommon for a person to have achieved some aspects of symbiotic relating or even to have achieved some more differentiated forms of relating and yet in selected (stressful) circumstances be living enclaves or pockets of organizing themes or experience.

This last point, regarding the potential presence of many relatedness themes from different developmental eras influencing a person differentially at different times and under various circumstances, underlines one of the fundamental features of the listening perspectives approach, which is that *the modes, patterns, and styles of previous developmental experiences are to be listened for as determining or influencing all subsequent relatedness themes and integrations*. The general underlying psychoanalytic assumption is that as a result of various transactions with the environment during the course of early childhood, various physical and psychological constrictions have developed that imprison the energies and transformational possibilities of soma as well as psyche, thus profoundly affecting subsequent relatedness potentials as well as future patterns of physical health.

One implication of this way of thinking is that different listening perspectives may be useful during different phases or moments in the analytic encounter. Another implication is that the more kinds of relatedness experiences a person has at his or her disposal, the more varied and flexible is one's living. For some people this can mean extensive freedom and richness. For others who have not learned how to utilize relatedness flexibility to best advantage in their daily lives, it can mean extensive interpersonal difficulty. The presumed outcome of the analysis of automatic and unconscious childhood patterns that restrict one's movement and freedom is increased flexibility in physical and psychical functioning. A person who has worked hard in cooperation with another person to free him- or herself of overuse or nearly exclusive reliance on restrictive patternings left over from previous developmental eras is generally motivated and capable of putting the newly gained freedoms and energies to creative and beneficial use.

THE ORGANIZING EXPERIENCE
AS A LISTENING TOOL

The term *organizing* has a curious origin. *Listening Perspectives in Psychotherapy* (Hedges 1983) discusses a fresh way of conceptualizing and working with persons living borderline personality organization, a term coined by Otto Kernberg. In discussing one of Kernberg's later papers on narcissistic disorders at a conference in Los Angeles, Jerome Oremland asked Dr. Kernberg why he spoke of narcissistic disorders when he could easily follow his own lead and speak of narcissistic personality organization. In *Listening Perspectives* I took this lead and then went further by writing about neurotic personality organization.

With these three listening perspectives in place (borderline, narcissistic, and neurotic), the question became what to call the fourth listening perspective to be used for studying psychosis. It seems important to think of listening to ways people have organized their personalities rather than to speak of pathologies. It became clarifying to consider all psychotic states as various personality styles whose apparent organization was spurious. Psychotic pictures could be seen as stemming either from a lack of organization along lines of self and other relatedness or from a fundamental internalized organizing experience that served to foreclose interpersonal relatedness, so that transformations that might produce growth and differentiation of personality patterns failed to occur. What was common to all psychotic states was withdrawal from the realities of the culturally shared interpersonal world. In different ways, according to various styles, an individual's personality remained relatively unorganized in relation to others or organized to block relations with others. His or her capacity to appreciate the realities agreed upon by others was left somehow undeveloped, impaired, or warped. The more obvious warpings showed up as familiar psychotic pictures.

Those individuals with impairments in self and other relatedness capacity tended to be seen more as borderline psychotics whose personal realities were at times internally confused with or entangled with the realities of significant others in idiosyncratic ways. But those individuals who were neither frankly symptomatic nor subtly entangled with others in peculiar ways were beginning to appear in surprising numbers in clinical practice. Kernberg speaks of such people as "asymptomatic psychotics." Hedges (1983) began speaking of them as "organizing personalities" or "personalities in organization."

It soon became clear that the fundamental processes common to all psychoses could be formulated more clearly in terms derived from listening to this less-obviously psychotic group. That is, the organizing experience could be clearly defined as a listening device derived from a developmental metaphor and helpful in understanding all psychotic states. It then became clear that the organizing experience as defined for listening purposes could be thought of metaphorically as a process common to all early human development. As a listening perspective, the concept of organizing could then be seen as a useful tool for receiving and responding to all people's most primitive transference experiences. The problem of "universal madness," long addressed by poets, philosophers, and artists, could now be systematically considered in psychoanalysis.

"ORGANIZING" RELATED TO FAMILIAR EARLY PSYCHIC MECHANISMS

Freud and the classical school of psychoanalysts have always been clear that the "talking cure," devised for the treatment of advanced-level oedipal neurosis, might be used to account for narcissistic or psychotic states, but that it does not provide viable treatment techniques for them. Hedges (1983) has reviewed the not very encouraging mixed results that have been reported over the years by dedicated clinicians attempting to utilize Freud's original free association technique with psychotics. Melanie Klein (1957, 1975) extends Freud's basic concepts developmentally downward. She formulates using the metaphor of the breast as the infant's first love object and has contributed immeasurably to the field with her concepts of projective identification and splitting (see Grotstein 1981b).

Winnicott (1958, 1965, 1971), as a pediatrician/psychoanalyst, contributes fundamentally to our understanding of the many early exchanges between mother and child in a way that few analysts without his background of experience could have done. Bion's (1962, 1963, 1977) studies of transformations of thought begin with the infant's sensorium and the maternal transformation of sensory experience through her thought. Bollas (1987) studies the transformational other as the infant's first experience of otherness through his or her own growing awareness of state transformations. Searles's (1979) studies of schizophrenia and Giovacchini's (1979b) studies of primitive mental states have all yielded valuable data and advances in psychoanalytic theory.

Sechehaye's (1951) invaluable work on symbolic realization, Tustin's (1972, 1981, 1986) highly original work with autism, Rosenfeld's (1965) illuminating formulations regarding psychosis, Ekstein and Motto's (1966) illuminating work with psychotic children, and Grotstein's (1981b) penetrating studies into the psychotic mechanisms all deal in one way or another with the earliest of human experience. But not until the present work has it been possible to conceptually isolate the organizing experience per se as fundamental to all psychotic processes, and as foundational to the human mind. All of the above distinguished contributors and many more have tended to reason downward from lines of thinking previously established in studies of later psychic development. In contrast, the concept of organizing experience begins by considering early mental states as the organism's natural, instinctual striving and questing to find a place within the safety net of the human environment through interpersonal attachment and attunement (subjects studied by Bowlby [1969, 1973] and Stolorow and colleagues [1982, 1987]).

This book does not focus on the human processes active in

attachment, or on those involved after connecting, or on those present in experiencing transformations, or on those essential to establishing an intrapsychic sense of symbiosis. Therefore, concepts such as projective identification, splitting, part objects, transformational objects, entanglement with the object, selfobjects, or any other concepts that imply that a connection has been found that serves to organize the personality will not be included in the present study. The purpose of this book is to isolate or to distill, as it were in pure culture, the organizing experience per se, because it is by conceptualizing the organizing experience in its most rudimentary form that the earliest forms of transference and resistance can be secured for analysis. Once a clinician can grasp the basic way that organizing transference can be observed and studied, this mode of clinical listening can be extended into all of the psychotic symptom pictures very easily. Further, as a tool for listening to all people's fundamental orienting operations in life, the listening perspective for the organizing experience becomes useful in sorting through aspects of all types of psychological experience and personality organization.

6

The Organizing
Transference

MIMICRY AS A BASIS FOR THOUGHT

The organizing transference arises from experiences the neonate or intrauterine infant undergoes in trying to organize reliable channels to the environment that insure the safety and continuity of physical and psychological life. When the child is reaching out or extending in some way to form a channel or path to the maternal body, either inside or outside the uterus, the interpersonal channeling or connection is facilitated if that extension is met (reinforced) in a timely and satisfying manner. Winnicott's (1949) formulation is that the infant needs to maintain a sense of "going on being." Any impingement on that sense prematurely activates the psychic system and forces the child to begin thinking precociously.

During the period from approximately four months before birth to four months after, the infant's neurological system alternates from rest to activity. The infant actively arranges numerous sensorimotor experiences, and he or she may be looking, listening, or experimenting with movement, sounds, or touch. Under optimal circumstances the infant is not required to problem solve in response to impingement, intrusion, or trauma. But when there is impingement into the sense of comfortably going on being, he or she is forced to react, no matter what the nature of that impingement is. Such things as an Rh factor, the presence of some undesirable chemical, or a shortage of food or oxygen in the placental blood could each provide a considerable impingement for a fetus.

Psychological studies suggest many ways that the mother's psychic life and her relation to her environment before the child's birth may impinge on the child's comfort and sense of safety, thus activating alerting mechanisms and thought processes. Any intense or prolonged environmental stimulus or deficit could impinge on the psychic world of an infant. Winnicott holds that impingement forces the infant to begin thinking, to begin problem solving, before that infant might otherwise have done so, before that infant may be fully ready. Under such circumstances, a child's basic thought patterns are responses to (persecutory) impingement. Winnicott had witnessed many childbirths and sees no reason to assume that birth per se need be traumatic. The baby has been in cramped quarters with limited possibilities for some time. The baby is ready to leave. There is an exit. The exit is usually large enough and the baby's musculature is adequate to traverse the birth canal. The process can occur and so the baby makes the transition from one sort of environmental circumstances to another. The baby is prepared for birth, already having experienced many tolerable frustrations with the intrauterine environment. Traveling down the birth canal may even be satisfying and positively stimulating in various ways. Midwives maintain that putting the infant on the mother's belly immediately and letting his or her own instinct to move to the breast occur, is also activating. In other mammals the licking of the baby's body seems to stimulate deep tissues and to enliven the newborn. So there may be many aspects of the birthing experience that are stimulating, soothing, and comforting to the infant.

However, says Winnicott, an unusually long or unusually intense birth experience may provide a trauma that can serve as a prototype in thinking about early impingements. If baby's first thought (in utero or postnatal) occurs in response to an actual traumatic intrusion, then the first thought mode upon which later thought modes are based is persecutory. Winnicott addresses the Kleinians who speak of observing persecutory anxieties in clinical situations. Winnicott believes that these anxieties exist because persecution (impingement) *has already occurred*. There is a fear that persecution will happen again. The child experienced primordial impingement or persecutory intrusion with the result that the basic pattern of the child's mind became interrupted and organized around anticipating or guarding against intrusion. The child scans the environment for more persecution because that is the foundational experience. Such a child was deprived of a secure "going on being" experience until the perception and motor equipment naturally evolved to tolerate gradually increasing frustrations, delays, and other maternal shortcomings.

In an optimal situation, by the third, fourth, and fifth months a mother and a baby are interacting in many ways. But a baby who has experienced traumatic intrusions perennially maintains a guard against further intrusion and in doing so has already lost much of its potential flexibility.

Even in optimal situations, Alice Balint (1943) still holds that the infant's first thought processes arise in relation to trauma, even if they be minor ones. The subtext of her paper is that primates have an innate capacity to mimic. Human babies mimic their mothers in order to gain understanding and mastery over what is happening to them. Before cause-and-effect thinking can occur, thought originates based upon primary identification at a gross body level (mimicry). An infant sees the mother smile and the baby smiles back. Mothers imitate the baby and the baby reciprocally imitates the mother in an endless circle leading to the mutual cuing process of the later symbiotic period of development.

Hedges (1983) speaks of the "mimical self" as an expectable aspect of psychic and somatic experience at the organizing level. People who retain organizing modes of interacting as a significant feature of their personalities live with mimicry as an important way of being in the world. One woman spoke of having a series of internal cassette tapes to tell her what to say and do in each situation of her life. To the extent that any part of the personality retains early modes of organizational striving, mimicry of human life and activity—in contrast to resonating emotional interactions—may predominate.

Anna Freud (1951, 1952, 1958) and Winnicott (1952) emphasize the role of maternal care in augmenting the protective shield during the period of early infantile dependency. Khan (1963) has introduced the concept of "cumulative trauma" to take into consideration early psychophysical events that happen between the infant and its mothering partners. The concept of cumulative trauma correlates the effects of early infant caregiving with disturbing personality features that only appear much later in life. Cumulative trauma is the result of the effects of numerous kinds of small breaches in the early stimulus barrier or protective shield that are not experienced as traumatic at the time but create a certain strain that, over time, produces an effect on the personality that can only be appreciated retrospectively when it is experienced as traumatic.

Research on infantile trauma and memory (Greenacre 1958, 1960, Kris 1951, 1956a, 1956b, Milner 1952, and others) demonstrates the specific effects on somatic and psychic structure of cumulative strain trauma. Khan (1974) holds that " 'the strain trauma' and the screen memories or precocious early memories that the patients recount are derivatives of the partial breakdown of the protective shield function of the mother and an attempt to symbolize its effects (cf. Anna Freud 1958)" (p. 52). Khan further comments:

> Cumulative trauma has its beginnings in the period of development when the infant needs and uses the mother as his protective shield. The inevitable temporary failures of the mother as protective shield are corrected and recovered from the evolving complexity and rhythm of the maturational processes. Where these failures of the mother in her role as protective shield are significantly frequent and lead to impingement on the infant's psyche-soma, impingements which he has no means of eliminating, they set up a nucleus of pathogenic reaction. *These in turn start a process of interplay with the mother which is distinct from her adaptation to the infant's needs.* [p. 53, emphasis added]

According to Khan, the faulty interplay between infant and caretakers that arises in consequence of strain reactions may lead to (1) premature and selective ego distortion and development, (2) special responsiveness to certain features of the mother's personality such as her moods, (3) dissociation of archaic dependency from precocious and fiercely acted-out independency, (4) an attitude of excessive concern for the mother and excessive craving for concern from the mother (co-dependency), (5) a precocious adaptation to internal and external realities, and (6) specific body-ego organizations that heavily influence later personality organization.

Khan (1963) points out that the developing child can and does recover from breaches in the protective shield and can make creative use of them so as to arrive at a fairly healthy and effective normal functioning personality. But the person with vulnerabilities left over from infantile cumulative strain trauma "nevertheless can in later life break down as a result of acute stress and crisis" (p. 300). When there is a later breakdown and earlier cumulative strain trauma can be inferred, Khan is clear that the earlier disturbances of maternal care were neither gross nor acute at the time they occurred. He cites infant research in which careful and detailed notes, recorded by well-trained researchers, failed to observe traumas that only retrospectively could be seen as producing this type of cumulative strain trauma. Anna Freud (1958) has similarly described instances in which "subtle harm is being inflicted on this child, and . . . the consequences of it will become manifest at some future date" (p. 122).

Psychological theory and infant research (Stearn 1985) are rapidly adding ideas to help us think about what the experience of the infant may be like during the organizing period. These concepts help us grasp the kinds of early mental structuring that can be listened for in the analytic situation: (1) basic primate mimicry and primary identification, which give rise to the "mimical self" (Hedges 1983); (2) later adaptation to the maternal environment giving rise to the "false self" (Winnicott 1960), seen most clearly in the later symbiotic bonding period; and (3) a kind of stimulation experienced by the infant as intrusive strain trauma causing an adverse reaction of the infant, which sets off an adaptation in caregivers resulting in what can be thought of as "an internalized vicious circle of mutual misadaptations" (Khan 1963).

In listening to a person living a pervasive organizing experience or to a person living out a pocket of organizing experience, how might we begin to identify aspects of his or her experience that might be considered transference from the organizing period?

CONSIDERING WHY SYMBIOTIC BONDING DOES NOT OCCUR

One way to begin thinking is to consider that babies come into the world ready to attach themselves to a (m)other. Bowlby's (1969) work on attachment has shown that human babies naturally seek attachments that make the human emotional exchange possible. If the child does *not* move toward bonding, if the child fails to bond in an overall way, or if parts of the personality are left out of the bonding dance, there must be a significant reason why this otherwise natural, expectable process did not occur. It is helpful to picture an infant extending through vocalization, perception, or movement, striving for a connection, seeking warmth, stimulation, nurturance, or a sense of comfort and safety. If the mothering person, for whatever reason, is not able to meet these extensions in a timely manner or does not know how to, or is unwilling to, or meets extensions with a negative response, the extensions withdraw and/or atrophy. The baby simply does not reach in that way any more because there is no gain, no percentage, or perhaps there is even pain associated with that kind of extension.

In Freud's (1895) earliest paper considering issues of primary repression at a quasi-neurological level, he suggests that an attempted pathway that goes unrewarded by pleasurable experience or that meets with painful experience is intentionally blocked against future extension, as though a sign were posted there, "never go this way again." Bioenergetics analysts (Lowen 1975) think in terms of various systems of involuntary muscular constrictions that become chronically fixated, creating body rigidities and blocks in the flow of natural energies so that future extensions are blocked because they are experienced as painful.

The reason all people, in various ways, can be said to retain psychic and somatic modes of organizing experience is that there is no

such thing as perfect mothering. Current infant research suggests that
mother and baby may only satisfactorily connect thirty percent of the
time (Tronick and Cohn 1988). In these earliest months every baby
has reached out, needing, wanting, and questing in various ways. His
or her quest may not have been met because no environment can
possibly meet all of these quests with perfect timing and empathic
attunement. So various experiences occur that teach the baby to avoid
or to withdraw from certain forms of contact where appropriate
environmental response is absent, missing, or negative.

It is helpful to picture a rooting baby who gets so far as to have
her mouth almost around the nipple when "something happens"
(internally) so that rhythmical sucking never starts. The receipt of
nourishment, comfort, and safety from contact with mother is foreclosed. The mouth stiffens and the baby loses the nipple, or perhaps
pushes it out or turns away, arching her back and screaming. This
image comes to mind when we hear of a person approaching a
therapist searching for human connection. The person extends,
reaches out yearning for human contact. Then "something happens."
She's suddenly just not there. Her questing personal presence in the
room has somehow vanished, although her mimical conversation and
activity may continue. Many if not most practicing therapists, presumably due to their own history of bonding experiences, fail to notice
for long periods of time that the person they are in session with has
essentially left the room, vanished from the interaction. Mimicry
prevails, so the person "passes" as interacting, when he or she is not at
all involved emotionally. It becomes helpful to distinguish behavior
that serves as grasping, clinging, or *attaching* from patterns or modes
of interpersonal interacting that constitute reciprocal emotional *engagement.*

Franz Kafka's literary work portrays organizing themes throughout. He himself must have lived significant organizing experiences to
be so exquisitely sensitive to them. In *The Castle* the hero searches
endlessly for a way to reach that nipple up on the hill, the castle. He
does not even have an identity beyond the initial K. He believes that
he has been sent for and that he is needed as a surveyor, one who
defines boundaries. But the castle is elusive, endlessly denying him
human recognition. K. extends himself in one way after another

attempting to reach the castle, to prove that "I was sent for, I am wanted, and I have a job here which involves living in the castle village and drawing boundaries." Kafka could not bring himself to finish the book, perhaps because this story was about his own life traumas. But in soirees he read it to friends and told them how the book was to end. All his life K. searches for a connection to the castle without finding it, always frustrated, always almost making it, just about having the castle within grasp. But each time suddenly and inexplicably "something happens."

The phrase "something happens" is of great importance because when people living organizing experiences extend themselves for contact it often lacks an explicit sense of agency, of "you" or "me." The experience is more one of, "I'm reaching, wanting, grasping, almost connecting, or attaining and then something dissolves, something happens." The subjective experience is more one of an impersonal force operating to attract and then, when the possibility of connection is felt or is within grasp, the attraction dissolves, vanishes almost imperceptibly. One woman talks about a wind coming up and all is lost.

In Kafka's proposed ending to *The Castle*, K., on his deathbed, has all of his friends gather around him. He still has never been able to directly contact the castle. Suddenly an unexpected messenger arrives from the castle with a cryptic note. The note, in effect, says, "You may stay and work in the village, but not because you were sent for, and not through any merit of your own, but for extraneous reasons." This is the essence of the organizing or psychotic experience: not feeling quite human, not having an identity, not feeling received by the human world. People living organizing experiences often say, "I'm weird. I'm different. I'm not quite human. I'm like a robot. I don't belong. I live in a glass bubble. I exist behind a glass wall that separates me forever from others." They somehow know that the experience they are living has never entered into an interpersonal bonding dance that lets people experience themselves as fully human. People living organizing pockets know that this part of their personality is strange, crazy, psychotic, or weird, and that it cannot find human resonance.

In Kafka's *The Trial* he poses the question, "What is my guilt?" In the end the protagonist bares his chest to the knife. His guilt is for being alive, for wanting more than his mother had to give him. In "On the Origin of The Influencing Machine in Schizophrenia," Tausk (1919) thought to ask his psychotically disorganized patient, "Can you draw me a picture of this machine which so unbearably influences you?" She drew a picture resembling a human body. Searles (1960) writes about the pervasive influence of the nonhuman in organizing experiences. There is not a resonating, rewarding experience of human life at this level. There are only objects, forces, operations, images, and powers, but not "I" or "you" as agencies.

IDENTIFYING ORGANIZING TRANSFERENCE

Identifying transference experience from this level of development begins with the assumption that if psychological attachment, the bonding dance, has not occurred or has only partially occurred, there is a reason. And whatever the reason, it occurred historically in the earliest months of life. Evidence of closed-off psychic channels for human connection and somatic constrictions that make extensions painful are retained in the personality and in the body structure in ways that can be observed in later life as the organizing or psychotic transference. This earliest of transferences represents learning experiences of the infant that occurred whenever he or she emotionally extended or reached out and was somehow turned away, not met, or negatively greeted. The questing activity was met with environmental response that taught the infant not to strive in that way again. The "never go there again" experience effectively marks organizing experiences that later can be identified as transference.

Psychoanalytic work has been characterized from its inception by its focus on bringing into consciousness previously learned, "automatic" or unconscious emotional responsiveness patterns. Psychoanalytic studies have aptly demonstrated how earlier emotional relatedness experience can be observed as structured modes of relatedness that become transferred into later interpersonal interactions. Psychoanalysts ask, What is keeping this person rigidly held within a certain almost compulsive way of being, of experiencing, and of relating to others? With people living organizing experiences, the transference structure can be seen as systematically functioning to limit or to prevent sustained human emotional contact. The person learned as an infant that emotional contact is dangerous, frightening, traumatic, and/or life threatening. Relatedness learning during the earliest months of life becomes organized around limiting the extension or reaching-out experience and preventing all forms of contact felt to be frightening, unsatisfying, or unsafe.

In sharp contrast to (borderline) people living out later-developed internalized symbiotic relatedness modes and who are terrified of rejection and abandonment, people living organizing experiences are terrified of interpersonal connection. At every moment of longed for and sought for contact, some (psychosomatic) image or experience of a traumatizing other suddenly intervenes to make sustained contact impossible. Alan Kirk's painting *Mother and Child with Teeth*, which appears on the cover of this book, portrays artistically the disconnected and threatening situation that is internalized in infancy and serves as internal motivation not to connect to others or to break connections as fast as they are formed. This is why the working-through process in analysis is accompanied by such intense physical pain. It is as though the minute the infant puts his or her mouth around the nipple and starts sucking, terror or poison was the experienced result. Overlearned aversion reappears later as transference. A person may be terrified of any human contact that is likely to cause him or her to reexperience that early massive and very painful trauma.

What follows are three examples of how an organizing experience can appear and how we as listeners can gain some grasp of the organizing transference experience.

TRANSFERENCE ILLUSTRATION 1:
RAGING AT THE THERAPIST

This case is from a woman therapist who has been seeing a female client for three years twice a week. An intense therapeutic relationship has developed. The client is a very bright and sophisticated woman, a professional. She lives in the world very comfortably in regard to everyday matters, but she suffers privately from having a multiple personality. The most troubling switch is when, without apparent reason, she goes into a rageful self. Her therapist sought consultation in a crisis after she received a telephone call from the client, who said, "I'm not coming in any more because there's something wrong with our relationship." The therapist inquired about the nature of the problem. The client responded, "I can tell you feel there's something wrong with my relationship with Naomi." Naomi is a lesbian woman with whom the client has developed an intimate relationship. She continued, "You don't think that it's right, or you think there's something wrong with Naomi. There's no point in our going any further so long as you think that way." She's angry, shouting at her therapist, and then she lists a number of other things. "You don't listen this way . . . and you're not that way . . .," a tirade of angry complaints and accusations leveled at the person and the practice of the therapist that the therapist had never heard before.

The therapist is very upset, feeling she may never see the client again. She is not even clear about what might have been said to set the client off. She cannot link the abrupt disruption to anything. The therapist asked, "What makes you think I don't like Naomi? I've always been supportive of your relationship with Naomi." But the client is certain she disapproves of Naomi and of the relationship.

So far as the consultant could ascertain the therapist has no such negative feelings about the relationship and has no personal biases against lesbianism. In fact, the therapist seems glad her client has found a friend. The therapist is in crisis because she has been able to schedule a telephone appointment with her but is anxious about how it may go. She tells the consultant that her client is basically not a lesbian. She's had three or four relationships with women but they have been relationships in which she is looking for soothing contact with a woman, possibly in order to feel mothered. She cannot develop relationships with men because she does not know how to relate to men. She is confused and frightened by men.

The client has talked at various times about how even though she is having a sexual relationship with a woman, she does not feel that she is a lesbian. She does not feel like other lesbians. The client feels certain she is really not a lesbian. At one point the therapist had said, "I really don't think you're a lesbian either." It occurs to the consultant that this could be where the organizing transference became attached, that is, in the therapist's attitude that she is not a lesbian. The consultant asks, "How have you developed your view? From all you have told me of her relatedness capacities, she's emotionally 3 months old. We have no idea what lesbianism means to her, and we have no idea what her future may be. She has developed no real sexual identification yet and therefore, no stable gender identity." The therapist immediately resonates with that. It seems the client is experiencing some breach in empathy. She has determined that her therapist has an attitude that she is not really a lesbian. Now she claims the therapist disapproves of Naomi and of her relationship with Naomi.

The therapist has learned how to work the organizing experience very skillfully. For many months the therapist and patient have worked over many connecting and disconnecting experiences in other relationships, although the client has not been able to work the organizing transference directly with the therapist, at last not until now. In a series of parallel transferences the two have been studying the ways the client connects and disconnects daily with people. She says, "I *feel* fully connected with people. I see people. I talk to people. I move in a social world. Superficially I do very well, but at some other level I know I'm not connected." She has the conviction that her mother "gave me away" in the seventh or eighth month in utero. And that what she has been striving for ever since is to be bodily reconnected to mother, to be sustained in a physical relationship. The suggestion is that there was once a connection, but that mother broke the connection. The analytic speaker has no idea how to make or to sustain mental connections.

The client has presented one critical traumatic memory. When she was perhaps 2 or 3, she and her mother lived in quite poor circumstances, in maybe one room with a bathroom down the hall. Her mother would often take her to the bathroom with her. The child witnessed her mother's miscarriage and watched as her mother pulled out the bloody fetus and flushed it down the toilet. It was a vivid memory.

The consultant asked the therapist, "Do you suppose her mother also tried to abort her, because that seems to be what's coming up in the transference? I remember one man who had an endlessly recurring dream of desperately hanging onto the edge of a cliff, clinging to one root, about to fall to his death at any moment. His mother later confirmed that she had used a coathanger several times in an attempt to abort him during the pregnancy. His struggle to stay alive was vividly represented in the recurring dream. Do you suppose her memory is a screen memory? Or is it something she actually witnessed? My hunch is that the memory stands out so vividly because she believes 'that's what mother did to me. Mother flushed me down the toilet. Mother broke the contact and flushed me down the toilet in the same way.' Perhaps that's what she experiences you are doing to her right now. She has somehow succeeded in experiencing in transference that you're aborting her. She is using something in your demeanor toward her friend Naomi in order to project the organizing transference wish to abort her into the therapeutic relationship."

The deceptive thing, and the reason this example is clear (and the next one even more interesting), is that when a therapist first starts tracking these organizing experiences in transference they frequently look like symbiotic (abandonment) material. The speaker says, "I'm leaving you because you failed me. You abandoned me and I'm never coming back." Yet, upon closer examination, we begin to realize that as the organizing transference begins to fit into place, the client waits for a moment in which she can re-create the organizing rupture in the relating. In this case she re-created it by screaming accusations at her therapist about her attitudes and how bad she is as a therapist. Her intensity and abruptness and her departure from ordinary reality appreciation have left the therapist shaken. The therapist says, "I've never been this shaken with this woman before. I'm worried I'll never see her again. I'm worried she'll never come back."

It is not too difficult to infer, under the circumstances, that an unconscious fantasy may exist on the therapist's part of getting rid of the client. She then says, "Oh, you know, there's another thing. I have been delaying all week returning her phone calls. She called me. I think to myself, I've got ten minutes and I can call her. No, no, no. If I call her tomorrow I'll have 15, so I'll call her tomorrow." So she's aware she's pushing her away. The therapist also said she had the fantasy of "Well, you know, she's threatening to be very difficult lately, and the truth of the matter is, if she didn't come back I suppose it wouldn't be the worst thing in the world for me." The client may have picked up some ambivalence in the countertransference that she reads as abortion fantasies, miscarriage fantasies. This is her way of accomplishing the disconnection, first inside herself and then with her therapist.

There are two ways we may study the presence of the organizing transference "rupture in relating": in its passively repeated form and in its actively mimicked form. In the present example we might first infer that when the baby needed something, mother attempted in some reasonable way to give the baby what she needed but it wasn't right. Mother's attempts failed somehow. So the baby began screaming. We then picture this mother, who with limited resources did not know how to respond to the baby's screaming. Maybe the child had an earache. Not being able to bear the tension, the mother leaves the scene so the child learns "When I scream mother leaves." So the analytic speaker now screams at her therapist with the expectation that she too will leave her. Her way of accomplishing the rupture is to scream. When the consultant suggested this to the therapist she quickly reviewed every relationship the client has had with a man. At the point in the relationship at which the client begins to feel connected to the man, suddenly she switches into this "other personality," which is a "screaming bitch," and starts screaming and yelling obscenities and accusations at the man and so he does not stay around. She accomplishes the break by screaming accusations.

But the activity of actually accomplishing the break belonged to mother and so is somehow identified with, mimicked. According to this line of inference, did mother scream at the baby for misunderstanding her needs in the relationship, for not being responsive to mother's attempts to care for her? We don't know exactly how the primary identification with the mother who broke the contact operates from this limited material but it provides clues for future analytic understanding. The therapist is still left worrying, "But what am I going to do with this disconnection?" Since the therapist has been traumatized, like the mother may have been with the child's needs, she too seems almost ready to flush her down the toilet.

An alternative formulation might use Fraiberg's (1982) notion of "pre-defense." In observing interactions of neglected and abused children with their parents Fraiberg noticed three almost biological reactions that serve to (defensively) control the stimulation: aversion (flight), freezing, and fighting. This client's screaming at men and at her therapist might be considered a fighting response in the face of anticipated abusive overstimulation and contact rupture that the organizing transference threatens to generate. (The following two vignettes illustrate the flight and freeze tendencies.)

These interpretive hunches connect immediately with the therapist, so that she is ready to talk with her client about it. The consultant warns, "Don't rush into this material, because one thing we know is that when people are in organizing states they can't handle much at any given moment that is abstract, that is verbal. Just be with her for now. You've learned from her rantings. You've seen the small window to her soul from your own shocked experience, which no doubt in some way represents her trauma as an infant. But if you start to talk about it too soon, you'll be introducing ego functioning into a space where ego does not belong—which may have been her mother's worst empathic error. If so, then you become her psychotic mother by trying to be too helpful!" On the way out, the therapist says, "You know, I just never know what to expect from these organizing people. I've been really gearing up for the worst." The consultant responds, "Well, maybe you will have a difficult experience when you talk with her on the phone. These people have a way of making it very hard on us." The therapist says, "But you know, it also occurs to me that maybe when I call her, at the other end, there will just be this still, quiet little voice that says, 'Hi, I've missed you.'"

The following week the therapist reports exactly that. She was able to stay with the client and help her feel how awful it was to think that her therapist in some way might disapprove of Naomi or think that a lesbian relationship was not right for her. The rupture had been repaired, the connection remade so she could continue to stay in therapy. But the crucial transference experience that appeared is by no means understood or worked through. This episode represents her first tentative foray into working the organizing transference directly with her therapist. Now the heat is temporarily over and the therapist has a clearer view of the nature of her disconnecting transference replication. The organizing transference seems to be worked through in a series of waves or episodes. She will be more prepared to act quickly next time. The interpretation will perhaps be possible in the non- or preverbal way the therapist stays with her in her rageful self and invites her (perhaps with extended hand) to stay connected and to live out together her terror of being with the therapist rather than to disconnect or rupture the connection with rage.

TRANSFERENCE ILLUSTRATION 2: FLIGHT FROM THE THERAPIST

This example of organizing transference involves a woman therapist who has been working with the client for three or four years. She talked about her work in a case consultation group. The client has been driving an hour and a half each week to see her therapist. The therapist says, "so there's a long umbilicus." The client has presented as tenuous in her ability to maintain relationships. In the last six months she has talked frequently about terminating therapy because of money and distance. She canceled her sessions in bad weather and during the winter holiday season. On several occasions the therapist has empathically tried, "Well, okay, I can understand how busy you are and how far it is. You have accomplished a number of things in therapy, so if you want to consider termination we can talk about that." She even suggested helping her find a therapist who was closer. But that all became taboo. The client was allowed to talk about termination, but the therapist was forbidden to talk about it.

On the occasion in question the woman called during the Christmas holidays and without any warning canceled all future appointments. Her therapist then made several phone calls, unsuccessfully attempting to reach her. She sent a Christmas card. She did everything she could to reach out to her. The therapist thought, "Well, maybe it's best that she stop and this is her way of stopping. Maybe I shouldn't be pursuing her." This *laissez-faire* attitude may be appropriate for listening to more differentiated forms of personality organization but is clearly not empathic when working an organizing transference in which the client cannot initiate or sustain connection. This therapist is an empathic and intuitive woman and so remained persistent in her attempts to restore the connection. They finally did connect by phone and the therapist found out what happened. The client said, "In the last session I was telling you about my friend Valerie and you turned away. Then I knew you didn't care for me so there wasn't any point in my coming back."

As the incident was discussed in consultation, the consultant encouraged the therapist to attempt a review of events in order to try to get some content about what was being talked about with Valerie. Concrete images about contact ruptures serve us well in understanding organizing experiences. It is often important to ascertain exactly what was being talked about, and why turning away to pick up a cup of tea was seen as a rejection. The client has been slowly backing away, but not letting the therapist back away. The therapist cannot talk about termination but the client was waiting for the moment when the therapist turned at a critical moment so that the rupture of the organizing transference can be attached to the therapist's turning-away activity. The consultant says, "She's found a way to live out the organizing transference of mother disconnecting. This is the window to the organizing experience we are waiting for. We wait for the moment in which the reenactment of the turning away, the breaking of contact, the rupture of experience happens in the transference."

This episode might be mistaken for a symbiotic-relating scenario or narcissistic breach in empathy—"just when I needed affirmation from you, just when I need something from you, you turned away." It could be seen as splitting; it could be seen as abandonment; it could be seen as selfobject failure. But the consultant had heard developments in the case several times before, enough to realize that there was a deep organizing component. In response to the consultant considering the rupture as disconnecting transference, the therapist said, "You know, she's been married for twenty years. So I had always thought of her as basically symbiotic or borderline in her object relations. But now I recall a number of instances with her husband in which she must have been in an organizing pocket and experienced her husband as the psychotic mother." But now the rupture of relating had actually been recreated with the therapist. She says, "It's funny, during this time period she had moved. She called my recorder to leave her new phone number on it. And, you know, I didn't take the phone number off the machine before I erased the message." So the analytic listener is ready in some sense to let her die, too.

The therapist was fired up with these ideas because they seemed to make sense and to organize in her mind many past incidents. She's ready to go back and talk to her client about all of this. The consultant cautioned her not to rush and told her why. The therapist tunes in quickly and says, "I feel like, where we're at right now, is we're both lying down in a play pen and I have to wait for her to come to me." The consultant reminded her the baby has to be allowed to find the breast. The transference to the psychotic mother will be reenacted again and again so there will be ample time to interpret. But she can use her new understanding to be with her client in new ways.

The therapist was reminded of what she already knew from her studies of the organizing experience, that abstract verbal interpretations per se will not touch this very early transference. Interpretation at the organizing level must be a concrete activity, often manifest in physical gesture or interpretive touch at the specific moment when the analytic speaker is actually in the act of pulling away from contact, of (transferentially) creating a rupture. Viable interpretation of the organizing transference involves an actual, physical, concrete reaching out of one person toward another in such a way as to communicate, "I know you believe you must break off our personal engagement in this way now. But it is not true. You have, as an adult, the ability to stay here now with me and experience your longstanding terror of connectedness. How can you manage not to leave me now? Can we manage to remain in contact for just a few more minutes?" Clients often deliberately and perhaps wisely conduct the early phases of therapy at quite some distance from the therapist by spacing appointments far apart or arranging long and difficult drives. They know that closeness can only be experienced by them as traumatic.

The therapist had arranged this consultation because she was concerned about her own anger. In the midst of all the client's coming and not coming, calling and canceling, connecting and disconnecting, the therapist had become enraged and said she was "just ready to kill her" when she sees her on Thursday. She even made a slip and said, "I have an appointment with her on Saturday." The consultation group laughed to think she does not want to see her so soon as Thursday. She is an excellent therapist, and she really does want to connect, but it is easy to understand the countertransference ambivalence. Ruptures in relating that organizing transferences necessarily entail stir up organizing experiences in the therapist.

TRANSFERENCE ILLUSTRATION 3: FROZEN IN IMPOTENT RAGE

In this example of how organizing transference works, an emerging theme of an otherwise very well-developed woman has been related to the organizing period. This example is from a much later working-through period of her analysis with a male therapist and occurs in a personality much more capable of verbal abstractions than the previous two. The woman's mother, during the baby's first few months of life, was afraid to pick up her baby for fear of "breaking" her. It has been discovered through several years of intensive psychotherapy that there were many strengths this mother was able to stimulate in the child, but at the deepest psychic level there are connecting difficulties. The emergent theme over several weeks was the analytic speaker's rage that occurs on a fairly regular basis in social situations when she knows that the person she's interacting with can indeed do more for her and be more there for her but somehow flakes out. In short, her rage is mobilized at people when they have more potentially to offer than in fact the person is actively living in the current relationship.

In a key session she develops the theme further. Early in her marriage, she says, her husband was far more warm, far more giving, far more available than he is now and how angry she is that he isn't more available when she knows he can be. She becomes exasperated to the point of feeling utterly helpless and frozen. With a close friend she indicates that what attracted her to the friend was that this other woman had so much to give. She is well traveled and well read. She is alive, active, versatile, a good conversationalist, and much more. But, in a recent example, when her friend had a bit of the flu and refused to get out of bed to go to the client's daughter's first softball game, "then I don't see her any longer as what she could be or might be for me. And I become angry and disillusioned with her. Now I know what has been bothering me so much lately about her in our relationship. Too often she cancels, flakes out, or blobs out when I know she doesn't have to, when I know she has far more to give but is choosing not to. I become completely immobilized in impotent rage."

In the discussion of various examples that have occurred with her husband and her friend, she said, "Now I'm finding that not only when I'm enraged at the other person for not living up to their potential do I not get what they have to offer me, but I also see that when I'm enraged I am totally unable to take in, to get, to make use of what they can in fact offer me." She referred to some examples from previous transference experiences in therapy where, in complaining bitterly about the therapist's seemingly endless unavailability over the holidays and weekends, she was so preoccupied in the sessions leading up to the holidays that she was unable to make use of whatever good experiences might be possible. Her comment is, "Something always happens." The emphasis here is on the subjective statement of the disconnecting experience being impersonal. It is not, "I'm disappointed with the other," or "the other lets me down," or "the other fails to live up to their potential." It is "we're interacting and then *something happens* and the potential that is there isn't being lived out, and I fall into a lost state of sadness and grief, which is usually manifest in instantaneous but frozen rage."

At this point in the session the client realizes she has lost or repressed a further insight regarding her husband and friend that she was very excited about only a moment before when she connected to it. But just as quickly as the insight came, it fled and she was very disturbed for some time about having lost this insight.

Late in the session she provides another example of some neigh bors whom, when she first began to get to know them, she experienced as somewhat available. Now she experiences them more as users than givers. And while, she acknowledges, the reverse is no doubt also true in ways, she cites several instances from the beginning of their relationship in which the neighbors were very supportive, very helpful, very outgoing. But the man in the couple began on occasion to have other things that kept him away from doing things with them. And the woman became unavailable to have lunch with the client often or visit over coffee. Before too long there were enough gaps in the relationship that it became unbearable to her. She says, "It's easy to say they aren't meeting my needs. I'll have to go elsewhere." But she realizes that this is not entirely the case. They do have some things to offer, but because they are not offering all that they can, she feels that "mysterious unbearable pain" again.

After a few thoughtful moments she said, "It sounds like a reason to break contact." The therapist quickly replied, "No, it's the *way* you break contact." She then said excitedly, "That's exactly what I lost. I was trying to formulate the problem with my husband and my friend in terms of how I break contact but I couldn't quite get there. If I'm always living in what a person could give me but isn't, then several things happen: One, I have reason not to relate to them. Two, I'm not relating to them at all but I'm relating rather to my fantasy. And, three, they do have something to give or I wouldn't be relating to them, but in my distress and frozen anger I'm completely missing what they have to give to me. I break the contact by being sad and enraged, complaining about what I'm not getting."

At this point she slowed down and indicated that she was emoting very deeply, that she feels she's reached a very profound point. "I know somehow that this can change my life if I can finally get hold of it. If I can find some way of fully knowing about this, I will be able to change many things." Her therapist said, "It seems as though you have located the mechanism regarding how the contact is broken and how it relates to the early experiences of your mother who, much of the time, was there so that you knew full well what things she could provide. But when she was preoccupied, or not able to give, or frightened about how she might harm the baby, she bowed out, leaving you stuck, knowing that she could give more but not giving it.

No wonder she reports that you were such a good baby and slept a lot!" The content of the transference is, You could be giving me more but you're not.

Then the client said, "Now I know why my daughter seems to be left out of this dynamic. You know how I've always said with her it's somewhat different? Well, the difference is that I'm not expecting to be given to by her. I understand that her role isn't to give to me and so I'm much freer to relate to her without this pain coming up. The few instances in which I do lose it with her, I may feel that she's not giving me her full cooperation as freely and fully as I know that she can. But, in fact, I am able to take a great deal from her by simply being with her—by being present while she is losing her baby teeth, or brushing her hair. I go to softball league with her and I receive through just watching." The therapist said, "You do take what she has to offer." She responded, "Yes, but it's often very indirectly, just by enjoying being with her. Whatever she does is so wonderful and beautiful that it's a very rich experience just being by her side."

She then comments about last week's session. "I was concerned that you didn't know about my feelings of caring for you and how grateful I feel to you for just being here with me. I get a lot from you by just being with you even if you don't have a lot to give on a certain day." (The therapist had a serious eye infection on that day and his spirits were a little off. It was something she detected and expressed concern about within the session.)

"Now," she continued, "I find I'm a little scared about knowing all of this. Things keep clicking in my mind—more and more examples. It's like my whole life is built on this single mechanism. No wonder I wasn't happy when John, my supervisor, failed to tune into me completely when I knew he could. If I finally identify this, I may be able to change. I am excited, but I think I'm mostly very scared. I think the scare is that I won't remember this, I won't be able to take hold of it. I won't be able to make it my own." The therapist said, "No. The scare is that you will remember it. You are in the process of deep change and as you are changing you are coming face to face with a terror you have avoided all your life. The terror of having to en- counter a real live person who has some good things to offer but who may not, for a variety of reasons, be willing or able to give fully in all areas. Sooner or later in every relationship you encounter this situation and it brings back the sad and rageful reactions you had to your mother during your earliest months of life. So you have been unable to continue relating or you have given up the relating when the conditions are not met right. What you are scared of is actually allowing yourself to negotiate the uncertainties of relationships and to survive the positive possibilities as well as the painful disappointments that are bound to be a frightening and powerful consequence of fully knowing and living out what you are now discovering."

Each of these three examples serves to illustrate how the rupture of the organizing experience is repeated in transference. In each instance multiple interpretive possibilities exist. The decisive moment of organizing transference interpretation is not visible in any of these examples—in the first two because the relationship had not yet arrived there, and in the third because the in vivo interpretations had already begun and the client was in a later stage of "owning" the interpretative work, although she expresses fear of losing it. Examples of the actual interpretive and working-through process are provided in a later chapter. The presence of Fraiberg's (1982) three "pre-defenses" of fleeing, freezing, and fighting is suggested in the three case vignettes presented and may be seen as the clients' ways of achieving a rupture in contact that, due to transference projections, is threatening to become overstimulating.

PART III

THE PATH TO ORGANIZING EXPERIENCE

7

Considering
Craziness

CRAZINESS

From the beginning of time all people have known about and have had to find ways of considering craziness. Today we find ourselves completely surrounded by all manner of craziness. Every day craziness of various sorts wells up inside ourselves. But how can we sensibly *think about* craziness?

To think or speak of anything at all, our language dictates that we decide on a subject and a predicate for each thought, each sentence. We must refer to some *thing* and then speak of some activity for that thing to be engaged in. Our language system itself compels us to consider craziness as an invisible, intangible thing. Attempting to define the nature of things that we cannot see, touch, or otherwise know about with our senses tends to make definitions more difficult to agree upon. "The weather is crazy this week," is a sentence that conveys a certain sense that most people would readily understand, although if the listener were not personally experiencing the crazy weather pattern firsthand, questions might arise.

"I'm going crazy under all the pressure from work this week," also has a certain readily understandable sense. But with people being so infinitely complex and unique, we immediately realize that the exact sense of craziness one might be experiencing under work pressure this week comprises a set of highly personal meanings that are by no means always clear from our statement. How are we to understand what meanings, what bodily and psychic sensations are involved for the speaker in this craziness? What would this person's craziness look like or mean to the person working next to her, to her employer, to her husband, to her children, to her Father Confessor, and so on? An entire text would need to be created by each person knowledgeable about her personal sense of craziness in order to express his or her individual understandings of what her craziness this week entails from many points of view. And even then we might wonder how acceptable each of these versions might be to her as demonstrating an under-standing of her this week.

But when she feels she is going crazy from work pressure this week, what does that say about next week? Does she feel or look as crazy in the morning as at five o'clock in the afternoon? Is this week's craziness the same as last week's? Does she frequently feel crazy or only occasionally? And does her craziness always feel and look the same? Perhaps her craziness at work is episodic and set off by different events. Perhaps her craziness, which she attributes to work pressure, has nothing to do with work but rather relates to emotional or physical stressors that might be attributable to other sources. Does feeling, acting, looking, or being crazy have any consistent meanings or contexts for this person? Is her sense of craziness an excuse for not being productive or a rationalization for carelessness or thoughtless activities? Perhaps she does not wish to be held responsible for her activities at work or elsewhere this week? Perhaps her complaint is a cover-up for something that she does not wish to speak of or think about.

From these most elementary questions about an everyday sense or frame of mind so intangible as craziness we can quickly see that the exact nature of and/or functions of the thing called craziness are certainly in question. In the old days would her craziness make people whisper that she was some sort of an evildoer, witch, or seer—perhaps involved in some black practices involving the supernatural? Would the intensity, frequency, or quality of her craziness qualify her as insane? And if so, as determined by whom? Perhaps we choose to think of her or to excuse her craziness on the basis of some sort of social, physical, or mental disorder or disease. Perhaps of greater concern is what will we *do* about her if this craziness persists or gets out of control somehow. Does she know just how crazy she is becoming? If she knows, what will *she* do about it? Is she seeing a doctor? Are medications likely to be helpful? Is she a candidate for psychotherapy? Does she need a support group? Or is she in denial, avoiding facing up to reality, self-medicating, or manipulating others so that she does not have to take responsibility for dealing with her problems herself? Perhaps we can understand her better by thinking that she comes from a dysfunctional family or that her parents were abusive or addicts of some sort. These sorts of comments and attempts at explanation that we hear frequently leave wide open the question of what we may mean when we speak or think of craziness.

The forms of considering craziness that we ordinarily employ indeed do conjure up many things that we might say we are looking at. Our accustomed thought modes further serve to suggest many ways of relating to whatever it is that catches our attention in craziness.

It does not take a genius to see that any close examination of the thing called craziness immediately and clearly reveals an elusiveness so great as to render the word *crazy* and all companion words unusable for systematic purposes because of their impreciseness and their endless array of possible meanings. And so, it has been thought, if we are to catch this beast called craziness in its lair we must lay a series of nets with which we hope to ensnare something that conforms more precisely to our sense of what is happening. Perhaps we have a series of different beasts qualified as craziness that we must systematically bring out of hiding. Speaking about such things as witchcraft, insanity, disease, physical deficiency, and mental disorders is one way people have historically tried to capture the elusive prey. Perhaps if we only knew more about the nature of the beast, or about how to take hold of it, or how to reform its disruptiveness, then we could find ways to make the human race safe from its dangerous intrusions!

All cultures throughout time have created mythical beasts in order to think more clearly about human "things" that cannot be seen or otherwise directly known by the senses. That mythical beasts are projected and concretized composites of human traits, qualities, and concerns is manifestly evident from any quick perusal of world mythology. Likewise, craziness has come to be thought of as something "out there" that we can more or less objectively consider and get some fix on so as to help us deal with it. This is the Western way of dealing with many human puzzlements—make them into things external to ourselves that we can then turn around in our heads in various ways much in the same way that we might turn a puzzling object around in our hands or mouths in order to discover its nature.

Our cultural heritage teaches us to think that whatever things we can agree upon as somehow existing must therefore have certain natures that are ultimately discoverable in one way or another. Certainty about the nature of mysterious things is believed to be attainable if we are just patient until we can know enough or until we can develop a technology or thought system properly conceived to reveal the beast to us. But history teaches us that the world's favorite mythical beasts, far from having been found to have an objective and discoverable nature, have turned out to be creatures of our rich collective imagination. Twentieth century thought is likewise reducing various forms of craziness from the status of objectively definable entities to a set of fantasies and mythic themes that spring from our own rich imaginations.

For ages humankind has considered lunacy an enigma as strange and as inexplicable as the erratic activities of the moon. But, as with humankind's discovery of the secrets of the moon, nineteenth century science set out to discover systematically the nature and patterns of human insanity. Now after more than a century of research into the nature of human craziness and its more chronic or stable forms referred to as mental illness, numerable mythic themes have been considerably clarified and codified. Not surprisingly, mental health professionals have come to categorize people according to the kinds of themes readily available for notice. The standard diagnostic manuals organize pathologies the way physicians classify illnesses, zoologists organize animals, and botanists arrange the species of plants. According to this medically based way of thinking, people are seen and referred to as things—hysterics, paranoids, schizophrenics, manic-depressives, schizoids, narcissists, autistics, *ad infinitum*. Mental categories serve to collapse the richness and uniqueness of people's individual lives into observer-convenient categories or species such that a person comes to be seen as a schizophrenic, a manic-depressive, a narcissist, or a borderline psychotic.

But aside from the very obvious humanistic concern for this obliteration of personhood when thinking and speaking about human craziness, we have to ask what distortions, limitations, and inadequacies are automatically introduced into our thinking and inquiry about craziness and what it means in people's lives when we use such descriptive thought modes. After all, aren't we all willing to acknowledge in various ways our own craziness? How is ordinary, everyday craziness to be distinguished from, say, what is called schizophrenia? These are the obvious questions that have been studied in various ways for the last century. It is hardly surprising that as various forms of craziness have been considered, a number of schools of thought have evolved. Nor is it surprising to realize that the ways in which professionals theorize so differently from one another are related to what they intend to *do* about that craziness.

One suspects that different ways of formulating the nature of craziness attract different kinds of people with differing personal, social, and moral biases—all finding ways to confirm their *a priori* biases through categorizing their observations of others. The proliferation of quasi-religious attitudes toward the "best" or the "right" way to consider craziness is well documented in the large number of competing psychological and psychoanalytic orientations, not to speak of the myriad of self-help organizations and doctrines. Is it so shocking to learn that large numbers of "truth seekers" have collected under different banners, each group hailing leaders with credos that spell out "the way" to understanding various forms of craziness? This would certainly be the longstanding human habit. Kuhn (1962) has demonstrated that over the millennia many areas of human thought have spawned variety and competition in approach, and that occasionally a revolution in thought occurs that he calls a *paradigm shift*. We are clearly in the midst of a paradigm shift in the way we consider our human relatedness, intelligence, and affectivity.

THE CONCEPT OF PSYCHOSIS

The term *psychosis* has been used in a variety of ways to describe the departure of an individual's way of organizing his or her private world and public behavior from the community's acceptable ways of organizing personal worlds. In extreme instances, the term *psychotic* has come to be applied to people who are actively hallucinating or having somatic delusions that depart from the nature of consensual reality, and thus the word has come to be a stigma for describing unacceptable people. It is not the type of stress or the developmental level of the concern people are experiencing that has been character- ized by the word, but rather the undesirability or the craziness of a person, so that the person is devalued.

In my work, I have found it useful to talk about the "organizing experience," relating it metaphorically to the earliest attempts of an infant to organize his or her sensorimotor world in mutually engaged connectedness with the maternal intrauterine environment and with mother's body and significant others in the extrauterine world. I am aware that many people, because their earliest experiences have been so traumatic, pervasively retain the organizing mode of relatedness in later life, although it may be masked by false self or mimical self formations. In many circumstances the person can "pass," or can adjust or adapt to the demands of society. But the person is by no means living fully within the interpersonal realities as defined by human culture. The person has, in some way or another, been left outside of the realities that human beings ordinarily appreciate and share. Most people only live "enclaves," "pockets," or "layerings" of organizing experience. Certain aspects or realms of every person's existence have not yet been fully integrated under the canopy of culturally defined human realities. In a psychoanalytic or depth psychotherapy experience, portions of any person's life dating back to earliest infancy may come under scrutiny as an organizing experience.

One person expressed the organizing experience in a dream of "just floating up in the air, seeing the stars and the moon, just circling. And something finally pulling me to the ground. But I was so little that I couldn't walk for myself. I could not do anything for myself. What I was experiencing was being lost in the universe. And with that, an extreme sense of absolute terror."

Another client, who was in a regressive moment of therapy, lived near the beach and was having oceanic experiences every day, actually in the water. In his analysis, he dreamed that he was floating above the beach and above the sand like a balloon. There was a string that was tied to a toilet on the beach. (The analyst's name was John!)

Another experience shared by a therapist was of a woman who had moved into an unorganized experience and desperately needed a sense of connection. Because the therapist took a total abstinence stance so far as touch was concerned, the client came one day with a piece of string. She asked if she could tie the piece of string around her finger and tie the other end of the string around his finger. The need for a concrete tie and her desperation are conveyed in this enactment.

As organizing experiences have yielded to systematic study from a therapeutic standpoint, two critical aspects have emerged. The first is the need to foster or to sustain connectedness. The second is the need to begin analyzing the appearance of modes of disconnection, modes of breaking or rupturing the contact moments as they occur within the context of the evolving connection and relatedness of the analytic couple. It has been useful, both in thinking theoretically and in interacting clinically, to use the terms *psychosis*, *craziness*, and *madness* loosely and interchangeably to point toward those experiences that arise in a person and force an interpersonal disconnection. At the point a disconnection is forced, the person is leaving human connectedness, leaving human realities, and moving into his or her own private psychotic world or organizing experience. My use of the terms *psychotic*, *crazy*, and *insane* to describe this moment has served for me to simply point to a way in which the person leaves human realities, human connectedness, and the spiritual aspect of human interconnectedness in favor of private, internal constructions based on early loss of the mothering connection or the mothering experience. Such organizing constructions have originated in infancy and stand to represent the need to find a way of surviving without that vitality that we ordinarily expect to come from the mothering person.

METAPHOR AND METONYMY IN STUDIES OF PSYCHIC FUNCTIONING

The metaphor of *structure* has traditionally been used to describe enduring aspects of psyche that could be logically and positivistically defined and, on the basis of inference, observed. This metaphor has served to distinguish the concept of enduring patterns of behavior or personality organization from the concept of "mental contents"— fantasies, images, urges, appetites, and other features that a person can experience and use language and symbols to describe. This structural metaphoric approach pictures human psyche as a "thing" that somehow resides "inside" a person. According to this view, psyche is an (invisible) construction of habits built from the results of a person's transactions with the environment as well as from a series of subsequent internal conflicts that have evolved between these structures or habit patterns. Psychic structures are thus supposed to make up an individual's personality and are usually endowed with qualities of agency. For example, "Your unconscious is telling you something," "The ego achieves mastery over the instinctual impulses arising from the id," or "The superego defends itself from id encroachments."

Those who have studied the workings of metaphor and metonymy assure us that it is only by virtue of comparison to the data of sensory experience that our language system arises, and that all complex thought relies on the interworking of the processes of displacement and condensation implicit in the concepts of metaphor and metonymy. (For extended expositions of these problems of language and metaphor see Schafer [1976], Spence [1982], and Lakoff and Johnson [1980]. Ryle [1949] and Wittgenstein [1953] provide philosophical analyses of these problems.)

Many thinkers about the problems of mental or psychic metaphors warn us about the recurrent dangers of clouding, and thereby limiting, our thinking by employing metaphors that cannot perform the work we wish them to. Furthermore, the general epistemological and philosophical reconsiderations required in responsible contemporary studies and implicit in the emerging relatedness paradigm of psychoanalysis point to the abandonment of many of our favorite limiting metaphors from systematic theorizing. Schafer (1976) and Spence (1982) have perhaps been the most outspoken in pointing out new directions that can most fruitfully serve to shift the modes of analytic theorizing as the future unfolds. (For an extended discussion of these points see Hedges [1983] on modernizing our philosophy of science, and Hedges [1992] on the epistemological, philosophical, and linguistic requirements of the relatedness paradigm shift.)

The *listening perspective approach* emerges from these critical and broadly based considerations. Far more than first meets the eye, the paradigm shift and the general listening perspective approach represent a truly radical transformation of our accustomed modes of experiencing, thinking, speaking, theorizing, and organizing our minds. One might well imagine that future explorers of psyche will define listening dimensions quite differently from those based upon the interplay of experiences of self and other. One might also imagine that even within the self and other listening dimension, the initial four logically based perspectives might give way to additional divisions or to creative redivisions. For example, one area that seems at present to be squeezed into the four perspectives comprises the experiences involved in separation from the symbiotic mutual engagement mode. Is the child's learning to say "no" enough to characterize the developmental shift that we call the "terrible twos"? In Freud's (1925) view "no" is not only the watershed that gives rise to the freedom and creativity in the individual person, but negation distinguishes among simple animal affirmations, reflexive responsiveness to the environment, and the human capacity for reflective thought. Are there not enough considerations involved in the psychological experience of negation, of independence, of separateness, or of relinquishment of the safety and rhythm of exclusive reliance on mutual cuing modes to justify the systematic elaboration of a logical perspective for listening and responding differentially to these experiences?

In analysis we observe entrenched resistance and extended periods of grieving as well as major disruptions in functioning as people begin discovering ways in which to relinquish overused habits that characterized their personal symbiotic relatedness modes. In the future we can anticipate many creative modifications, revisions, expansions, elaborations, and reformulations of the general listening perspective approach to analytic work. But the focus of this book is on a developmental experience that comes much earlier – an experience of reaching for necessary connectedness with the human environment and finding or not finding it.

8

The Quest for
Reliable Connection

REACHING FOR MOTHER

In forming a listening perspective for the organizing aspects of personality, a convenient metaphor suggests itself. Let us consider the baby's experience as one of trying to form a connection, a link, a path along which to extend herself, perhaps toward some needed or exciting feature in the environment, or possibly simply to flex, to extend, to organize the perceptual-motor apparatus.

We might begin asking why the baby extends herself at all. But to do so would lead us into an infinite regression to the point of asking why amoebas extend their pseudopods. Animals and humans move, extend, flex, contract, and relax, and in the process bring nutrients into their systems and evacuate wastes. The constructionist view of evolution speaks of the "autopoesis" (self creation) of "observing systems" (Maturana 1970, 1972; Maturana and Varela 1972; and Von Foerster 1984). Bowlby (1969) has spent a lifetime studying the processes of attachment in mammals and human infants, reaching the conclusion that baby's instinct for survival insures that she hold on to mother for safety and comfort. (For an excellent overview of Bowlby's monumental work see Karen [1990].) Tustin (1986), in speaking of the "rhythm of safety," observes, as a metaphor for the mother–infant relationship, that both mouth and breast are active in the suckling process and that with successful nursing neither baby nor mother feels safe or comfortable until an acceptable mutual rhythm is established between the two. We might then think of the quest for reliable contact as including (1) the search for comfort and safety, (2) the relief of bodily (instinctual) tension, and (3) the pursuit of stimulation that leads to learned patterns of seeking satisfaction and avoiding pain.

Franz Kafka expresses this incessant search in his writings (1926, 1937, 1979). Patrick Suskind (1986) in his novel *Perfume* writes of a boy named Grenouille whose monomaniacal search is olfactory—the search for the smell of perfect beauty. Jerzy Kosinski (1970) portrays the organizing search in his novel *Being There*, which he also adapted for the screen (starring Peter Sellers and Shirley MacLaine). The heroine in David Hare's (1985) play *Plenty*, played by Meryl Streep in the screen adaptation, is a beautiful, sophisticated, and wealthy organizing personality.

In psychotherapy consultations it is common for a therapist working with an organizing personality to express something like, "I don't quite know why this person comes to see me. He has never missed a session, is always on time, and pays his bill promptly. We don't talk about much and he doesn't seem to be able to make much use of what I have to offer, but he comes anyway. Somehow I don't feel we're quite connected. Sometimes I feel he doesn't even know who I am or that I'm in the same room. I worry if therapy is doing him any good or if I'm the right therapist for him. At times I have attempted to broach such questions but he becomes quite distressed so I just hang in there with him. He clearly wants to be here, he feels I am important to his life. But I don't know where we are, what we're doing, or where we're going." Such therapy clients are searching, endlessly hoping that some day in some way it will be possible to find a niche in the human world, a connection that will enable them to feel human, to feel real.

It is like an endless search for an elusive nipple that can be used for stimulation and growth.

It is my impression that many good-natured and sincere therapists have been working with unorganized people in their practices for years, doing their best to be kind, supportive, and empathic. But until now there have not been sufficient thought tools to know how to approach these people so that the *analysis* of their limiting inner blocks could be accomplished. It has not been possible using previously practiced modes of psychoanalysis to touch the barriers that these people have erected in infancy that have prevented movement into human bonding (symbiotic) experiences. While there is certainly compassionate, humanitarian value in being available for such people, in treating them with good will, and in supporting them in their life experiences, without initiating a clearly framed analytic process the breakdown of limiting organizing level structures is not possible and transformation of organizing states cannot occur.

THE THREAT OF DEATH

Another aspect of this search that comes up regularly in the clinical situation is the emergence of some form of survival fear. That is, implicitly or explicitly the organizing experience always contains the "threat of death." Many people in analysis are at first reluctant to voice this death fear, thinking it will sound weird, manipulative, or overdramatic. Others continuously live out this fear of death in threats, gestures, and ruminations. In virtually all cases of blocked or limited organizing experience what is at issue is reviving an infantile memory of a time when death was (from the infant's point of view) actually imminent. It may be difficult for a person living states of more differentiated psychic organization to grasp the subjective impact of such an ominous threat.

All mammals are equipped with some genetic message such as, "find the warm body and cling to it or die." A newborn mammal will move immediately into wild searching spasms and vocalizations if the warm body cannot be found when it is needed. When an organizing state exists, it lives on in the person because at some point in his or her early history the physical connections that might have led to psychological bonding could not be made. The necessary warm nurturing body was terrifyingly not available and *the person has internalized that nonavailability*. Sometimes the nonavailable environment is represented internally by the sensation or fear of emptiness. For this to happen the nonavailability of the needed warm body and the death threat had to be experienced acutely.

When considering this early level it may be our wish to distinguish between somatic connection to mother's warm body and psychic connection to the mothering person who brings warmth and nurturance. But the infantile human organism is incapable of such clear-cut distinctions. Psychic functioning at this level is somatic and somatic functioning is psychic. The distinction we later make becomes possible by virtue of the symbiotic ties that form—the mutual cuing, the establishment of perceptual complexes that "mean" that mother is coming or that represent the firm knowledge that "I have the power to call out when I need warmth and sustenance and it will come to me." Prior to that time the situation is a stark one of life or death depending on the availability of the needed psychosomatic contact.

The fundamental biological instincts of the child demand the availability of a maternal body (or some acceptable surrogate). This means that in listening to organizing experiences, there will always be in the background the fear of the loss of the needed other upon whose presence life itself depends. People are often able to voice a fear of developing a dependency on the analyst. It is not dependency so much that is feared—we are all dependent on one another. What is feared is the threat of death (in a myriad of forms) and experiencing the agonies associated with fearing death that lie beyond failed dependence. The fear of breakdown, death, and emptiness resulting from the breakdown of somatopsychic channels to survival sources is an ever-present (and often deeply repressed) memory of any person reliving an organizing state. In early experiences that blocked the path to further organization, the infant experienced an environment devoid of responsiveness. The formation that remains in psychic structure is emptiness, fear of breakdown, and/or the threat of death (Winnicott 1974).

CASE ILLUSTRATIONS
OF THE ORGANIZING QUEST

One woman was told by her mother that she was a good baby, that she did not demand much, and that she slept a lot. When this came up for transference review in analysis, the sleep urge on the couch became overwhelming at times. It was discovered that each time she faintly perceived that the analyst would not or could not be optimally responsive, death threatened. By becoming still and sleeping, the terrorizing trauma could be numbed out and the death threat avoided.

One man learned late in analysis that he had been born with blue limbs and required physical therapy daily for the first six weeks of life; when the threat of failure or loss of the other in actuality or transference arose, there would be a cramping pain in his extremities. This same man considered himself a workaholic. This tendency became related to his prenatal desperation to stay alive by working his heart and lungs, trying to get sufficient supplies of food and oxygen to his extremities. Horrible chest pains, heart aches, and struggles in breathing suggested the prenatal effort of the soma to stay alive during life-threatening situations. Interestingly, this man was born a month late. In analysis the experiences that emerged suggested that when he was awake he was always somehow obsessed with the fear that "the bottom is going to fall out," that something will happen to make life collapse if he does not work tirelessly to prevent it. It was difficult to get out of bed in the morning in dread of the effort that would have to be put out in getting through the day. The metaphor emerged of his terror of "being born" into the day or into life. Evenings were self-medicated into sleep—overriding the fear that "if I go to sleep, I may die in my sleep from lack of effort." The various somatic pains, crampings, and constrictions that appeared during the analytic study of this prebirth experience suggested that, paradoxically, the infant responded to the subjectively experienced danger that he would die from lack of food and oxygen, that "the bottom would drop out."

The body constrictions and stiffening apparently actually interfered with and delayed his being born. His fear of being born into life was reenacted each morning and every Monday. Needless to say, there was a lifelong depressive picture, because internalized was the dimly perceived prenatal fear of not having enough so that death would result. As this fierce will to live disintegrated through analysis, the wish to die expectably emerged (Lowen 1982). While with other people living in organizing states we may have known evidence of fetal alcohol syndrome, arteriosclerosis of the umbilicus, or other forms of anoxia or toxemia prior to birth, with this man we only have the postbirth circulatory pattern to alert us to his struggle. He did, however, during his analytic study of these experiences, have a frightening and vivid dream of a twist in the umbilicus that cut off the blood supply.

Another man experienced near death due to the toxins his mother was actively inserting into his body due to the Rh factor in his genes. He knew his mother had always abused him with "I almost died when you were born." But not until late in his analysis did he receive from his mother the actual information that they went through forty hours of labor, were packed in ice and separated at birth. He was put in an incubator and she was sent to another hospital for six weeks of lifesaving procedures. After this information was available, a series of previously enigmatic dreams suddenly made sense. One involved his skin crawling with pain and desire while in a bathysphere with the eyes of deep-sea creatures coming and going at the windows. The dream was accompanied by the olfactory sense of the smell of metal— all now interpretable as memories of the steel incubator, the nurses coming and going in the windows, and the horrible painful longing for skin contact. This man had suffered his entire life with an intractable and painful skin disorder that flared up unbearably during this phase of his analysis.

In another case encountered in consultation, there was a history of "terrible twos" kinds of experiences in life and in analysis. But the woman's unusually warm and intuitive therapist had been able to lead her to quieter, more intensely painful experience. No matter what the therapist said or how she tried to empathically intervene or comfort her, the woman remained intensely fussy, unhappy, and in pain. Fortunately, her therapist's narcissism was intact enough so that the constant devaluation of her could remain within a transference context, and her therapist did not have to react in exasperation or counter anger. While listening to the interaction, the consultant encouraged the therapist to think in terms of some picture involving a mother and an infant. "What would this whole interaction look like if we saw it?" The picture emerged of a baby lying in a crib unattended and in pain, distressed, fussing, and at some level afraid of dying. The therapist had earlier learned that if the woman lapsed into painful and angry silences, not to let her stay there without response. All her life her friends and family had learned to give her "wide berth" for fear of being snapped at. But that had the effect on her of leaving her totally alone, which she hated, so the therapist found ways of enduring the difficult task of being present while being constantly snapped at.

After more than a week of bitter silences, with the therapist maintaining presence and attempting to make empathic comments amidst a barrage of attacks and dismissals, a day came in which the therapist in one way or another looked at her until she caught her eye and called her name in a playful, peekaboo fashion that caused them both to smile and laugh. The following day, still unable to speak, the woman brought a fifteen-page outpouring she had written the night before, addressing her daughter who was grown and living an infinitely better marital and family life than she herself had ever been able to muster. She had the therapist read her outpouring aloud since she, herself, felt unable to speak. What was contained in her words to her daughter was essentially her own mother's organizing level message to herself. That is, after the therapist had been successful in "holding" the traumatic infantile state for an extended period of time and then calling her into contact, the woman was able for the first time to represent—in a displaced form addressing her daughter—her internalized mother. "I was so preoccupied with my own pain that I know I could not give you what you needed. With your father I was afraid he would leave me, that he would find someone else and be happy." These two sentences illustrate how the displaced transference theme was stated in both the active and passive forms of the relationship with her own mother. That is, actively stated, her mother was preoccupied with her own pain so that she could not attend to the baby's needs, and, passively stated, the baby's fear that when she could not fill mother's needs mother would leave her and find someone who would. In a set of moving statements to her daughter the analytic speaker vacillated from blaming mother for what she could not give and blaming the baby for not being able to hold onto mother by providing mother with what she needed.

Searles's (1979) comments on psychotic guilt are relevant here. He formulates that guilt at this level takes the form of something like, "I feel guilty for not being a good enough or adequate enough baby so that I could provide my mother with what she needed to make her whole, so that she could mother me in the way that I needed." Because of this woman's best efforts not to do to her daughter what was done to her, she had succeeded, by bringing in auxiliary resources, in raising a daughter who was considerably less disturbed than she was.

The written outpouring gave representation to transference themes likely to follow in the working-through period. The internalized picture of the infant in the crib began to fill in. If the mother left because the baby was fussing, that was wrong. But if the mother stayed, no matter what she did, since it sprang from her own preoccupations rather than from attunement to the baby's needs, it still left the infant fretful. No ministration could soothe or comfort. In transference no matter what the therapist did, no relief or comfort would be possible. Fortunately, the therapist was able to let herself simply be with the woman, acknowledging that this pain must be lived out together, sorry that no matter what she offered, it could not bring relief, but all the while speaking a firm resolve that, "we have to live this awful situation out together." It was, of course, this determined holding attitude on the part of the therapist that allowed the transference, the perennially fretful disconnection to be relived and, after a safe and reliable connection was made, to be represented in displaced form in the letter.

A man in the consultation group, as we were trying to imagine what the interaction that was occurring might look like in an infant and mother interaction, volunteered that he thought of his retarded daughter's attempts to relate to her baby. Wanting to be the best mother she could, but not having a firm grip on how to empathize with the baby, she always approached the baby with her own well-intentioned agenda. But her agenda did not match the baby's needs and he fussed and fretted. Somehow infants may understand the good, loving intentions of mothers who cannot be fully empathic, and that may be helpful to the baby. But the bottom line is, the child does not have an opportunity to coalesce an inner sense of agency from which to reach and experience the work of figuring and the joy of finding connection to the essence of the mothering person.

It may be further instructive to note that, in the case conference in which these troubled silent hours of this woman with her therapist struggling to survive were presented, other therapists, well-schooled in Kleinian object relations theory and ego psychology, attempted to understand the interactions in terms of projective identification and ego interactions. They had some familiarity with the three years of previous therapy work with this client, including the long periods of the "terrible twos" scenarios to draw their experience from. But the consultant was able to show that, although prior experience may have been optimally listened to as symbiotic scenario, that is, as borderline level material, the present experiences afforded the woman an opportunity to experience and then to represent pre–object relations experience, experience prior to the time in which projective identification or basic ego functions could be said to be effectively in place. At this most rudimentary of psychic levels, the person is working on understanding the problem of finding mother – how it could and could not be accomplished, rather than the vicissitudes of that relating.

What made possible this particular experience was the prior willingness of the therapist to hold steady through a series of rebellious attacks and silences. Once trust had been established that the therapist knew what the requirements of being together were, the woman could bring up for study the underpinnings of the borderline scenario, the fretful baby with a preoccupied mother. How easy it is for a therapist in his or her more differentiated state with training in listening and interpreting to more complex interactions to miss completely the need for experiencing the quiet patience of a mother who has a child with a feeding difficulty, a constitutional difficulty of some sort, or the need to coalesce a rudimentary personal sense of agency before opening up to stimulation from outside.

The ways in which an infant searches for mother are infinite as are the difficulties that may arise in the process. The task of the therapist who wishes to work with organizing experiences is great. Instead of meaningful schemas involving mother–infant interactions, it may be best to imagine, to picture what the current state of affairs in the analysis might have looked like in early infancy. What does the infant do with her needs? What experiences with the other are inadequate? What are the anticipated responses from the other? How is all of this being re-created as a result of a solid holding situation that the analyst is providing? What might have been the nature of this baby's earliest frustrated search, as known through the here-and-now interaction of the analytic hour? Through early internalization processes how does the baby persist in not finding or in finding and losing or rupturing the connection? What does the other do or fail to do in order to meet baby in a way that should be satisfying—but because of internalized blockings the baby cannot receive or make use of? The search for contact and how it is being reenacted in the analytic relationship is the first thing to listen for on the organizing path.

9

The Experience of the Reflexive World

CONTENT VERSUS STRUCTURE

When a person allows organizing states to appear in the analytic interaction we generally wonder what the person is trying to tell us. What is being expressed or represented? The person may be speaking in terms of multiple selves, faraway kingdoms, adventures on Mars, machines inside that control him, magical and mechanical forces operating in his life, affects out of control, black holes, strange happenings in body parts, exotic tales of ritual abuse, or experiences while having been abducted by aliens.

To remain empathically connected, the analyst must be willing to engage in conversations about all manner of psychic content; but experience tells us that it is a cardinal error for an analyst to become swept away by the details of organizing content. It is also an error for an analyst to be concerned with whether the content is "objectively true" or not, that is, whether a traumatic event did or did not "really happen," although this may be of crucial importance to the client. The analytic value of the content relates to the paramount importance of studying the transference of the contact moment.

The psychological and psychoanalytic literature is replete with accounts of therapists and analysts immersing themselves in organizing content for long periods of time with limited results. What experience makes clear is that it is not through a detailed understanding of a person's traumas or recovered memories per se that the critical therapeutic work occurs. Rather, we know that deep traumas, however represented, serve to cut the person off from various kinds of self and other experiencing. The crucial aspect for the therapist to tune into is not the molest, the ritual abuse, or the abduction content per se, but rather the subtle ways in which, whatever trauma may have occurred, there remains an internalized psychosomatic block to free, open, and flexible experiences of self in relation to others. That is, whatever rupture of contact with the nurturing and safe human environment the person has experienced, the result is an internalized blockage. The content of the trauma is of intense subjective importance to the person in analysis. But no amount of content analysis will enable the analyst to make the decisive move toward bringing the internalized contact-rupture structure into view for analysis (breakdown).

Organizing experience occurs in the earliest months of life. Ruptures in early organizing experience are universal. The clinical question is, How pervasively is the person affected and in what ways by the early trauma? It is well known that later experience that is massively intrusive and disorganizing (such as war traumas and sensory deprivation experiences) stirs one's deepest organizing experience. This means that the organizing *content* may come from any of life's episodes; but the personality structure tapped by the trauma and remaining affected is the person's basic orienting and organizational strivings. Analytic therapy views transformation of personality as a matter of interpretive interventions in the structure, not the contents, of the personality.

THE DISCOVERY OF THE CONTACT RUPTURE

The first insight that enabled the present thinking to transcend the problem of psychotic content was provided by psychologist Dolly

Platt, who was participating in a case conference with me in 1980. In the first draft of *Listening Perspectives in Psychotherapy* (Hedges 1983) I had not intended to include a consideration of psychosis. But the draft was read by many therapists who felt the text would be incomplete without at least an outline for a listening perspective for psychosis. So during the last year of text revision an "organizing" seminar met weekly to brainstorm about problems involved in treating psychotic states. Each therapist in the study group was actively engaged in working with one or more people living pervasively disorganized experience. Linda Reed, who was well known to the group as a superior therapist for her deeply empathic and connecting work with a number of symbiotic (borderline) patients, agreed to present ongoing process notes of her work with a deeply disturbed and disorganized woman.

Martha was in therapy with Linda twice weekly. She had met Linda initially at a local yoga center where Linda was an advanced instructor. Martha had come from another state where she had participated in some exotic experiences with a splinter yoga group known for its esoteric approach. Martha walked the streets wildly hallucinating, but refused all talk of a visit to a psychiatrist or the possibility of medications to limit the hallucinations. Although gravely disabled in terms of being able to put her good intelligence to work in employment, with boyfriends, or in roommate situations, Martha liked her hallucinations and contextualized them within a cosmic union that gave her a sense of safety and purpose. Those were the days before responsible practice would have insisted on psychiatric monitoring, so her refusals to be evaluated for medication were questioned but accepted by Linda.

Fortunately the group had Linda's good sense and training in yoga to guide them through the strange material involving Martha's cosmic thoughts and esoteric practice of yoga. There were days in which Linda, after reporting a series of bizarre verbalizations of Martha about the nature of the universe and her yogic understanding of it all, would turn to the group and say, "This isn't yoga, this is crazy!"

One day Martha came to therapy and began by requesting a "treatment." In their earlier experience at the yoga center, Martha had requested acupressure treatments from Linda. Linda was trained and equipped to offer acupressure in her consulting room. However,

Linda's experience with Martha was that the physical contact of the acupressure was not helpful, but rather disruptive and disorganizing. The group had heard Linda report on several occasions in the preceding weeks her discussions with Martha on how, as much as Martha believed she needed and benefited from the acupressure, there were times in which it clearly did not help, and how Linda did not want to enter into any more "treatments" without first discussing where Martha might be at the moment, and what the potential meanings and possible benefits and drawbacks of acupressure might be. While these talks had been skillfully managed by Linda, neither she nor the group was convinced that Martha grasped the broader picture she was being given. This doubt was confirmed when Martha began the current session by asking for a "treatment."

Linda read her notes to the group, which showed how she had dealt with the request by reminding Martha that some unpleasant consequences had followed several previous treatments, that she (Linda) cared for Martha and wanted to be with her in positive ways, that she felt protective of Martha, and that she would not want to rush into any activity that had the possibility of not being good for her. The group listened as Linda worked her way out of the somewhat tense situation of refusing Martha's request. There were expressions of support, admiration, and relief as everyone in the group heard how well this empathic sequence had gone. Linda's notes continued, "Then the Heavens opened and giant white clouds billowed up into blue skies and heavenly light. Golden edges outlined the clouds as the throne of God appeared and a great bejeweled sword dipped from the Heavens from the hand of God and rested meaningfully on the head of Martha's therapist. Martha knew at once that this sign from God meant that indeed I was the therapist for her." The group gasped and murmured recognition of the content, which declared that Linda had indeed made an empathic connection and that the client was acknowledging it in her own somewhat bizarre way.

Everyone breathed easier and Linda continued reading her notes. Suddenly Dolly Platt blurted out, "Wait a minute! That wasn't a connection. That was a disconnection! Martha left Linda entirely at that moment in favor of God, she left the room entirely in favor of Heaven, she wasn't acknowledging a connection and responding or resonating with it—she split away from reality, she disappeared, she left the object relations scene and went to a psychotic construction." We were all taken aback, but the critical discovery that has fueled our research and theorizing since that time had just been made. Psychotic (or what we shall soon label "reflexive") content appears when object relations threaten.

Similarly Tustin (1981) has reported decoding the meaning of the often-appearing "black hole" in psychotic content. One day one of her little autistic boys called it "a black hole with a nasty prick." In context, Tustin immediately knew that the often used symbol of the black hole represents in autism the place where mother once was. It is the black hole of relatedness with others that threatens to suck the organizing person in. Its origin is possibly the open mouth where the nipple was once experienced as part of one's body and is now missing. At all costs connectedness and relatedness must be avoided and there is a lifetime of experience organized around never again allowing oneself, one's body to feel connected to another in the ways once experienced as traumatic. This is why in listening to organizing experience, there may occasionally be some value in considering projective identification, or splitting, or the passive and/or active scenarios; but by and large it is the developmentally earlier search for connection and the compulsive (internalized) rupture of connectedness before it takes, that make up organizing experiences.

FREUD'S REFLEX ARC

After Dr. Platt's insight it seemed that an entirely new model of primary mental functioning would be required in order to handle this new discovery about how psychotic content operates—which was now evident in many other cases as well. But it turned out that Freud was well ahead of us! In Chapter VII of *The Interpretation of Dreams* (1900), Freud had already formulated exactly what we were learning how to observe in studying organizing experiences. According to Freud's formulations we might describe the *content* of our reaching baby's organizing experience as "reflexive."

In attempting to account for a special class of "hallucinatory" dreams, just the kind of vivid experience we might imagine our organizing baby having, Freud formulated a model of an early formed or basic reflex arc operating at best with only rudimentary memory traces and *without* the later developed preconscious or unconscious functions (represented in Figure 9–1). Images in earliest mental states, according to Freud's thinking, can be thought of as passing *reflexively* forward and backward along the reflex arc from perceptual to motor experience and from motor to perceptual experience. That is, in primitive or hallucinatory experience it is not subjectively clear whether the perception of the breast precedes reaching and putting one's mouth around it or if the instinctive reaching and sucking give rise to the perception of the breast. Winnicott (1971), in picking up on this theme later, remarked that we do not ask the baby if she created the breast or if the breast was there for her to find. In organizing or reflexive mental states, sensorimotor processes are not fully separated or governed by cause-and-effect thinking, so that almost any content might appear "out of the blue" as perceived and/or hallucinated. That is, the distinction between what may be considered to be objectively real and what is subjectively real is not reliable. Reality testing as ordinarily considered is not stable.

In contrast to this early reflexivity, which is bidirectional, leading from motor to sensory and from sensory to motor experiences, a subsequent buildup of memory traces causes the reflex arc to gradually become unidirectional (Figure 9–2). That is, according to Freud's formulation, in more complex or more organized mental

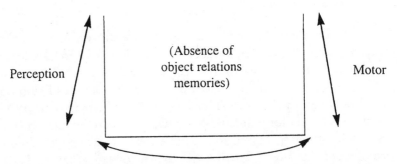

Figure 9–1. Unorganized Psyche: organizing images pass reflexively into and out of consciousness with hallucinatory vividness.

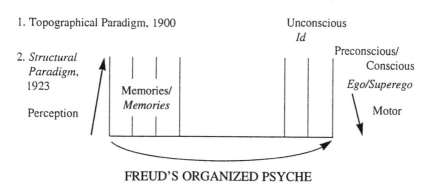

FREUD'S ORGANIZED PSYCHE

Figure 9-2. The Topographical and Structural Paradigms.

functioning an energy charge may be thought to pass regularly and predominantly (unidirectionally) from the sensory to the motor end of the arc, thereby giving rise to more stable and reliable perception and more directed motor responses—making reality appreciation more reliable. In more advanced stages of mental development, Freud (1900) postulated a mental apparatus capable of preconscious and unconscious functioning so that the conscious speaking state was systematically determined by various regulating and censoring processes.

Freud's 1923 structural theory (Figure 9-2 (see italicized words)) likewise postulates that the buildup of ego and superego functioning serves to limit the instinctual energies of the id, thereby establishing a unidirectional flow where reflexivity once prevailed.

In keeping with the parameters of the third paradigm of psychoanalysis (discussed in Chapter 2), we may now formulate the memory traces that filter and guide mental life toward full linguistic and cultural integration, toward triangular relatedness, as organized and integrated in an ongoing fashion along lines of self and other relatedness representations (Figure 9-3). That is, whether one considers Freud's reflex arc along topographic (unconscious, preconscious, and conscious) lines, along structural (id, ego, superego) lines, or along self and other representational lines, learned psychic structuring serves to transform the original organizing, reflexive mental states into more organized, directional, causative, and purposive psychic states that function to orient the person to a wide variety of realities more reliably.

Though Freud's model for early mental life is positivistic in its mode of formulation, the metaphor of a bidirectional, reflexively

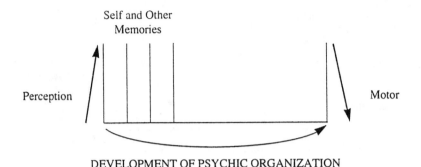

DEVELOPMENT OF PSYCHIC ORGANIZATION

Figure 9-3. The Third Paradigm of Psychic Organization.

operating arc does prepare the listener for *sensorimotor experiences passing into and out of awareness with hallucinatory vividness.* Restated, the ordinary expectable modulating (ego) and inhibiting (superego) processes or mnemic (memory) traces in mental functioning cannot be expected to be fully operative in the orienting attitude of organizing level experience. Likewise, even (id) impulses that are thought to be represented and repressed at later levels of development will not be present in organizing states. Therefore, it makes no sense with organizing experience to formulate in terms of "drive and defense" or to listen for "repressed unconscious" manifestations, since such mechanisms only appear with clarity in more complex mental states. Regardless of how well other personality functions such as intelligence and socialization may have developed, a person actively experiencing at the organizing level of relatedness is not at the moment integrating or consolidating the reflexive aspects of personality through more complex forms of self and other relatedness. Instead, psychotic content appears, forestalling the possibility of relatedness experiences that might otherwise permit the person to organize in a more advanced human context. I call this content "reflexive."

THE REFLEXIVE WORLD

Early psychic development has thus been thought to lead from reflexive sensorimotor experiences (the organizing listening perspective) toward the establishment of complex "splitting" and "projective identification" experiences (the symbiotic listening perspective), and later toward experiences of self consolidation (the selfother listening perspective), and yet later to experiences of ambivalence, internal conflict, unconscious (repressive) defense, and object constancy (the constant self and other listening perspective). When a person is actively involved in orienting and organizing an approach to the world, intervening regulatory influences cannot be assumed to be operating. The experience is of a world of sensations and activities that pass reflexively into and out of awareness with hallucinatory vividness. Winnicott (1949) observes that the earlier the mental state being lived at the moment, the less the individual is able to focus on or deal with at the time. Advanced-level organizations and memory are not available when reflexive experiences are being lived out.

Observation of reflexive mental processes may be obscured by confusional experiences often seen as psychotic symptoms or obscured by various forms of mental development such as mimical and false self constructions. So-called psychotic symptoms are often referred to as segmentation, disorganization, fragmentation, or secondary restitution. These kinds of experience are perhaps best thought of as remnants of the infant's attempts to organize cognitively and affectively outside of an object relations context. That is, when the infant cannot organize satisfyingly around mother's body and/or adequate surrogates cannot be found, the mind may be organized around experiences of persecution, depression, mania, or whatever other kinds of experiences are available.

Tustin's (1981, 1986) brilliant studies with autistic children illustrate how, in the absence of a sensuous experience with mother's body, the child becomes preoccupied with "autosensuous" experience. Her now classic example to illustrate what she means by autosensuous shapes that give rise to autosensuous experience is to ask you to notice the shapes formed on your body by the chair you are now sitting in pressing up against your body. Then shift your position and note how those shapes on the surface of your skin change. The autistic child, according to Tustin, has become preoccupied with manipulating these shapes for autosensuous purposes—for seeking interest, pleasure, comfort, and safety.

Forms of development spoken of as mimical and false self (to be discussed more later) may give the appearance of good adaptation or mental health, but represent ritualized and/or convoluted attempts to imitate and/or to adapt to environmental standards or demands. Little (1981) has pointed out that what psychiatrists often call "health" represents a poor attempt at adaptation, while what is often called "illness" is the truly healthy core of the personality from which future growth may spring.

One example of what might be called "reflexive" comes from a therapist who reports on a highly intelligent speaker who fills her hours with complicated talk about a particular school of psychotherapy, hardly permitting the therapist to get a word in edgewise, thus using jargon to prevent contact. Other examples are of people who speak incessantly about colleagues at work, or the vicissitudes of some relationship, or the details of some technical field such as computer, television, children, or movie trivia. In Kosinski's *Being There* the hero is able to speak only about gardening and watching television, regardless of what he is asked about. *The organizing experience can be clearly identified on the basis of content that fails to engage the other mutually and meaningfully.*

The literary works of Kafka (1926, 1937, 1979), Kosinski (1970), and Suskind (1986) illustrate vividly that reflexive mental states, with their quasi-obsessional emphasis on selected content, tend to continue *ad infinitum*—like a baby's solitary crib babble—but without transformation, without progression in character, and without signs of differential development. Contact with or relatedness to another human is required for the analytical and transformational processes to occur.

The frequent error of attempted therapeutic intervention in the past has been to work on understanding, or living inside the subjective content world of the reflexive state. Such understanding has no end and fails to lead out of the organizing state. Organizing content, according to most known approaches, tends to be decoded according to the kinds of guidelines that Freud, Jung, and others have provided for symbolic analysis of advanced neurotic states—but with little, limited, or no success. (See Hedges [1983, Chapter 12] for a review of psychoanalytic studies of psychosis.) Careful scrutiny of case studies that demonstrate transformational development of persons living organizational experiences suggests that the gains that may be attributed by the analyst to decoding and analysis of the symbolic content of the psychosis are more likely attributable to the personal immersion and dedication of the person of the analyst rather than to any understanding of the content involved. A brilliant example is Sechehaye's *Symbolic Realization* (1951) in which she feels that it is by two developing and making real a symbol that the progress in the case was made. It seems to me that it was the reality of the available object relation offered by the immersed therapist that accounts for what the client was able to accomplish. That is, it was not the realization of a symbol that was transformational; rather, *relatedness* became realized and then could be represented in a mutually understood symbol.

CONCLUSIONS

I have found it important to think of most of the content of the analytic hour with organizing states as reflexive in nature, harking back to Freud's first published theory of mental functioning. Whether the client is discussing hallucinatory experiences, delusions, or personality switches, or obsessing about people, events, affects, abuse, abduction, body parts, or whatever, by regarding the content as flowing back and forth on a reflex arc from sensation to motor response and motor response to sensation, we can avoid becoming overly caught up in any of it. We can seek to be free of the reflexive content in order to study the relatedness process *as it is actually occurring in the here and now.* We can respond to content mainly for purposes of empathy as well as for noting the symbols and imagery being used, which we will no doubt later come to understand in quite different ways from how they are currently being presented (this point is further elaborated in Chapter 10). What interests us in the reflexive flow of content is how that content is being actively used in the service of connecting or rupturing connectedness in the moment, because it is the analytic study of transference and resistance operating in the contact moment that permits psychic transformation. That is, if in normal, expectable human development the reflexive flow diminishes as memory traces of object relations shift the arc to a unidirectional, causal progression from sensory perception to motor response, then we ask why this person has not made that shift and remains somehow stuck in an organizing experience. There are undoubtedly clues in the content, but locating them and deciphering them is a difficult and challenging task (to be discussed in Chapter 10).

In contrast to unorganized experience, which passes into and out of consciousness with hallucinatory vividness, organized psychic activity is thought to start with the perception of a stimulus (externally or internally generated) and to end with some kind of purposeful motoric innervation. In unorganized or undifferentiated experiences there may be little or no reliable, causal, or purposive distinction between such things as (1) inside and outside, (2) bad and good, (3) male and female, (4) self and other, and/or (5) adult and child. Regarding organizing content as reflexive in nature, rather than causal or purposeful permits the listening focus to remain on the contact moment, that instant in which organizing transference can be framed and analyzed.

10

The Idiosyncratic Use of Symbols,
with a Case Illustration
Provided by Frances Tustin

ORGANIZING SYMBOLS

Organizing experience is expressed by an array of unusual and often strange, puzzling, or even bizarre-appearing symbols. But efforts to decode organizing symbols in the way analysts are familiar with fail to elucidate their meanings in the expected ways, because symbols that express the organizing experience do not arise in human experience in the same ways as other symbols. The experiences to be expressed are presymbolic. There is no capacity to symbolize experience during the organizing developmental period. Memory traces are left in the body's extension and constriction habits, which tend to govern a person's later automatic comings and goings in relatedness experience, but they have not been lived out in shared experience with another, nor are they subject to displacement and condensation processes, which are usually involved in symbol formation.

Freud and Jung teach how individual experience may be expressed and repressed in collective forms—symbols, images, and archetypes. That is, our cultural/linguistic system has a set of complex rules and codes for expressing private experience in public terms for the sake of communication and self reflection. An oedipal-age child is initiated into the complexities of that cultural system through his or her struggle with triangulations in which the ultimate third party is language and culture, the structuring symbolization process itself. Kohut (1971, 1977) teaches that preoedipal individual self experience is not so much symbolized as such, but is represented in various self to selfother resonance patterns that are actively sought and lived out. Stolorow and Atwood (1982) explain that symbols at a borderline or symbiotic level represent unique patternings of self and other experience. That is, affective interactions established during the symbiotic period are represented in retained affective interaction patterns, or in modes and patternings of self and other relatedness. Thus, in narcissistic and borderline levels of psychic development, symbols are used to represent forms of relatedness with their accompanying affects. In the symbiotic and separation-individuation experiences, a young child is learning about shared experience and one's similarities and differences from common experience.

Symbols used in organizing states attempt to express experience that is prerelationship. Organizing symbols cannot represent anything relational since a symbol cannot stand for something that does not quite exist. Therefore, organizing experiences, as such, are unrepresentable in any ordinary sense of the word. So how can we understand the symbols that are presented by people living in organizing states in an attempt to express themselves?

When we think of symbols, we ordinarily think of metaphor and metonymy, of displacement and condensation. A symbol stands for something, it expresses personal meaning in consensual terms. When we consider a psychological symbol, it invariably symbolizes some aspect of interpersonal relatedness experience. If it does not, it remains at the level of a sign. Ordinary symbolic analysis begins with an understanding of the public code and proceeds with a decoding so that the personal experience expressed by public symbols can be understood in its specificity. But a century of experience in studying psychosis has demonstrated the futility of starting with the heavily laden social symbol and attempting to decode its personal meaning in the way that is possible in advanced-level psychological constellations. Nor can we consider the organizing symbol as a representation of self or self and other interactional experience as is possible with self states and symbiotic states.

Understanding organizing-level symbols cannot proceed from considering the rules of the code and then decoding to arrive at personal meaning. Rather, we must begin by understanding the person's idiosyncratic prerelationship experiences in their specificity — as expressed in here-and-now relating. The critical experience that will point to the way a person is utilizing a symbol at the organizing level is the experience of searching for contact, approaching the other expectantly, having that possible or real contact ruptured traumatically, erecting barriers to ever having such contact experiences again, and/or arranging a retreat. Only after we become skilled at seeing the individual's prerelatedness experience can we then take a look at the symbols being employed to express that experience. We then see that social forms (symbols) have been (imitatively) impressed into expressive service, which, in the mind of the person, privately captures some aspect of his or her organizing experience. But the person's *use* of the symbol remains idiosyncratic, unlike the way better-integrated experience is expressed.

In contrast, the oedipal experience is, *par excellence*, an experience of embedding one's private experiences into the symbolic order such that one remains forever alienated in ways from the somatic self that are mirrored by the system of language and culture (Lacan 1977a,b). Complex psychic life is lived in a set of cultural and linguistic mirrors. Preoedipal self experience is more personally expressive in the sense that one is using common language to represent (rather than to symbolize) self experience and patterns of self and other experience. But organizing symbols stand as personally chosen, arbitrarily employed bits of a complex system that the person has not learned to fully integrate or to assimilate into his or her somatopsychic experiencing. The organizing symbol serves to express personal experience, but its use is so idiosyncratic and arbitrary that it is simply not subject to the usual decoding processes to which a symbol ordinarily lends itself.

How can we understand this presymbolic use of symbols? In ordinary, expectable human experience a mother's handling moves the child's experiences toward broad social consensus as the two share in ordinary human realities, as the two learn to express personal realities in socially established forms—gesture, sign, and symbolic expression through language, image, and metaphor. But if a mother, for whatever reason, is experienced as too intrusive, too distant, too bizarre, too destructive, too depressed, or otherwise lives outside of ordinary human consensual realities, the infant's experience may not be brought into that common realm that characterizes the human symbolic order. That is, meaning will not be shared, but will be idiosyncratic. The child may learn to mimic or to conform to shared realities, but she will not know how to be an integral part of them in relatedness situations herself. Her symbols will then come to *express* (1) the search for and the fear of contact, (2) reflexive consciousness, (3) nonhuman forms and forces, (4) body preoccupations, (5) disorientation in time and space, and/or (6) the yearning for and fear of human contact (touch). She will find or invent symbols to express how contact for her has the power to transform as well as the power to traumatically rupture contact.

Summarizing, symbols as we ordinarily consider them, express our personal relatedness experiences in interpersonal, agreed upon forms. When the critical experiences that govern a person's life are prerelational, there will be a deficit in the capacity to experience social consensus and in the capacity to appropriately utilize symbols that abound in human consensus. But the person may learn to imitate human life or human symbols and then to use imitative understanding to express his or her concerns. Analysis of such an expressive process is not subject to the usual decoding of symbolic expressions. Organizing symbols are idiosyncratic. Attempting to understand them apart from prior understanding of the nature of a person's basic prerelationship experience is bound to be misleading and futile.

A CASE ILLUSTRATION FROM FRANCES TUSTIN

To illustrate the way in which people living in various organizing states develop and utilize private symbols for expressing themselves,

Frances Tustin and Marion Solomon have graciously permitted me to print a transcription of a presentation Tustin made for Continuing Education Seminars to a group of Southern California analysts led by Solomon, who visited London in the summer of 1985. Therapists who view the videotape (available through Continuing Education Seminars, 1023 Westholm, Los Angeles, CA) of Tustin presenting this session with Peter are awestruck and envious at the power and depth displayed in her understanding. What follows is a transcription of her spoken presentation and a brief commentary directing attention to Peter's idiosyncratic use of symbols.

I will tell you about a boy called Peter. He came to me age six years. Since he lived in the North of England, he only came twice a week. This was much less than I ordinarily saw these children. I usually saw them at least four times a week and usually five. But this little boy came just twice a week.

To bring Peter to his session the parents used to drive down to the little country village in which I lived in Buckinghamshire, and would leave him with me for an hour. Then they would go on to London to stay with relatives. Then on a Sunday, (that was on a Saturday), they came back by my little village (so Peter could have another hour with me) and went off to the North Country where they lived. They were very devoted and dedicated parents as you can see. And they didn't make it a trial at all to come such a way. Later they even bought a caravan and put it in a field in the next village to mine and they used to bicycle as a family up to see me. This was when Peter was getting very much better.

Well Peter was a classic example of Kanner form of autism. He had been seen at age two and a half by Anni Bergman. Now many of you will know Anni Bergman. It was at the time when she was Margaret Mahler's senior therapist. She is now running her own unit in New York University. I won't go into how she told me about Peter because it is a very interesting story, but it is a bit anecdotal and gossipy and I want to get on. But she told me that she had seen Peter, aged two and a half, and that he was one of the worst autistics she had ever seen. People in England say, "Autistic children cannot be treated." Then I say, "I have got them better." Then they say, "But they can't have been autistic." It is a lovely syllogism. But obviously Anni Bergman was very experienced in the diagnosis of autistic children. Also I was very fortunate in having Dr. Mildred Creak of Great Ormond Street who sent me most of the children that I have treated. I don't think anybody in this country or in the rest of the world would dispute Mildred Creak's diagnosis. She was a superb diagnostician of psychotic children. She always said, "I'm no therapist, but I can send you children that you can treat." And she did. I think with this audience I don't really need to establish the fact that the children were autistic, but in England it does need to be established.

Well Peter had had some educational therapy and the parents were grateful for this, but they felt that it didn't go far enough. This was why they sought out psychotherapy. They had seen, so they told me later, several people before coming to me, but they thought that I talked common sense. I think it was perhaps because I have a slight North Country accent which gives everything you say a feeling of being down to earth and very commonsensical. They were used to the North Country.

In the early sessions Peter behaved like most autistic children do. He walked on his toes. And he walked as though he were floating. He was beautifully formed, as these children are. He had a lovely physical body. He touched objects with a featherlight touch. He had a very few words which this educationist had helped him to acquire and, as I began to realize later, how he touched these objects was very, very significant. But I didn't understand as much as I do now, at that time. He rubbed his bottom and his whole body against the walls.

What was unique to Peter was that he carried a large keyring. Yes, I have written about this little boy in *Autistic States in Children* (1981). But the session I am going to give you is not one that was recorded there. Well Peter had this huge keyring. He was nearly bent over double when he first came to see me carrying this keyring. In the early sessions he would finger these keys in various ways. I think Peter responded more quickly to psychotherapy than most of the children, autistic children, I have had because I think he had been helped by his educational therapy. It was behaviorist. It was by a man who evolved his own peculiar methods for treating handicapped children of all kinds, physically as well as psychologically handicapped. I don't know whether to call him a genius or whether to call him a way out weirdy, but he certainly brought his own particular methods to educating the handicapped. He had helped Peter to be with cognitive things, but Peter's feelings were absolutely nonexistent, and his relationships with people were just nil. He didn't look at you, you know the way autistic children avoid looking at people. Well, he was very typical in this. I would feel that I didn't exist for him, that I was a nobody, that I was a non-person. I would feel that I just did not exist. I knew that this was the most difficult time in the work with these children. I think it helps if we can understand something of what is going on in that very early time with these children. It helps us understand those patients who are silent. And adult patients or neurotic patients who are so difficult to reach if we get some idea of what is going on in the child's mind. Because even at this stage the child has a mind. If we have some idea of what is going on in that early stage, it can help us to understand our very difficult to reach adult patients. I only realized later much of what was going on in those early days.

I should say the keys didn't have any purpose other than their idiosyncratic purpose to Peter. As I realize now, they were at some times autistic objects and at other times they were autistic shapes.

After about three months, and that is very quick, of this type of activity in which I felt useless and shut out, there was a breakthrough in that Peter started to draw around the outlines of the keys. He did lots of them. He kept on doing it. Then after about a month of this, there was the wonderful day when Peter came in and drew another picture. That was a wonderful day because he drew the chest of drawers in which the children's toys were kept and there were keys against the keyhole of each drawer! He drew a key against the keyhole of each drawer. So now, you will understand why it was so remarkable. Keys had a realistic function which could be shared with other people in the outside world. They had a shared function. We all use keys in that way and so they were no longer used in his idiosyncratic, peculiar way, as an autistic object to keep him safe or as an autistic shape to help him to feel comforted. They were now real keys used in the real world and they were related to the chest of drawers in which the children's toys were kept, which was very significant to him. A relationship to me was now developing and I no longer felt such a non-person. I really felt that I was a presence in the room to Peter.

The session I am going to present occurred when this relationship was developing well and Peter was talking, laconically but personably. This gave me insight into the strange world in which Peter lived. I want us to stand within that strange world this morning to give us a slightly new perspective on our work with adult patients and with neurotic child patients too. The session is going to be presented just as I recorded it after the session. It is by no means a perfect session, but I am presenting it warps and all. I am sure you will be able to help me understand it more fully.

The session occurred four months into therapy. Father had been away. He often went away. He was due back the next day after this one and I knew this. His (Peter's) mother had told me as Peter came into the room with me that Daddy was coming back tomorrow.

Peter entered the room carrying a banana encircled by his hand proudly and triumphantly saying, "Look what I have got!" As I looked at it, it seemed to be much more than a mere banana. It seemed to be growing out of his hand and to be part of his body. It was the way he held it and the triumphant gleam in his eyes which gave me this impression. Well, he peeled the banana and he ate it voraciously with great greedy gulps. He hardly chewed it, but he let it slip down his throat, rolling it round on his tongue as if it were part of his tongue. It was gone in three bites and gulps. As soon as it was gone his triumphant look and stance collapsed. He looked tired and old. He looked at me pitifully and said, "I've got a sore place." As he said this he touched his mouth and then said, "On my arm." He offered his arm for me to look at and there was, indeed, a small sore place. He said, "Susan," that's his sister, "did it to me. She scratched my thing away from me." He then went on to say, "He," he said "he" instead of "she," "Is younger than me and she doesn't know any better." It seemed as though he was repeating what his mother had said to him. He continued, "He scratched me." It was a small, round sore place which looked to me to be more like a bite. The whole speech was somewhat confused. I said I thought that while Daddy was away he and his mother had become very close to each other like when he was a little baby. Daddy coming back tomorrow stirred up the time when he had felt that the lovely sensation thing in his mouth, which connected him to the Mummy had been snatched away from him by Daddy and later on by Susan, his sister. He felt that losing it left a sore place. He said, "What's a dinosaur?" These children, when they begin to speak, you know, have a very wonderful vocabulary. I said that he felt that if he knew a lot of long words, like dinosaur they would plaster over the sore place.

When I have presented this hour to therapists, some have not been satisfied with that interpretation. They have suggested he might have been saying that he had to "dine off a sore"—dinosaur. These children do play with words. It is not punning. They really think that the meaning is embedded in the word. You know like the nominalists and the realists, I'm never sure which one it is that think that. Or he might have been saying "die now sore." Well anyway, I didn't say that to him. He said, "Daddy gave Mummy the keys so that she could lock up the factory so that no one could take anything." I said that it made him feel very unsafe when he found that his mother wasn't joined to his body. He was afraid that his mother was no longer locked up and that his things weren't safe. He gave a strange reply to this saying, "When the stopper came out of the bottle, I fell and fell and there was no bottom." I said, "Yes. It was very frightening when you found the nipple thing wasn't in your mouth like the key to lock it up."

Peter went to the mirror and looked at his mouth and gazed at the gaps where his milk teeth had been. I said now that his first teeth were coming out, it reminded him of the time when he felt that he had lost the nipple stopper from his mouth and he had felt that there was a gap, an empty space. He said, "I'll teach them to grow!" I said, "There is a part of you that knows that you can't teach them to grow. That it is not under your control to make them grow. That you have to wait for them to grow." He said in a forlorn way, "I *am* the manager!" I said, "It is hard for you to have to learn that things happen to you which you don't arrange yourself. You so much want to feel that you are in control of everything so that nasty things don't happen like finding that you and Mummy aren't joined together and that you have to share her with Susan, your sister, and with Daddy." And then, he always called my husband Arnold, I said, "Similarly you also have to share me with Arnold and with the other children. All that hurts you and makes you feel sore." He was still at the mirror and he extended his tongue. As he looked at his mouth he said, "Boiler." He had talked enough about boilers in other sessions. I hadn't found the significance of this, of the word to him. Suddenly, at this point in the session I had a flash of intuition and I said, "Oh, I know. Do you think that boiler is a boy with an extra bit to his body? Is that it?" And he nodded very pleased that I had at last understood. You see autistic children use words as though they are concrete objects. They are not abstract words. Words are physical, material things. And boiler—that had a boy with an extra bit. You can see why they find it quite difficult to learn as the normal child learns because they are living in this very magical, strange world.

I went on, "When you were a baby you felt that the feeding thing on Mummy's breast or on the bottle was an extra bit to your tongue. Like you felt like the banana was an extra bit just now." He came and stood beside me because I think he felt I was really understanding him now. When he felt that, he had what he later called "a conversation." He stood beside me talking to me in a conversational way. He said, "I used to go to see Uncle Tom." Uncle Tom was his former teacher. He then said, "What is a partition?" I asked him what he thought it was. He said, "Something that divides one room from another." You see they are very bright really. And he then said, "Do you know what an intersection is?" I asked him to tell me what he thought it was, to which he replied, "Where the road divides." Well, I said the obvious thing. I said, "I thought he was feeling that he had to accept the fact that he was no longer part of Mummy's body, part of my body, but that we were divided from each other and that made him feel very sad."

However, at the end of the session the realization of our separateness was too much for him. I was sitting on the sofa with my arms folded, one on top of the other. Peter looked at my posture very carefully and then tried to copy exactly the way my arms were folded and my posture. I said that I thought when the session came to an end it was hard to bear the thought that we were divided from each other and went our separate ways. He felt that if he looked exactly like I did and copied exactly what I did, then we were identical with each other and we were not separate from each other. He nodded sadly. When I said it was time to go, Peter went to the door with heavy steps. Later Mother told me that Peter seemed very tired following his time with me. In the light of this session I believe she meant depressed.

COMMENTS ON TUSTIN'S SESSION WITH PETER

Peter's fierce attachment to his ring of keys, which serves no practical purpose, has been enigmatic to everyone. He carries them around, at times holding them tightly or brushing them lightly against various parts of his body. Tustin alludes to her general understanding that autistic children may use things as "autistic objects," holding them tightly, which functions to give the child a sense of safety, as we are told Peter has done at times. Or autistic children may use things as autistic shapes, lightly passing them over various skin, mouth, anus, or other surfaces to achieve a sense of comfort through manipulating the shapes that form on the sensorium, which we are told Peter also has done at times with the keys.

When Peter draws an outline around them, their importance seems to shift as they are no longer merely used as a part of his body but now are represented on a piece of paper in the same way that people represent themselves in drawing or writing. Shortly thereafter, the keys are drawn according to his recognition of their function in interpersonally shared realities. His drawing placing keys against each keyhole of each drawer in his drawing of the chest of drawers where children's toys are kept, introduces not only the shared function of keys but his awareness that her husband Arnold and other children have private relationships with Mrs. Tustin. In the countertransference she feels now more present in the room, no longer a nonperson but a real presence in the room.

Prior to the session Peter's mother informs Mrs. Tustin that Peter's father has been away and will be returning tomorrow so the stage is set for what we are about to witness. Peter enters triumphantly holding up a banana that somehow seems to be a part of his hand saying, "Look what I have got!" But no sooner than he has downed the banana in greedy gulps, after rolling it round on his tongue as if it were a part of his tongue, his triumphant look and stance collapse and he looks tired and old. Peter's theme as Tustin reads it goes: "I become depressed when the nurturing object that I perceive as a part of myself disappears." Pitifully he says, "I've got a sore place," touching his mouth but saying, "on my arm." The theme: "My injury involves my mouth and is related to when my sister came to take my mother's feeding place away, just like what will happen again tomorrow when Daddy comes home." Peter confuses "sister, she" with "he." Tustin interprets: "While Daddy is away you and Mummy have become very close like when you were a little baby. Daddy coming back tomorrow reminds you of the time you used to feel that lovely sensation thing in your mouth which connected you to Mummy and when it was snatched away by Daddy, and later by your sister, Susan. You feel that losing that left a sore spot in your mouth."

Peter clearly feels understood and responds, "Daddy gave

Mummy the keys so that she could lock up the factory so that no one could take anything." Suddenly the mystery of the keys comes out of hiding. *If he had just had the right key he could have locked the nipple to his mouth and no one could have taken it!* Tustin: "You felt very unsafe when you found that your mother wasn't joined to your body. You are afraid that mother is no longer locked up and your things are not safe." Peter: "When the stopper came out of the bottle, I fell and fell and there was no bottom." This is what happens when a child suddenly loses a nipple-stopper that rightly belongs to the bottle mouth, the bottom drops out, the baby feels endlessly dropped. Alice Balint (1933) writes about this primitive anxiety of being dropped.

At the mirror Peter locates the gap between his teeth and Tustin comments that the loss of his milk teeth reminds him of the time when he lost the nipple stopper from his mouth and felt there was a gap, an "empty space." Peter, feeling threatened with a loss of power, determinedly announces, "I'll teach them to grow!" Tustin: "There is a part of you that knows that you can't teach them to grow, that it is not under your control to make them grow, that you have to wait for them to grow." His forlorn response registers his sadness at being unable to control events that affect his mouth. He insists, "I *am* the manager!" Tustin: "It is hard for you to have to learn that things happen to you which you don't arrange yourself." She is resonating with Peter's sense of events "just happening" that destroy human connections. Suddenly he says, "boiler," a nonhuman word he has repeated somewhat nonsensically over the months. Tustin's intuition is quick as a flash because she knows how autistic children play with words as though they were things with meaning embedded in them. Another idiosyncratic symbol is suddenly unmasked, *"Boiler is a boy with an extra bit attached."* How much Peter longs to be a boiler once again with that nipple securely locked in place and under his control. Tustin: "When you were a baby you felt that the feeding thing on Mummy's breast or on the bottle was an extra bit to your tongue. Like you felt like the banana was an extra bit just now." Peter moves close for a conversation. But no sooner than he feels a connection, he thinks of Uncle Tom, his (now lost) former tutor whom he used to visit like he now visits Tustin. He may also sense that there is not much time left in the session and he will have to leave. Peter asks, "What's a partition?" Another idiosyncratic symbol becomes unmasked. He knows that *a partition divides one from another*, and that "intersection" is where *the road divides in two*. Tustin: "You are feeling sad that you are no longer part of Mummy's body or a part of my body, but that we are divided from each other."

At the end of the session we see physical primary identification (A. Balint 1943) at work before our very eyes in response to Peter's lifelong traumatic internalization of the unwanted division that Tustin has just voiced. He bodily imitates her posture in an effort not to be different from her, in hopes that if he is her he will not have to be divided by the end of the hour. Following the session his mother sees him as "tired," which Tustin interprets as "depressed." Peter has certainly made contact with his experience of connecting, which stirs the terror of having something that makes him feel secure taken away so that he feels as if he is falling endlessly.

In this magical session Frances Tustin sees exactly how Peter has impressed keys into expressive service as a personal symbol to express his passionate search for personal security, which was taken from him when the nipple revealed itself traumatically not to be under his control. The way he manages the banana and considers his milk teeth are all images or symbols that express his idiosyncratic need for his boy to have that extra bit to him. "Partition" and "intersection" are traumatic private symbols that express the sadness of no longer being part of mother's body, or of Tustin's body (and perhaps of Uncle Tom's). He attempts to master the trauma provided by Tustin's interpretations and the impending threat of loss of Tustin at the end of the session by physically identifying with the traumatizing (separating) object in the manner Alice Balint (1943) has written about. Through mimickry Peter *becomes* Tustin with her arms folded who sends him away. This identificatory posture at the time of separation may also express the reasons for the autistic state itself, and how it was internalized in the first place by feeling closed out and/or sent away.

We are indebted to Peter, Mrs. Tustin, and Dr. Solomon for this most illuminating example in which Peter impresses public symbols into personal and private expressions in a most idiosyncratic way.

11

Nonhuman Imagery, Focus on Physical Sensations, and Orientation in Time and Space

NONHUMAN IMAGERY

Beginning with Victor Tausk's (1919) paper on "the influencing machine," psychoanalytic literature on psychosis has highlighted the dominance of nonhuman imagery in the organizing experience. Harold Searles's monograph, *The Nonhuman Environment* (1960), clarifies the kinds of relatedness that tend to characterize organizing experience. His careful delineation of mechanical, impersonal, and supernatural forces that govern the nonhuman world prepares the listener for a special nuance of observation and interpretation that operates in attempts to organize sensorimotor experience. Searles's attention to the mystical, totemistic, and animistic sheds light on an entire range of possible interpretations that are likely to figure in one way or another in many people's efforts to organize their sensorimotor dimensions of the world.

Listening beyond the reflexive aspects of the clinical hour to the nonhuman content in organizing experience provides the possibility of increased empathy with the mechanical, nonhuman way in which a person may experience his or her body or thinks about diverse features of the world. Persons living organizing experience employ expressions in which people and human interactions are viewed essentially as complicated "things," powers, machines, trends, devices, forces, diseases, or robots. Talk of humans and their interactions may obscure a person's experience of impersonal movements and forces that must be reckoned with, controlled, or avoided.

Studies conducted by psychologists interested in the Rorschach Inkblot Test frequently focus on the projection of inanimate movement onto the inkblots. Experts generally do not expect people to project inanimate movement responses (e.g., spinning tops, swirling clouds, divine forces, dripping blood), the reason presumably being that humans tend to identify with animal or human movement. It has been thought that hyperactive children and manic individuals may project inanimate movement responses as a representation of their experience of the world whirling impersonally around them. Paranoid people may give inanimate movement responses, projecting fears of impersonal forces persecuting them—often interpreted by clinicians as hostile and sexual impulses that they dimly perceive inside and project outside. One fascinating study was conducted by a Canadian Navy psychologist (reported in Exner and Weiner [1982]) who rushed about a ship during a life-threatening storm asking sailors what they saw in the inkblots. That they projected vaguely ominous and threatening nonhuman movement seemed to reflect the raw, impersonal, threatening reality that they were having to deal with at the moment. Psychotic populations of all kinds have been known to score in this category of inanimate movement, presumably reflecting their predominant psychic involvement in a prehuman world governed by inanimate forces, strange happenings, and persecutory signs.

We often find the imagery that people use to describe organizing experiences is nonhuman. "I am held back by a prison wall, an iron cage, a glass door. When I almost reach to others so I can be real 'something happens,' a connection is melted by fire, the forces of the universe explode inside me, a bridge is pulled away, the road to the castle dead ends." In early discussions of the disconnect event in analysis, the person may feel blamed as if the disconnect is something that he or she is thought to be doing or is being held responsible for; but this is not the person's subjective experience. "I am trying, seeking, almost finding, and then . . . something happens; but it's not me, I'm not doing it. And you are just as bad as everyone else if you think so."

A FOCUS ON PHYSICAL SENSATIONS

Early organizational strivings, which form the core of what is to become known as the self, inevitably involve the sensorimotor apparatus. Studies in childhood psychosis (Mahler 1968) regularly observe preoccupations with and exaggerations of various bodily and sensory experiences. Auditory, tactile, visual, olfactory, and gustatory sensations, delusions, preoccupations, and hallucinations are to be expected in the course of listening to organizing experiences. Bodily sensations or hypersensitivities represent more than simply symptoms, and can usefully be listened to within the context of developing potentialities for personality functioning. Tustin (1981) reports the development of hallucinations, primitive phobias, and mood swings as regular and reliable indications of forward movement in psychotherapy. Her autistic children report not only fears of losing body parts and size (e.g., height or weight), but the belief that growth comes from snatching bits and pieces from the bodies of others. A preoccupation with body parts and sensations is basic to the organizing process and to be expected in psychoanalysis.

Freud in his study of Judge Schreber (1911) holds that no theory of psychotic processes can be trustworthy unless it covers hypochondriacal symptoms. He believed that hypochondria stands in the same relation to paranoia as anxiety neurosis does to hysteria, that is, as foundational, fundamental. At this point in history when we are able to locate the origin of functional psychosis in the earliest months of life, we understand that psyche is simply not distinguished from soma at this level of experience. As the baby reaches into the world with her body, her psyche takes the same path, is essentially the same process. So that when organizing experiences present themselves for study the experience is *always* a bodily experience. When people are analyzing the barriers to making and sustaining contact with the analyst they experience intense physical pain, and shake with terror, bodily terror—their head hurts, their heart pounds, their skin crawls, their blood runs cold, and so on. Likewise, when a satisfying connection can be made, the sense of comfort, safety, and well-being is physical as well.

Alexander Lowen (1971, 1975), originator of bioenergetics analysis, makes clear throughout his work that "we *are* our bodies," and "there is no change but body change." He states experience that tallies with that of any psychoanalyst who continually observes physical symptoms coming and going, who watches people writhe, shrink, scream, laugh, and weep—all with a body intensity that defies any sort of mere rationalization. We are our bodies. Our experience is our bodies. We reach and find with our bodies and suffer horribly on a physical level when we fail to find the relatedness to others that we need, or when we are reliving or remembering early failures through our bodies.

Hypochondriacal and psychosomatic symptoms are a regular part of an early fixation on body sensations and indicate a failure to represent experiences in psyche. Hypochondriacal preoccupations and psychosomatic symptoms are generally most usefully listened to in the context of organizing experience that has not yet found a way of being represented in psyche. In contrast to the general psychiatric view in America, which follows the model for neurosis (Alexander and French 1946), that psychosomatic illness involves a "body language" with "organ selection" and "symbolic displacement," Joyce McDougall (1986) and Andre Green (1986) have written most clearly on the prevalent continental view that psychosomatic preoccupations are somatic representations of experience that has not been represented in psyche.

In listening to organizing experiences the traditional search for the meaning of the somatic symptom, as with the psychic symbol, seems doomed to failure, since body and linguistic signs at the organizational level of experience have not been integrated within the cultural system of signifiers. Baby's focal experiences at the organizing level are predominately those of her body and those of her mother's body, which she seldom has occasion to differentiate from her own.

ORIENTATION IN TIME AND SPACE

An infant learns about time and space through orienting to mother's body and to her movements and activities. We find that many people who pervasively live organizing experiences often have persistent difficulties in their time and space orientation. It is surprising to do a survey of a random grouping of people in terms of how they find places on the map, how they determine compass directions, and then how they know where they are and how to get to where they are going. People have different ways of keeping oriented. One 9-year-old boy persistently drew maps in his therapy sessions. He would map out his special education school and its grounds so he knew where to eat, what teachers would welcome him at their door at any time, where his favorite books and videocassettes were located, and where the director's office was located, "just in case you have any important questions." Maps for weekend excursions all over Southern California included freeways and exit directions to Disneyland, Knott's Berry Farm, Sea World, the San Diego Zoo, and its Wild Animal Park, among other critical destinations. Finally it became evident that the boy could barely stay oriented to cross a street, so he and the therapist begin walking the neighborhood getting directions straight from the sun's shadows, the ocean breeze, and the occasionally visible mountains. Finally he and his therapist traversed by bus his route to and from home including how to transfer, buy a soda while waiting, and how not to confuse landmarks. All of this activity was accompanied by a profusion of maps and step-by-step directions he made up as he learned orientation. The critical dimension to all of this, however, was not merely the instructions but the working through of what prevented him from reaching his destination, from finding his teachers, his therapist, and his home. Child psychologists note all manner of emotional disturbance in the Wechsler Preschool and Primary Scale of

Intelligence (WPPSI) Maze Test in which the lost chick must find the mother hen!

Our time sense is also deeply personal—what time means to us, how we relate to promptness, delay, rush, others' time versus our own time, and so forth. Since time and space are so highly personal, and social forms of time and space are learned later than the organizing period, an analytic listener can expect to hear many references to unusual, confusing, or frightening experiences of time and space and of the perceptual modes involved (seeing, hearing, smelling, touching). The first ground is mother's body (Keleman 1975). The first map is of mother's breast and face followed by her unconscious response system. Sight, sound, warmth, cold, smell, and touch are all involved in this early map making. Time is also an essential learned ingredient in all relationships. Organizing states are highly varied with regard to personal use of time and space. (An extended case illustration entitled "Lost in Time and Space" appears in Hedges 1994b.)

12

Transformation Through Connection

TOUCH: THE FOUNDATION OF HUMAN EXPERIENCE

In the Bible we are told that while God created the other animals, he breathed the breath of life into Adam. On the ceiling of the Sistine Chapel Michelangelo portrays the conveyance of Divine spirit from God to Adam through extension and touch. In Madonna paintings the spirit of the Divine on earth is nurtured through swaddling, holding, suckling, and tender attentiveness. A recently published interdisciplinary symposium entitled *Touch: The Foundation of Experience* (Brazelton and Barnard 1990) explores in depth the meaning and impact of touch in human life. Several of the philosophical contributors to this symposium trace the study of touch from Plato and Aristotle through twentieth century commentators. The general consensus of opinion corroborates the Michelangelo conclusion that the human sense of Logos is passed down the generations through touch. Whether touch or laying on of hands is actual or metaphoric, what is consistently seen to be of importance is the *desire* or *intention* on the part of the initiated in human spirit to "reach out and touch" the uninitiated. Mutual enjoyment of the touch may be a critical ingredient for many.

Traditional analytic approaches have eschewed physical contact of any type as being a violation of the fundamental stance of analytic neutrality practiced so rigorously in the treatment of neurosis. The notion that people have reliable and fixed interpersonal boundaries has been used to justify uncritically the psychoanalytic dread of physical contact. The willingness on the part of an analyst to engage in physical contact of any sort, even a gestural handshake, has generally been considered an acting out of some need on the part of the analytic listener to intrude into the analytic process. Yet we know that a wide variety of kinds of physical contact, from token and situational to deliberate and systematic, play a regular part in psychotherapy with early developmental organizations as practiced today, not only in nonanalytic schools, but in analytic work with preneurotic constellations.

Heinz Kohut's (1981) deathbed legacy to us involves a vignette in which he extended his fingers for a desperate woman to hold on to, and a commentary on the need to study a developmental line of the faculty of empathy from concrete physical forms to more abstract mental forms. Vignettes like Casement's (1986) agonizing experience of being begged for hand holding until both he and his patient were able to establish that in this instance it was unnecessary, are highly instructive in considering how an analyst might go about differentiating a compelling request for physical contact that might be unwise or unnecessary from an instance in which some form of touch might be unavoidable or even indicated. The famous Lipton (1977) incident in which he permitted one of his patients who had a fever to use his office thermometer has been bandied around in the psychoanalytic literature endlessly with many feeling that this form of contact was too intimate, that "whistling Dixie" in a session is not an appropriate form of analytic contact. One quickly surmises that a major problem with the traditional so-called frame technique is that it introduces a systematic morality into the analytic encounter that may keep things tidy and may serve to bolster the defenses of the analytic listener, but may not lead to optimal responsiveness to the client at the moment.

We now know that without involved and attentive human contact the baby would die of marasmus. We are now equally clear that quite apart from genetic and biological considerations, functional psychotic conditions are directly attributable to missing, defective, erratic, inappropriate, or intrusive early human contact. From studies of childhood psychosis and dynamic psychotherapy with psychotic states in adolescents and adults, it is also clear now that human contact, usually accompanied by or manifest in some form of physical touch, is requisite to transforming reflexive mental states into symbiotic bonding patterns. The foundation of human experience is now understood to be generally related to contact, to touch in some form by an other *who is well motivated to achieve and sustain the contact in an enlivening manner.*

The ongoing technical controversy rages around whether some form of literal, physical touch may be requisite or unavoidable. While I am sympathetic to the wishes of many that actual physical contact is avoidable in analytic transformation of organizing states, in persons whose lives are lived in predominantly organizing reflexive mental states I have yet to observe a single instance in which major psychic transformation has been accomplished in an atmosphere of total abstinence of physical contact. On the basis of observations, and flying in the face of the many therapeutic, legal, and ethical concerns, I cannot assert or assume that this work can be done without, at some point or another, in some way or another, *interpretation by way of human touch* being necessary or optimal. Those who believe otherwise will be known by the success of their work with psychotics. It may seem theoretically plausible, but practically highly unlikely, that long-term transformative work can be accomplished without physical contact of some sort. There are obviously many difficult issues involved in an analyst's attempting to engage in timely, nonintrusive, nonacting out, and responsible *interpretive* analytic touch. When and how to engage in personalized therapeutic contact of any sort, much less actual physical touch, requires extensive training and supervision to insure that it is engaged in only sparingly, in proper ways, and at proper moments for a specific interpretive purpose.

People who have difficulty knowing how to distinguish sensitive, nonintrusive touch that is of interpretive and therefore of transformative value from other forms of touching clearly should not engage in this type of work and should avoid touching altogether. From an ethical or legal standpoint it is advisable for an analyst or therapist not to engage in touching unless a consultative or third-party case manager or case monitor is involved, as a protection for the analyst as well as for the client. The issue of physical contact inevitably involves the analyst's personal and professional integrity so that personal comfort in this area must be achieved before using interpretive touch in transformational work with organizing aspects of personality. An appendix to this book contains a model informed consent form that may be helpful when therapists are considering touch as a part of their interpretive work.

TRANSFORMATION THROUGH CONTACT

Basic organizational aspects of personality are not thought to be readily accessible for analytic study via the usual verbal-symbolic, introspective modes of investigation that have characterized the analysis of neurosis. Nor are organizational issues available for analysis through the mode Kohut has called "self to selfobject resonance." Nor are they available through interactive modes of investigation or systematic countertransference studies commonly used in understanding the symbiotic and postsymbiotic transferred relatedness modes encountered in borderline personality organization. The investigative mode *par excellence* for listening to organizing aspects of personality necessarily becomes that of interpretive contact and "interception" (Hedges 1983, Chapter 12). Organizing features must be met (intercepted, contacted) during moments of sensorimotor or cognitive-affective extension in order for the impact of the inconstant configurations of the (part) other to be experienced and registered in the emerging personality formation, along with various contrasting experiences of (part) selves.

The crucial implication of this line of thinking is that therapeutic connection with early organizational aspects of personality will not be possible through extensive analysis of symbolic or symptomatic representations since these manifestations are mimical or secondary constructions arising in reaction to early faulty object relations. Overtly psychotic phenomena represent abortive attempts at self stabilization or self nurturing and soothing, which only seldom include representations favorable for realistic relatedness to others. Grave therapeutic limitations have been repeatedly demonstrated through exclusive reliance on (1) extensive analysis of the symptomatic or symbolic content of the psychotic life, (2) therapeutic immersion in the subjective "psychotic world," and (3) utilization of countertransference reactions to (the fragmenting/withdrawing aspects of) psychosis.

The infant, child, or adult whose personality is arrested at, or who is temporarily living with, early organizing issues is usually seen as living in "a world of his or her own." The nurturing, soothing, pacifying other must patiently wait until the infant or person is momentarily oriented for contact with the other. The child Celeste, reported by Ekstein (1979), played quietly every day in her analyst's room for many months until at last representations began to emerge in the form of small Kleenex figures that related silently to one another until the magic day when one special Kleenex figure approached and came to rest on the analyst's shoe. Had the analyst intruded into her play before she was ready to acknowledge his presence, he would no doubt have been repeating the intrusive trauma of her infancy.

The analyst's work consists of creating an atmosphere in which sensorimotor extensions can be met or intercepted when they occur. Only then is the frame established in which the organizing or disconnecting transference can be studied. In Bollas's (1979) language, the task of the mother/other is to be available to assist in the transformation of various self states.

During a diagnostic study of one severely disturbed boy, it emerged that his maternal grandmother had died only days after he was born. In her agitated and fragmented grief, his mother was frequently unable to sleep. However, by waking the baby to feed, rock, and talk to him, she would become soothed enough to sleep herself. Her ministrations were thus related more to her own comfort than to the child's need. In these and other ways, the infant's vacillating need states were not adequately responded to at moments when *he* was extending in sensorimotor readiness. The therapeutic task became one of encouraging the emergence of early need states and intercepting or transforming them along lines that were comforting to the child.

As baby gazes and plays timelessly at mother's breast, mother must herself be prepared to enter into a reverie or altered state of consciousness and to wait for a moment when contact becomes possible. Momentarily eyes meet. Then follows the smile, the gentle caressing and rocking that brings (reinforces, seduces?) baby into relatedness. Her small hand stretches aimlessly until suddenly it is caught by her own gaze. Then comes the squeeze, the gentle tones of mother's voice, the many signals that reinforce and transform the nature of the connection between the hand in the visual field and the hand being stroked. This connection occurs against the background of mother's smile, gentle voice, and soothing motions. Stimulating experiences produced by internal states, as well as experiences produced by impinging external stimuli, are intercepted with attention and reinforcement by maternal intelligence and preoccupation, thus "teaching" (by classical conditioning processes) the possibility of altered or transformed states. Adequate empathically guided interceptive experience leads toward a mother–child mutual cuing and bonding process, which characterizes the "protective shield" of the symbiotic envelope or canopy (Khan 1963). Subsequently, overwhelming states are only experienced during the absence of the symbiotic partnering experience, whether that absence is manifest in the actual external partner or in various internalized counterparts.

As the analytic listener first assumes a place in the psychic life of the person living with organizing issues it will likely be in a transforming role. Bollas's (1979) discussion of the "transformational object" contributes fundamentally to an understanding of the listening context of the analytic situation. Earliest experiences of parenting involve the transformation of bodily functions and mental states. Bollas points out that Freud (forgivably) failed to take note of the fact that the analytic situation itself constitutes an "acting out" of the early transformational experience.

A person arrested in an organizing state is presumed to have suffered deficits and/or traumas in the early transformational processes. While the person may sometimes be quite ready to have the deficits (usually various dependency needs) responded to by the analyst, the traumatized areas pose more of a problem. Presumably early parental omissions and/or commissions missed their mark, resulting in various affective and cognitive constructions (i.e., the so-called psychotic symptom constellation). In other (more favorable) cases, persistent searching, orienting, and *organizing* processes mark personality development.

An awareness that the transformational processes themselves may enhance the analytic connection with organizing states suggests a new set of listening concerns. The analyst must be content to set aside verbal and even interactional approaches in deference to the more subtle but crucial role of being present for or witnessing transformation of various early developing self states through empathic connection or interception until mutual cuing can become an important factor.

Bion (1962) has contributed fundamentally to our understanding of this contact process with his theoretical concepts "container" and "contained." For many years his basic research question was, "Why does one monkey think and the others do not?" His ideas have resulted in an elegant and complex theory of the origins of human thought. One of Bion's key ideas is of use to us in understanding the *function of actual interpersonal contact as reflective interpretation* of baby's flexions or extensions. Bion speaks of "beta elements," which roughly correspond to sensory experiences. Baby experiences beta elements and, in one way or another, she expresses or her mother intuits some experience or state such as hunger, gas pains, or drowsiness. Baby is essentially helpless to *do* anything about that state but baby's mother using her relatedness intelligence thinks and acts in such a way as to transform baby's state. After a series of similarly repeated sequences, baby, through processes we might consider almost as classical conditioning, comes to link together the beta sensations with a rudimentary alpha element, which is a primary thought process involving the transformational mother. Bion labels this maternal function vis-à-vis baby "the container and the contained" to indicate a circular process from baby's sensory experience through mother's thought system, through the resulting physical and mental transformation of the experience, and returning to baby's sensory experience. Note how Bion's model of a circular thought pattern from baby to mother's transformational activities and returning to baby's sensorium is distinctly different from, and marks a decided progressive complexity over, the basic reflex arc model (see Figure 9–1) that Freud believed characterized the earlier and original situation.

From this rudimentary beginning more complex forms of thought develop, leading to the acquisition of high-level abstractions. The key feature of Bion's argument is that the emergence of thought requires that another person first think for the infant. The sequence leading toward the development of complex thinking only becomes possible when some subtle flexion or extension of baby's is met, contacted, or intercepted by the thoughtful caregiving other.

Confirming this general line of thought is the work of the Soviet neuropsychologist Vygotsky, who has demonstrated in a variety of ways that human learning is governed and aided by cultural tools that the individual contacts in his or her immediate social environment.

At this point in our hypothetical path toward connection with the human environment we will proceed as if baby has extended in some way and has been successfully contacted by mother. But soon we will return to this point on the path to connection and consider what happens when baby is not met.

THE ESTABLISHMENT OF MUTUAL CUING

Empathic, noninterfering, enlivening contact with a person's organizing processes may be expected to lead toward a mutual cuing process between basic personality dimensions of the analyst and elemental organizing extensions of the person in analysis. Searles (1979) has depicted psychoanalysis with unorganized mental states as consisting of the formation of a "therapeutic symbiosis" followed by successive phases of separation and individuation. According to Searles, both analyst and patient have the eventual task of individuating from the union enriched in such a way as to be able to honor the

other's separateness and individuality. Searles's notion of the therapeutic symbiosis can prepare the analytic listener for the gradual
emergence of a mutual cuing process based upon the establishment of
ways of handling personal needs and preferences that each has in the
relationship. Only after the holding and containing functions are
smoothly in operation as a symbiotic relatedness pattern can the
separation-individuation processes be expected to go forward.

By the time baby can reach and her extensions can be met in
such a way that psychosomatic states can become transformed and
mutual cuing with significant caregivers begins, it is possible to
consider the operation of psychic mechanisms such as splitting and
projective identification. (For a thorough discussion of these processes, see Grotstein [1981 a, b].) Freud's formulation of the earliest
"purified pleasure ego" relies upon a presumed subjective understanding that "what is pleasurable is me, and what is unpleasurable is
not me." As this pleasure–unpleasure principle begins to give way to
the reality principle, the infant (sometimes with great reluctance)
begins relinquishing simple organizing experiences that contrast pleasure and pain, and begins more complex ego understandings of self
and others. At this point in our imaginary schema of baby's growth we
would begin listening with another perspective, one designed to
highlight affectively interactive experiences rather than reflexive experiences, one that recognizes complex self and other relating rather
than simply searching and reacting to finding or not finding. So our
journey into finding relatedness as a possibility ends here and is dealt
with elsewhere (cf. Hedges 1992). We now return to the contact point
in order to think through some of the consequences of baby not
finding suitable connections.

13

Transference Psychosis: The Rupture of Contact

CONTACT FAILURE

As previously acknowledged, no mothering situation can provide baby one hundred percent timely and empathic responsiveness to her perpetual extensions. Winnicott (1953) speaks of "good enough" mothering to indicate that a certain minimal kind of responsiveness is required for ordinary development. Others have spoken of such things as the "average expectable environment." But whether by accident, fiat, or parental intention, many infant sensorimotor or cognitive-affective extensions go unresponded to. Recent infant research (Tronick and Cohn 1988) suggests that infants and mothers may only satisfactorily connect thirty percent of the time! We do not know the exact effect of occasional lapses in attention or minor deviations in maternal preoccupation, but clinical studies of psychotic states demonstrate clearly the effects of chronically and/or traumatically failing contact — whether due to some shortcoming in the environment or to some inborn factor in the infant that precludes experiences of contact that might stimulate object relations development. We can only assume that lesser failings have a lesser, but no less real effect.

Failed contact is a universal human experience that has been neglected in considering internalized or retained emotional responses to not being connected with in the analytic encounter during periods when people are remembering by living out organizing experiences.

Thus far in our examination of the issues that the baby encounters on the path to connection we have seen what appears to be natural, instinctually determined extensions that have been met and thereby reinforced by someone in the environment who was attuned to the subtleties of the baby's physical and psychological existence. The path that is met by an attentive, enlivening other becomes circular so that the baby is reaching, exploring, finding, and *creating* satisfying and stimulating transformational experiences for herself. "Look, now she's smiling, now she's reaching to me, now she's concentrating on her bowels—she's becoming a real person!"

In the literary work of Kafka, Kosinski, and Suskind we see their heroes doing much the same thing as the baby we are following on her path to connection—searching, reaching, and in ever so many ways striving for connection with the potentially stimulating, tension relieving, and need satisfying environment. But with each of their heroes we notice something else. They never quite find the stimulating connection that leads to transformation. Their heroes never quite feel satisfied, never experience relief, never are able to transform their needs beyond the basic searching that our baby knows so well. Something has happened to foreclose further development of ordinary human relatedness. Kosinski and Suskind describe infancies that were understimulating, nongratifying, depriving, and traumatic. Kafka's work is largely autobiographical. In numerous places in his writings he accounts variously for the persistence of organizing states: to a prima donna, narcissistic mother in "Josephina, the Singer, or the Mouse Folk" (1924, in Kafka 1979); to an unconcerned and blaming father in "Letter to His Father" (1919, in 1979); to family dynamics in which he is regarded as a thing in "Metamorphosis" (1915 in 1979); to monstrous noises from the outside world pursuing him in "The Burrow" (1923 in 1979); to not having been sent for and not having been allowed a basic identity in *The Castle* (1922, in 1926); to feeling guilty for not being a good-enough person to satisfy the world in *The Trial* (1914, in 1937); and to a host of other defects and causes.

IDENTIFYING THE CONTACT MOMENT

The central thesis of this book is that the organizing experience revolves around the contact moment. The analytic listener's first task is to sort through the reflexive content to determine where potential points of real interpersonal (affective) contact may be possible. Then the analyst learns to track the person's movement toward contact moments that seem as inevitable as any mammal searching for a breast. But somewhere just before, during, or immediately after contact "something happens" to make contact or sustained contact impossible. *It is the specificity of the contact-rupturing experience that must be brought under analytic scrutiny.* The person's internal, idiosyncratic way of rupturing contact is understood as the organizing or psychotic transference and can be fruitfully studied in the psychoanalytic setting. Resistance will come to be understood as the person's all-out efforts to avoid dealing with (1) the contact experience itself and (2) the traumatic life-and-death transference issues that terrifyingly must be relived if one is to sustain the contact. As resistance and transference analysis proceed, the transference psychosis will gradually become established. This is a complex state of affairs in the analytic relationship in which the earliest mother–child relationship that prevented the person from developing further is being lived out. This same listening tool is as useful for people living pervasive organizing experiences as for people who may be much better developed in many or most ways, but who need to explore some aspect of early organizing experience in their analysis.

Freud's fundamental concept of cure in psychoneurosis is the establishment of the transference neurosis, meaning the full and conscious establishment of the oedipal-instinctual attitudes of childhood in the here-and-now psychoanalytic relationship. That is, neurotic attitudes are created through repressive maneuvers of a

young child. The analysis of defense and resistance allows for the full
return of the symbolically repressed in the present (adult) relationship.
The analyst's task ends with the establishment of the neurotic attitudes in the analytic relationship—that is, when the ordinary neurosis
is replaced by the transference neurosis. There is nothing further to
resolve, work through, or strengthen. The parts of the self that had
been subject to repression have been liberated, the repressed (sexuality
and aggression) has returned in full force to contemporary experiencing by the mind of a conscious adult in full light of day. (For an
elaboration of Freud's notions of the curative value of the transference
neurosis see Hedges [1983, pp. 39–40].)

However, in preneurotic, preoedipal states, more than merely
experiencing a return of the repressed in the analytic relationship is
required for personality transformation. Kohut speaks of processes of
resonating understanding and of the benefits of human empathy
(beyond mere observation of another). Psychoanalysts who write
about borderline and symbiotic states speak of shifts in the ego to
accommodate new modes of relatedness. At the organizing level the
establishment of the transference psychosis has often been seen as the
ultimate place where the treatment may go, but it has not been
considered curative in itself as is transference neurosis. The reason is
clear: the establishment of the transference psychosis marks the
appearance of somatopsychic memories that have never been represented in psyche. It cannot fade harmlessly into the past unless
something in the present replaces it as a way of being.

The transference attitude that is brought forth for analysis of
organizing experience relates to the way contact has been ruptured
traumatically in the past. But the effect of the infant's internalizing
and subsequently continuing to live out the rupture experience is that
personality fails to develop in significant ways. We might think that in
the wake of the dissolution of a psychotic transference attitude the
person is ready to learn a new skill, that of sustained relating. But in
practice it does not work this way because the person has been so
terrified of failed contact that the psychotic manifestation, the organizing transference, does not yield completely to analytic work unless
and until the analytic speaker feels clear that he or she can indeed
safely connect with the real person of the analyst.

The organizing experience that is internalized can only be fully brought for analytic scrutiny when there is enough belief established that other ways of surviving the internalized infantile trauma are possible and available within the analytic relationship. It is only within the context of reliable analytic holding (Modell 1976) that a person dares reexperience the life-threatening infantile trauma of the organizing period, which is still silently alive in the personality. Only as the analyst offers a new and better way of relating in the here and now can the ancient disconnecting traumas be relived and actively relinquished in favor of actualizing in the analytic relationship more complex and flexible relatedness modes.

The fatal flaw that has destroyed analytic work of this sort since its beginning is that psychotic or organizing experience entails, by definition, a loss or alteration of appreciation of ordinary and consensual reality definitions. When this happens a negative therapeutic reaction (Freud 1918, 1923, 1933) may result and the therapy may end abruptly and prematurely, often with the analyst being experienced in the same way as the original traumatizing other. For this reason it has been a matter of routine that when a classical analyst encounters a psychotic pocket, regressive analysis has been ended in favor of supportive psychotherapy. In a later section of this book I take up the practical issue of securing a case manager or monitor for a variety of reasons, not the least of which is that when a negative therapeutic reaction threatens, a third party with whom the speaker has already gained some measure of comfort can be on hand to help guide reality testing by serving as an auxiliary ego while the transference psychosis is forming and is being analyzed. Whatever else cure or transformation may mean with organizing experience, it involves the full establishment of the transference psychosis and the subsequent renunciation of it in favor of other possibilities more in keeping with human consensual realities. But various transferred and realistic dangers and surprises may await the analytic listener in the process of framing and analyzing the organizing experience.

BREAKING CONTACT: THE NEGATIVE THERAPEUTIC REACTION

Occasionally emerging with the new freedoms, we observe an underlying destructive or self-destructive theme that threatens to obliterate or severely limit the flexibility of the relatedness gains that might otherwise be possible. Freud (1918, 1923, 1933) discussed this kind of event as the "negative therapeutic reaction." In his experience, an excessive idealization of the analyst that is persistent and resists analysis may give way to an overwhelming outbreak of denigration and destruction directed toward the analyst and toward the treatment process. The underlying motive Freud attributes to excessive "moral masochism," the compulsion to suffer righteously, and the obstinate refusal to give up a martyred, moralistically determined suffering, presumably based upon a primordial bonding and/or prebonding rupture pattern that was overlearned. "In order to be loved and to feel safe and fulfilled I must be in extreme pain, must feel abusively treated. I dare not find a way to comfort and relieve my agony or I will lose the cherished sense of righteous indignation I learned from my earliest experience with my mother."

When this type of severe earliest relatedness pattern is mobilized by the analytic work, the person may abruptly and aggressively abandon the analyst and the treatment (Freud 1918, 1923, 1933). The negative therapeutic reaction can now be seen as implying that the person has touched the organizing level of experience, has touched upon the agony of failed connection that he or she is obligated in love to endure, but that the person is held captive by a primary relatedness pattern that demands some kind of lonely suffering attributable to bitter and repeated failure of sustained contact. The person will likely be able to say exactly what form of (idealized) contact is needed from the analyst, but the entrenched determination to suffer and to punish the other for causing the suffering is the primary form of sanity and quality of relatedness experience that the person adamantly refuses to relinquish. Developmentally "below" or "historically earlier" than this long-suffering destructive and self-destructive relatedness pattern are various forms of agony related to extensions and yearnings for contact that have not been met. Agonizing, painful, unending, confused, convoluted, unsatisfying, and unrelieved wandering in search of connections that can be utilized for safety, soothing, and stimulation characterizes the organizing experience that may later color the bonding experience and is vividly depicted by Kafka in his voluminous writings.

An additional feature of the idealization and masochism implicit in those who are at risk for a negative therapeutic reaction is what might be called a "yearning for nirvana." By nurturing the belief or fantasy that everything should be, nay must be, perfect, ideal, blissful, happy, or totally cured these individuals insure ongoing and unending unhappiness, misery, suffering, and unrest. The ideal state of mind and being, like the ideal analyst who provides all that is necessary for comfort and safety, is a fantasy that is difficult to relinquish, especially if it is accompanied by an attitude of entitlement, the right to a perfect analyst, to a perfect analysis, and to a perfect and blissful outcome. Perfect trust in a perfect analyst is demanded so that "basic trust" (Erikson 1950) in an "optimally failing analyst" (Kohut 1977) cannot be achieved. When this foundational righteous entitlement and indignation become activated, an abrupt and angry termination of analysis is in the making. Freud spoke of a will, a determination to remain ill that under such conditions cannot be transcended. The analyst has now become the psychotic object who is either hopelessly overwhelming and must be painfully fled from or who must be pursued for revenge.

PSYCHOTIC TRANSFERENCE

With all the effort and devotion focused on the quest for human contact, how is it that the person living organizing issues is so often unable to find or to create ways of establishing the required connections? Every organizing issue or pattern that a person retains and actively lives on a daily basis is held firmly intact by a psychotic transference structure. Every organizing mode, regardless of its presumed cause, its thematic variety, or its pervasiveness in the person's life, owes its entrenched futility to a learned pattern of withdrawal from or avoidance of all or specially selected contact situations. The person has come to live in terror of the pain that in earlier life experiences was associated with contact and/or contact failures.

This fear of contact situations contrasts sharply with the fear of abandonment long familiar to analysts working with people living symbiotic or borderline interaction patterns or scenarios. At the earlier organizing level the fear is of contact. After the establishment of a firm holding and mutual cuing process (of whatever character) becomes established, the fear is of separation, loss, or abandonment of the other. But what exactly is meant by "psychotic transference" and how can the problem be analytically approached?

The pathway to becoming initiated and integrated into the psychological structures that characterize human cultural life as we think of it passes through the symbiotic bonding experience. The feeling of being real, of feeling human like other people, of sensing an aliveness and cultural attunement with the human race is cultivated and achieved by two in a mutually engaging symbiotic exchange where each learns about how to *relate to* the humanness of the other. When the young child has an opportunity to feel, to experience, to know about, to cultivate, and to live out her physical and instinctual endowment within an empathically attuned human relatedness pattern governed by considerations derived from the human cultural and linguistic community into which she was born, she has the opportunity to feel real, alive, and human.

Depending on the degree to which a person was deprived of this opportunity for organizing a self in tune with environmental, cultural, and linguistic possibilities, her daily living will remain restricted to prehuman or nonhuman relatedness capabilities. The efforts that the person made in infancy to reach out, to seek human contact and bonding were somehow ineffectual. Perhaps the baby's efforts were inadequate to draw the needed attention from caregivers. Perhaps her overtures fell on deaf ears, or worse, were met with sadistic, erratic, inappropriate, or traumatizing intrusions that caused her to withdraw from emotional relatedness situations of a certain variety or from human contact situations altogether. What is learned and overlearned by virtue of its primacy in experience or its intensity of deprivation or abuse, is *"never go there again."* Freud in his "Project for a Scientific Psychology" (1895) accounts for this absolute withdrawal in terms of the operation of the Psi System.

With strong or persistent negative reinforcement at contact moments, we might surmise that one or another of the mythic themes of psychosis (schizophrenia, manic-depressive, autistic, etc.) will come to characterize the forming personality, although it may not be altogether evident until much later, due to the development of adequate intelligence and socialization skills that mask the underlying object relations difficulties. Historically, the psychoses were known as *dementia praecox*, precocious dementia, because the disorganization showed up only in adolescence, childhood adaptation being adequate to mask the organizing themes and patterns. Later the term *schizophrenia* was used, that is, "split personality," to denote an early, masked premorbid personality and an ill personality taking over after puberty. It is now generally believed that the childhood ego is usually able to adjust adequately until the biological and social pressures accompanying puberty create an overload so that the basic object relations deficit that has been present in masked form since infancy becomes more readily visible. The ego, which mimics and/or adapts, may carry the person through life "passing" as normal or ordinary, or a life crisis or an analytic experience may bring the organizing experience into view.

With less traumatizing but less than optimal orienting and satisfying responsiveness from the environment, the more dramatic psychotic themes may fail to develop as a substitute for satisfying object relations. But an inadequate, ineffective, wandering, "organizing" life-style may develop, which could take on any kind of appearance. Regardless of how good the organizing life-style looks, or how well the person is able to pass as normal, upon close scrutiny the object relations deficit is discernible. With many organizing personalities even expert scrutiny is not needed to see the inefficient, ineffective, unrewarding life the person is living. Psyche or soul in the ordinary sense has simply not undergone the emotional relatedness transformations of symbiotic bonding and subsequent separation-individuation and it shows up in his or her everyday lackluster, chaotic, confused, or restricted personal life.

The emotional bond that characterizes human life and that serves *character*istically to orient the person to other people, according to a personally forged emotional style, has not been made. The person is perpetually engaged in orienting to the realities of the world without any consistent, reliable, or integrated relatedness style, interpersonal relatedness patterns, or modes of interpersonal exchange. Analytic workers may refer to such life-styles as "masochistic" but this notion is inadequate since there is no motivation to retain an attitude of suffering as there might be in an overlearned symbiotic, narcissistic, or neurotic pattern. The person is simply not equipped, by virtue of not having had a symbiotic bonding experience, to deal with the relatedness complexities and nuances of human social and cultural life. Such individuals, like Kafka's characters, pass through the world of people, not comprehending human relationships and being continuously bombarded by misunderstood intentions. One wonderful character in a short story of Dostoyevski is totally devoted to his office duties but will not, and we later realize that he cannot, deviate from his known daily rituals as a copyist to satisfy the more diverse demands of social life. The mimical self prevails with some false self conformity patterns but true instinctual, bodily, and psychological self-integrations are absent, leaving the person vulnerable to the winds of fate.

Those whose infancy was traumatically encroached upon have developed lives organized along stereotypic patterns or common symptomatic themes that do not serve to establish creative, flexible, and efficient ways of sustaining relationships. These people may be extremely intelligent, may be highly adapted to the social order, may hold good jobs, may contribute in significant ways, and may have friends and family. But throughout, there is an absence of some essential human ingredient—the flexibility that comes from meting out a deeply personal emotional relationship with a significant other in infancy. After infancy the person either learns to passably disguise the deficit from view of others or finds ways of enduring the humiliations offered by others for his or her lack of understanding and faulty emotional finesse. Or the person may develop an emotionally isolated or defensively covered life-style, always sensing that "something is wrong with me, I'm different from other people, not quite human somehow, I'm strange or weird." Many, if not most, of the people currently reporting "recovered memories" in altered states of hypnosis, chemically induced interviews, and/or psychotherapy seem to be producing "flashbacks" that operate like dreams on the basis of condensation and displacement.

It is this psychotic or organizing transference, the expression of and the embodiment of ruptured contact, that appears just at the moment interpersonal relatedness becomes a realistic possibility. The resistance to experiencing the traumatic rupture again can be expected to be fierce. Instead, the person (defensively) shifts into her mimical self.

THE ORGANIZING PERSONALITY AND THE
MIMICAL SELF

As research into all types of organizing states progresses, what becomes more clear is that organizing issues or organizing aspects of personality are by no means limited to the more obvious forms that have been designated "psychosis." Elemental organizational strivings can be observed to form the foundations of all personality functioning to a greater or lesser degree. More importantly, what has emerged in clinical practice is a surprisingly large group of persons whose personality functioning is limited in various ways by their continuing to live on a daily basis various organizing, searching, and orienting patterns, but who demonstrate little overt psychotic symptomatology. These "closet" organizing personalities fail to make full use of shared realities, although they are able, often quite successfully, to mimic the behavioral and sociocultural standards of the world surrounding them and thereby to lead often quite successful business, professional, social, and family lives. Psychiatrists are now referring to such persons as "asymptomatic psychotics," although they are commonly diagnosed as borderline or schizoid character disorders. "Normal"-appearing organizing personalities function on the basis of a "mimical self," a psychic capacity for imitation, ritual, and/or compulsive mimic of human behavior and interactions. Eccentric, idiosyncratic, or constricted functioning may be displayed in these elemental states regardless of what mythic themes the person may be living or whether he or she is simply imprisoned in an endless searching and orienting mode imitating others to get along in the world.

The hero of Jerzy Kosinski's *Being There* is certainly a prototype of the undifferentiated, unorganized person able to get along in the world by virtue of mimicry. In Hal Ashby's film version we see Peter Sellers always glued to an available television set and bodily mimicking the gestures he sees portrayed there. Kosinski's irony serves to further suggest how universal the mimicry is as we watch our world of everyday reality function likewise on the basis of sophisticated mimicry. Our difficulty in distinguishing good mimicry from sophisticated personality organization and integrated relatedness flexibility is pointed to by Kosinski when at the end Chance is seen as the most viable candidate by the party for the presidential nomination! Although he clearly identifies himself as Chance, the gardener, people insist on seeing him as Chauncy Gardenier, eminent world economist, further emphasizing our tendency to fill in the gaps for people, to see what we want to see, to overlook mimicry if it is well done. I have observed in consultation numerous analysts completely taken in by effective mimical selves, so wishing to be related to as a real person in the analytic role that they fail to notice the imitation of object relations. Sometimes analysts, in their eagerness to be known for their personal qualities, fail to notice that they are not at all being responded to as living, breathing human beings, but rather are being perceived as some object or obstacle in the environment to be dealt with.

The notion of the "mimical self" would be the developmental precursor to Winnicott's (1952) concept of the "false self," which relies on at least a preliminary recognition of the (m)other in order *to adapt and to conform to* her demands. Winnicott's formulation of the false self is a function of conformity to demands of a symbiosis, while I have defined the mimical self function as arising in consequence of patternings that preclude or exclude more than a rudimentary recognition of the separate existence of others (Hedges 1983).

14

Countertransference to the Organizing Experience

Empathic contact with elemental organizing processes inevitably entails a certain regression, or what Furman and Katan (1969) have called "ego flexibility," on the part of a mother or an analyst in order to attend to infantile psychic movements. Furman and Katan prefer to call the normal processes of maternal adaptation to the infant "ego flexibility" to avoid the pathological connotations they feel are present in the word *regression*. Narcissistic injury is frequently felt when a mother or an analyst is responded to at best as a need satisfier or at worst as a dreaded enemy, unreliable caregiver, or nonhuman intrusion.

Giovacchini's (1975, 1979b) penetrating focus on the disruptive effects that "primitive mental states" regularly have on the personal and professional integrity of the analyst points to very special listening problems. Giovacchini speaks of the "impact of the delusion" to refer to both the positive and negative effects that the patient's experience of reality have on the comfort and identity of the analyst. His discussions of the problems involved in maintaining, losing, and regaining the analytic stance prepare the clinical listener for disruptions in his or her own personality functioning when working with organizing experiences. Giovacchini discusses interventions and maneuvers undertaken by the analyst so that the analyst can continue functioning as an analyst. Anticipating disruptions in the analyst's personality functioning and being prepared to undertake tactics or maneuvers designed to maintain the analytic position and/or to shore up the personality functioning of the analyst constitute important contributions to clinical listening with organizing issues. Winnicott (1949) prepares the analytic listener to experience hate in the countertransference as an appropriate response to being exposed to hostile primitive introjects.

Different forms of countertransference experience, that is, emotional responsiveness on the part of the analyst, are to be expected depending upon the developmental level of the issues currently being presented for analysis. (See Hedges [1992] for a study of the variety of kinds of countertransference responsiveness.) Thus far, four distinct forms of countertransference have emerged with clarity that characterize therapists' responsiveness to organizing experience:

1. *The belief that the person is somehow so defective that he or she can only be treated chemically, physically, or supportively.* This belief is not confirmed by my studies and is directly opposed by many analysts with similar experience (cf. Sanville 1992). In my view this is a wholesale writing off of human potential and fails to take into consideration that these individuals possess full human capabilities that have been stopped short by infantile experiences that can be analyzed. There are certainly psychotic pictures that have as their basis an organic reason that human connectedness fails, but the vast majority of psychotic states are considered functional and therefore amenable to treatment with the proper environmental resources and psychological tools.

2. *The fear of psychotic energies being directed at the person of the analyst.* Melanie Klein is cited in Strachey's classic paper (1934) on the therapeutic action of psychoanalysis as having observed psychoanalysts' reluctance to make mutative interpretations (ones that have the power to transform). It was her belief that analysts fear encountering the full force of id energies directed squarely at themselves in the

transference, which interpretation promotes. We can now say that in the analyst's finding the good contact moments and seeking to bring the internalized modes of contact rupture into full emotional re-creation in the analytic relationship, the full power of a lifelong history of psychosis is being invited into the analytic consulting room with the analyst as the target of powerful psychosomatic energies. This prospect can be frightening and, indeed, with many organizing or psychotic states it is dangerous and inadvisable to attempt to work with it on a practical basis. Later I will consider practical issues regarding encouraging the emergence of the psychotic transference when it cannot be managed, and some of the factors that necessarily limit the safe emergence of psychotic transference. But aside from critical practical considerations, there is no reason in principle why emotions of whatever nature and intensity cannot be experienced in analysis and directed at the analyst. The analyst simply has to be prepared to tolerate the strength of their emergence.

3. *Organizing transferences stimulate the analyst's own organizing yearnings, traumas, and fears.* When an analyst repeatedly reaches out to someone and is not responded to or is responded to in intrusive or frightening ways, it tends to activate his or her own most primitive experiences when reaching out to mother and not finding her. Analysts may wish to keep the relating on a superficial level so as not to have to reexperience their own most primitive selves.

4. *An analytic listener may break contact out of empathy with the analytic speaker.* Well along into the therapy, after (a) suitable contact points have been identified, (b) interpretive contact has occurred, and (c) sustained contact is beginning, the analytic speaker is often quite excited by the accruing results. He or she has never before been invited to relate in a way in which it was possible to respond. Nor has the person living in an organizing state ever been effectively shown the nature of how he or she ruptures contact. Soon the person excitedly begins catching on, bringing in numerous examples of loss and regaining of contact in daily life. At this point we watch analysts become preoccupied and drowsy—clearly in an attempt to put the damper on the relating. This is usually an unconscious reaction on the part of the analyst that registers his or her knowledge that all of this contact is indeed dangerous for the analytic speaker and possibly for the listener as well. It is as though the speaker, in an enthusiastic move

to rush ahead, is in danger of biting off more than he or she can chew and the analyst is instinctively finding a way of slowing things down. This can be noted and spoken, however, so that two can discuss the dangers of developing sustained contact and work on them together.

SUMMARY AND REVIEW

Part III began with a consideration of the dilemmas that human craziness has posed for the development of human culture. Newtonian science in a medical context was employed in the nineteenth and early twentieth centuries to study the "things" called craziness as varieties of "mental disorders." The last three decades have witnessed a gradual shift in thought paradigm from the models employed in Newtonian science and medicine. The paradigm shift highlights (1) a commitment to consciousness raising, (2) an elaboration of systematic subjectivity, (3) an emphasis on narrative rather than historical truth, (4) an acknowledgment of quantum uncertainties, (5) a shift from "thing" study to a more general listening perspective approach, and (6) a variable responsiveness technique.

Freud's first two paradigms of psychoanalytic thinking were based upon the assumption of (1) the dynamic unconscious and (2) the definition of an internal tripartite structure of personality (id, ego, and superego). The emerging third paradigm relies on the assumption of psychological organization in humans revolving around slowly developing experiences of self in contrast to experiences of others. The general listening perspectives approach calls for the systematic elaboration of a series of vantage points, derived from self and other merger and differentiation experiences, from which to study the narrations and the narrative interactions of the analytic encounter.

Considering the ability to make and to sustain human contact as the prerequisite for the development of the human symbiotic bonding experience, I then set out to form a listening perspective for receiving and responding to presymbiotic organizing experiences.

In considering the infant's path toward human contact and the varieties of possible experience if that contact is successful or if it fails, the following issues were considered:

1. The universal quest for human contact, which serves to orient and organize all psychic activity;
2. Freud's formulations regarding the reflexive nature of primary, non-realistic, "hallucinatory" experience, which render most psychotic content useless for analysis;
3. The role that the nonhuman plays in early development;
4. The peculiar and idiosyncratic ways in which organizing symbols operate;
5. The prominent role that body parts, physical sensations, and bodily functions play in early life;
6. The special ways in which disorientation in time and space affect organizing experience;
7. The crucial place of concrete touch in the foundation of human experience and its interpretive value in analytic work;
8. The transformational experience, which is possible only through human contact;
9. The function of mutual cuing processes in the formation of the symbiotic bond;
10. The ways in which contact experience can fail, giving rise to various mythic themes (of psychosis) that come to characterize personality functioning;
11. The extreme form of contact break formulated by Freud as the "negative therapeutic reaction";
12. The ways in which psychotic transference becomes structured and serves to foreclose the possibility of human contact;
13. The formation and social roles of the mimical and false self constellations;
14. Disruptions in the personality functioning of the analyst (countertransference) as a result of attempting to achieve contact with organizing states.

With this basic orientation in place it is now possible to move to a consideration of the technical processes actually involved in transformation of organizing states.

PART IV

TECHNICAL AND MANAGERIAL ISSUES INVOLVED IN WORKING THE ORGANIZING EXPERIENCE

15

Overview of Technical and Theoretical Issues

ANALYSIS OF DIFFERENT KINDS OF RELATEDNESS ISSUES

Freud's writing borrows the term *analysis* from nineteenth century chemistry. In chemistry, complex compounds are treated in various ways to break them down, so that component elements can be identified. In using this metaphor for psyche, Freud focuses on the treatment of neurosis and the Oedipus complex. That is, Freud's models of psyche were developed for the purpose of analyzing mental structures that a child forms from ages 3 through 7 in which symbolic repression of sexuality and aggression holds center stage. Freud's doctrine of (secondary) repression, which is the hallmark of neurosis, holds that the child, possibly consciously, definitely unconsciously, makes an active decision not to think or act in sexual and aggressive ways because the world around her forbids it. At this level, the emotional and cognitive life of the child is embedded in words and symbols so that repression is accomplished by means of the verbal-symbolic language system. In the traditional analysis of triangular or oedipal neurosis, verbal interpretations have been demonstrated to have the power to stimulate unconscious repressed material so that the repressed returns as a result of correct *verbal* interpretations. This is the classical theory of psychoanalytic technique to be applied to the treatment of psychoneurosis. [For a fuller elaboration of the theoretical and technical issues in this listening perspective see Hedges (1983, Chapters 3 and 4).]

But in analyzing the three levels of preoedipal psychic structure formation, different and more helpful theoretical and technical ideas exist. For issues originating predominantly from the level of secondary narcissism, the work of Heinz Kohut (1971, 1977) has been most clarifying. Kohut teaches that self-to-selfother (or selfobject) resonance is the critical variable in establishing the cohesiveness and temporal stability of the self. That form of emotional resonance is at its zenith between 24 and 36 months, although selfother needs span the entire life cycle. Kohut demonstrates that mirroring, twinning, and idealization are the chief interpersonal features involved in self to selfother emotional resonance. Kohut formulates that when narcissistic issues are being presented for analysis, self to selfother resonance begins to fill the analytic relationship according to the same personal style once learned by the toddler in seeking certain kinds of affirmation, confirmation, and inspiration from its significant others. But the particular modes of seeking selfother resonance that are learned at this young level and retained in the personality tend to be limiting to the adult. Kohut teaches that we need various kinds of selfother affirmation, confirmation, and inspiration from birth to death, but that early learned modes represent the limited mind of a child. There are many more different and effective ways to seek affirmation, confirmation, and inspiration as adults.

Kohut's technique is to let the search for emotional resonance develop in analysis according to the way that it was once learned. When the analyst fails to resonate according to the needs of the self, expectable narcissistic injury and rage result. Then a process of discovery can begin. The early learned particular modes of seeking selfother resonance can be uncovered by two working analytically. In time, the person in analysis begins to have more empathy with him- or herself, and with personal selfother needs, so that whatever the selfother needs are, the person learns to manage them in a variety of different ways.

With Kohut's technique the structure that is "breaking down" through analysis involves the personal and characteristic modes through which the self seeks affirmation, confirmation, and inspiration. Just as when the inhibiting influences of the neurotic Oedipus complex break down and the person's sexuality and aggression become free to engage in more flexible modes, so at the narcissistic level, when the archaic modes of selfother resonance begin to break down, the person is free to search out selfother modes that are far more flexible than the ones previously experienced. [For a fuller elaboration of the technical and theoretical issues involved in this listening perspective see Hedges (1983, Chapters 6 through 9).]

At the age of 4 to 24 months the period Mahler (1968) has called "symbiosis," the fixations that clinicians generally refer to as "borderline" or "character" form a different kind of somatopsychic structure. Special techniques for analyzing or breaking down overlearned symbiotic structures have evolved in psychoanalysis. This is a level of preverbal representation that is primarily experienced by the growing child in terms of affects and affective (somatic) interactions with significant others. True, children are learning language during this time, but the salient issues of their interpersonal emotional lives are not yet embedded in the verbal-symbolic language system, so verbal interpretation cannot be expected to be useful. This means that the most relevant material for analysis of the symbiotic structure is the personal affective interaction that develops in the analytic relationship.

For purposes of analytic listening we might think of certain stylized modes of affective interaction between a mother and a child as a "scenario" (Hedges 1983). We observe scenarios as regular or ritualized interactions, games, or dances that a mother and a child learn to do with one another. We can watch the roles switch back and forth from passive to active. Mother does this; child responds accordingly. Child does that; mother responds accordingly. Certain stylized ways evolve in which the emotional interaction comes to be *character-*

istically played out by each mother–child dyad. These symbiotic rules for emotional interactions become internalized in the personality. They serve as the person's basic expectations in intimate interactions, and color emotional relatedness throughout life.

As the child passes through this symbiotic or mutual cuing period mother begins to help the child individuate from these modes that have been shared by two. The child begins to refuse mother's rules with "No." Mothers call the ticket out of the symbiosis "the terrible twos." Mahler (1968) speaks of "separation-individuation." Freud believed that civilization in a historical sense as well as in individual life begins with "negation" (1925). Only after "the terrible twos" have been successfully negotiated with mother, can the selfother resonances begin, which Mahler (1968) formulates in terms of "rapproachement," the child reapproaching mother for self confirming responses. But during the zenith of symbiotic scenarios, the emotional interactional modes become fairly stylized or fixed.

All people retain, to a certain extent, internalized affective modes from the symbiotic period. We become aware of these modes most painfully in our deepest love relationships, when we find ourselves having knee-jerk emotional reactions to one another. Even when we stand back, seeing that our reactions are quite irrational and inappropriate to the present intimate situation, we can still feel their emotional power over us. We realize that these patterns of emotional responsiveness come from our earliest love relationship with mother, or whomever was functioning in the mothering role for us at that time.

In the analytic situation, there is no way that a person can simply speak these relatedness modes that need to be analyzed because they are nonverbal and preverbal. They must, in some way or another, be lived out in the emotional relatedness interaction of the analytic couple. As they are lived out in analysis, an actual interpersonal interaction pattern develops that is stronger than what is expected in oedipal neurosis or narcissistic selfobject resonance. Blanck and Blanck (1974) speak of a "replicated transference" so that in some real way, or token way, the emotional bonding experience (or bonding dance) of mother and child actually becomes replicated or emotionally reexperienced in the knee-jerk interaction of two people. Searles (1979) speaks of the formation of a "therapeutic symbiosis" to characterize the emotionally realistic interaction of two personalities that naturally emerges in this kind of work.

The analysis of the replicated symbiotic transference then proceeds in several ways. The material from the symbiotic period must be allowed to come alive in the analytic interaction. Then, once seen, it usually takes two forms: (1) passive, with the analyst being experienced in the parental role and the analytic speaker living out the child role; and (2) active, with the analyst being mothered or parented by the client in the same way that the client was once parented. This second form of replicated transference is thought to reflect how the client, through primary identification, has taken in modes of relatedness from the parent that have caused the child trouble, and has identified with them (Balint 1943).

In this active form of replicated transference the person in analysis actively lives out the parent role in his or her symbiotic scenarios vis-à-vis the analyst. Through countertransference experiencing (the emotional responsiveness of the analyst) the analyst thus becomes the recipient of the emotional life or relatedness experience of the infant self of the client.

After the replicating transference comes alive in analytic relating, the verbal and nonverbal interpretive work typically takes the form of trying to demonstrate how "at times you experience me as your mother or some other early caregiver. But at other times you treat me as you were once treated and I feel it is somehow alien to me. You're treating me the way your mother (or some other early significant person) once treated you. When you were two, you couldn't speak up for yourself. You didn't know how to make effective protest. But I can speak up for myself and I'm having trouble interacting in this way that you seem to be asking of me."

Much of this work is nonverbal and interactional. That is, the actual interpretive confrontation of symbiotic scenarios is often done more through presence, being, and deed rather than through words. Restated, a certain mode of *emotional* (not necessarily behavioral) interaction is being foisted upon the analyst. The analyst goes along with it as much as possible until there is some understanding of it. Then, at some point, verbally or nonverbally, the analyst finds a way to stand against the emotional mode of relatedness and refuses to interact any longer in this way because it does not reflect accurately the present interpersonal realities of the dyad. The other person is thereby given an opportunity to relinquish compulsive adherence to those particular internalized symbiotic modes, in favor of establishing other interactive modes more appropriate to his or her contemporary life.

As in the analysis of neurotic and narcissistic structures, the possibility of developing increased flexibility through transformation arises as a result of analyzing or breaking down the structured object relations, or the interpersonal emotional structures that were formed during the 4- to 24-month-old mutual cuing period. (For a full elaboration of the issues in theory and technique see Hedges 1983, Chapters 10 and 11; for discussion of the symbiotic listening perspective see Hedges 1992.)

At the organizing level, psychic structures may begin to form in utero, three or four months before the child is born, although structures developed in the first three or four months of life are usually more easily inferred. In the optimal situation, in utero and in the early extrauterine environment, the child's needs are adapted to almost entirely so that intense or prolonged frustrations do not occur.

Winnicott (1949) has spoken of the child's sense of "going on being," and the importance of the child's maintaining a sense of continuity of being. He holds that it is the task of the people in the child's environment to assure that impingements into the child's sense of continuity remain minimal. Slowly, as the perceptual and motor apparatus begins to mature, the child begins to show an ability to tolerate frustrations and to adapt more freely. But during the earliest period, if an impingement on the child's sense of "going on being" is introduced, the child is forced to react or to think prematurely. Many infants are forced to begin reacting or "thinking" even in utero, when there are prenatal deficiencies, toxic substances, or unusual circumstances in the womb such as a twisted umbilicus or hardening of the umbilicus artery. There are many possible impingements in the extrauterine environment that might force an infant to begin thinking before he or she is ready.

The primary task of the infant, both in utero and in the early extrauterine months, is to form channels, in a very lively and active way, to the nurturing, stimulating environment. The visual, auditory, and tactile senses, as well as the child's intelligence, neurological system, and all other systems that the child possesses, need to be nourished, protected, and stimulated by others in the environment in a variety of ways. Children who are not stimulated die of marasmus. Current infant research is demonstrating many other devastating things that happen to children when their maturing sensory apparatus and their emotional needs are not adequately stimulated and cared for. Khan (1963) speaks of cumulative "strain trauma" to denote stresses in infancy that are not the product of gross negligence or abuse but that nevertheless have cumulative long-term damaging effects.

In order for the child to form adequate channels to sources of environmental nurturance, stimulation, comfort, and safety, the child, in a variety of ways, extends or reaches out to the environment. The human environment must meet the child's extensions for the cycle of nurturance, stimulation, and comfort to be safely completed. Unfortunately, in both in utero and extrauterine experiences, there are many times when these channels of potential stimulation and growth cannot be completed or are actively disrupted by environmental influences. If the disruptions are too long or too intense, we have what Winnicott has called impingements on the nascent psyche. At that point, the child reacts from an instinct to survive. When the child is thus forced to react, the *way* that the child reacts will form the later foundation of that child's mind. Subsequent mental life is bound in various ways to be fearful, angry, and paranoid because the child was early on forced to react to realistic intrusion or trauma. Frustration, anger, dread, and fear are appropriate responses to impingement. An anticipatory sense is laid down in psyche that says, "a danger is going to come from the outside and hurt me or intrude or deprive me in some way." That sense caused by early impingements then constitutes the primary mental formation and will appear as a persecutory pattern in the organizing transference. All other mental structures of that person will be built upon that initial thought paradigm and influenced by it.

We can think about organizing experiences pervasively lived by people who have undergone massive unfortunate early experiences. We can also consider organizing experiences more universally, in the sense that no child is ever fully met in all of its ways by environmental caregivers. Pockets of organizing experience are therefore universal. Sometimes the pockets are rather large and provide major areas of defect or disturbance for people. At other times organizing pockets are small and only become visible under conditions of extreme stress. But, whatever the nature of the experience, and to whatever degree it was experienced, in these areas where the child is traumatized the child no longer reaches out.

There are an endless variety of ways in which a child may seek stimulation and responsiveness from the environment. In whatever ways the child was traumatized, the child will pull back from all future experiences that are emotionally related. What becomes internalized is the child's fear of or *refusal* to make human contact in those ways ever again. It is as though the child reaches out with a hand, the hand is burned, and a message is sent to the brain, "Never go there again." And that message along with its emotional imagery, is internalized permanently in the child's primordial mind, so that whole areas of potential cognitive, emotional, and behavioral activity are stunted. When we see people later in life in an analytic situation, we can be sure that larger or smaller portions of their earliest psychic potentials have been limited in certain ways and that early organizing structures are blocking further development in major or minor ways. The analytic task is to analyze that block so that greater psychic and somatic flexibility can be developed.

ANALYZING THE ORGANIZING OR PSYCHOTIC TRANSFERENCE

Considering the analytic task at the level of the organizing experience, there are two major areas of concern. The first area is that of trying to maintain a holding environment and fostering emotional contact between the two participants—whenever possible, in whatever way possible. Fostering contact entails indentifying the contact moment, developing ways of encouraging it, and learning how to begin bringing the person (who is so afraid of contact) into actual emotional contact with the analyst.

Shortly after the person begins to move toward the analyst or to establish various forms of contact, a second concern emerges, which is the appearance of the internalized terror of contact. This aversion to contact is retained from infantile trauma and arises in any of a variety of forms to block or to foreclose the possibility of subsequent dangerous contact. This internalized organizing structure is transference from unsatisfying, frightening, intrusive, or otherwise traumatizing others in infancy. In terms of present-day realities, it is essentially delusional in nature.

One way I have developed of speaking about this transference event is the "appearance of the psychotic mother." That is, as soon as the person begins to reach into the forbidden zone, the prohibition long ago set down that said, "Never go here again," reappears, and the person breaks the contact. What has to be analyzed is the ways, the times, and the manners in which the person compulsively breaks whatever contact is just beginning to be made.

So the two faces of analytic work with the organizing experience are (1) encouraging the person into contact, and (2) waiting for the moment in which the psychotic mother appears to destroy that contact. Analyzing the organizing transference entails finding ways of staying with the person through that frightening, agonizing contact moment, of trying to analyze, of bringing to light, the exact nature of the organizing structure that prevents sustained interpersonal relatedness. The resistance to allowing transference situations to arise must first be studied analytically. What are the fears? What are the terrors that accompany the contact? And how do these manifest in somatic and relational realities? Transference cannot be studied without studying the resistance to its establishment. Resistance cannot be studied without the person taking decisive steps toward staying in contact; interpretive holding and touch are the chief technical tools.

IDENTIFYING DIFFERENT KINDS OF TRANSFERENCE

The central tool of psychoanalysis, since Freud first enunciated it in 1912, has been transference. The basic notion is that overlearned emotional experience from the past has formed certain enduring patterns of emotional responsiveness in the personality that are regularly relived in significant relationships throughout one's life. In the analytic relationship the goal is to bring these emotional experiences to light so that they can be seen, understood, and anlayzed, so that they lose the power and impact they once had as a result of childhood experience.

At the neurotic level, transference can be secured for analysis through the illusory process of the verbal-symbolic free association technique that Freud invented. That is, as the ghosts of the oedipal drama reappear in the room they are projected into the analytic relationship and onto the person of the analyst. These patterns of triadic emotional relatedness dating from the third to the seventh year of life can be known about through these transferred projections and the free associations that give rise to them. The attitude toward transference that has characterized classical psychoanalysis has been that transference is basically a distortion of the realities of the analytic hour. The problem with this view is that it implies that the analyst knows what reality is!

Kohut (1971, 1977), in defining narcissistic or selfother transferences, points out that transference does not occur in a vacuum and need not be seen as a distortion. Rather, transference represents a person's unique experience of something that actually does or does not occur. Schwaber (1979) holds that whenever transference occurs, it is important interpretively to start off with something like, "When I did such and such, you had such and such a reaction," so that the interpretation always begins with the element of reality that the person is reacting to. Transference interpretation at the level of selfother resonance thus refers to the person's experience of the immediate reality of the actual activities, or failure of activities, of the analyst in the analytic interaction and what kinds of fragmenting activities ensue.

In the replicated transference from symbiotic experience, the realistic presence and engagement of the analyst are particularly important to consider. Interpretive activity centers around the way in which the two engage each other and how the client experiences the analytic interaction in ways similar to one's early experience of mother or some significant other. The interpretation ultimately shows that when two engage in a particular way that replicates the characterologically based past, it is actually somehow destructive to the speaker's overall experience in the long run since the symbiotic engagement is overly merged with an other and therefore is self-limiting in nature. The interpretation highlights the speaker's desire to move out of the familiar but limiting mode of relating that we have discovered together. When the person does begin relinquishing long-held modes, there is grieving for a lost (m)other and a lost self that once related to (m)other in certain ways.

At the organizing level, it becomes critical to realize that contact and breaking of contact can occur on an almost minute by minute basis in subtle ways. That is, the ebb and flow of the analytic session itself will actualize for the speaker the ruptures in contact occasioned by the appearance of the internalized psychotic mother. As the analyst moves into interpretive activity about the transference, there is a great danger that the interpretive activity will be received as blame. "You're experiencing me in such and such a way," is going to be heard by the speaker as blaming, distortion, or being held responsible for some kind of a misunderstanding. It becomes particularly important to keep all interpretive activity in terms of, "when I left you in such and such a way, the fear that you experienced was very similar to the fear that you've known all your life."

RESISTANCE AT DIFFERENT
DEVELOPMENTAL LEVELS

The second central tool of psychoanalysis throughout its history has been the analysis of resistance. When Freud first encountered resistance to the flow of the analytic material, he felt that it was an obstacle to analytic progress. Later he realized that *resistance is a critical relatedness memory.* Considering resistance in this manner is particularly important since there is a tendency, in the therapeutic community, to use the term *resistance* to mean that the client is resisting me, or the client is resisting my interpretations, or the client is resisting the therapy. A more proper understanding of resistance is that the speaker in analysis is resisting having to reexperience a prior related-ness trauma in the transference context of the current relationship. What is being resisted is being resisted on the basis of there having been some overwhelming experience that one does not want to reexperience in transference within the present analytic relationship. Resistance serves in its own way to represent the nature of that dreaded relatedness experience.

At the neurotic level, resistance is to the revitalization of re-pressed sexuality and aggression. At the narcissistic level, resistance is to uncovering one's narcissistic attitudes, such fundamentally uni-versal narcissistic beliefs as, "I am the center of the world," "The world owes me a living," "Everyone should love and admire me and my ideas," and "My ideal leaders should rule the world." Shame enshrouds the resistance, "I'm ashamed to acknowledge my narcissistic self and my hopelessly self-centered ideas." At t he symbiotic level, resistance is to relinquishing "Mommy and me" scenarios. That is, the relatedness modes of the scenario must be held onto at all costs, because the scenario was the way in which the child first loved, and was able to be loved in return. The resistance is to letting go of the scenario, because an archaic love will be lost, an old self will be suiciding, and an old mother-structure will be killed off. What always follows in the wake of relinquishing symbiotic modes of relatedness is massive confusion and grief. The resistance is to loss of that sustaining sense of dual unity implicit in "Mommy and me" scenarios. Often early resistance is manifest as a fear of dependency on the analyst, or a reluctance to consider the emotional relatedness of the therapeutic couple. Later resistance tends to take the form of "I can't do it by myself. Don't abandon me and don't expect me to individuate or be independent."

At the organizing level, the resistance is to dealing with the psychotic mother transference structure, to dealing with the breaking of contact and the rupture in relating. The breaking of contact guards the door to keeping the person from reexperiencing primitive over-whelming trauma and breakdowns that once occurred when contact was sought and had to be painfully withdrawn from.

Working with organizing experiences is extremely difficult and often very taxing on the therapist, because the therapist is required to stay in a specialized mode of interacting, sometimes for long periods of time. A danger, then, is that when the therapist is trying to broaden the perspective, elaborate the interpretation, contextualize something that is currently happening within a broader framework, the speaker's reluctance to follow the listener's thoughts will be seen as somehow being uncooperative. The speaker in analysis may indeed manifest resistance by feeling hurt or angry for being blamed, and feeling held responsible. But what is usually happening is that the listener is not, at that moment, staying at a level where the speaker can feel coalesced. And what is being resisted by the speaker is the experience of having to drop once again into the trauma of the abandoning psychotic mother, which at that moment the analyst is being for the client.

A similar tendency may occur when the analyst is feeling taxed by the work, feeling an internal depletion or resistance to staying in the place that is being required by the work. In this frame of mind, the listener interprets the speaker's needing to be in a certain place as resistance to the analyst or resistance to the therapy. But this attitude, once again, re-creates for the speaker, in actuality, the experience of the psychotic mother who could not be in the needed place at the needed time and saw the infant's needs as overwhelming.

Speakers are often very vivid in the way they describe their experience of the analyst not being present with them at a given moment in time—such as feeling lost and alone. They express this experience as not being able to locate mother or to find her. They express it as an inability to come out of the transference. They express it as floating in the universe with nothing to connect to. One client expressed it as feeling like she was about to explode and be annihilated. Another client expressed it as feeling "anchorless," another as "endlessly falling." There accompanies this sense of being lost a terror of being in a world in which there is no connection, in which there is nothing to bring a sense of being solid, or in direct solid contact with someone else. The agonies to be reexperienced in the organizing transference are not only confusing and frightening, but usually severely physically painful body memories that want to be avoided at all cost. Another client represented this experience as having "a picture of a uterus attached to an umbilical cord on a placenta, but not inside of anything." There was no wall of the uterus, no sac, nothing around it that was feeding it or maintaining it. It was a totally free-floating, terrorizing experience.

ANALYZABILITY: THE TECHNICAL APPROACH OF EACH LISTENING PERSPECTIVE

It is appropriate to continue to use the word that Freud coined, *psychoanalysis*, to indicate that what distinguishes psychoanalytic work is defining and isolating enduring emotional interactional structures that are retained in the personality from different age periods, and then, through varying techniques, finding ways of bringing those structures to light so that they can lose the power (through analysis, understanding) and the impact that they have carried in that person's life. The spirit of Freud's original psychoanalytic work with oedipal-level neurosis can now be extended to a variety of preoedipal relatedness structures.

Classical psychoanalysts, following Freud, believe that only neurotic structures are analyzable using psychological or verbal methods. That is, in order to analyze an Oedipus complex, the prerequisite is an intact ego and the capacity for effective use of the verbal-symbolic system, and ultimately the capacity to detach psychologically at termination. Thus preoedipal conditions have been considered by classical psychoanalysts as unanalyzable. That is, it has been believed that without an intact ego structure the transference could not be resolved so that the person could terminate the analysis as an independent, whole self, as an independent and separate center of initiative.

Kohut demonstrates that the 24- to 36-month-old level of self-other resonances are indeed quite analyzable. Using the metaphor of a bipolar self with two opportunities to develop, Kohut (1977) demonstrates the capacity to terminate. Although a different conceptual approach is required from the classical one and different technical tools are required, the same basic psychoanalytic process occurs. That is, narcissistic structures are brought into analytic focus so that their impact can be diminished, and greater flexibility in personality functioning becomes possible.

Analysis of the 4- to 24-month-old symbiotic or borderline structures that were overlearned in the context of "mommy and me" interactions and retained in the personality can likewise be transformed, and/or relinquished rather than being compulsively lived out (Hedges 1983, 1992). Eventually, a cohesive self can form and independence be achieved so that termination can be experienced in analysis.

At the organizing level of the infantile search for reliable channels to the nurturing and stimulating environment, the internalized structures for analytic focus serve to prohibit interpersonal contact. As moments of breaking contact are brought into focus in the analytic relationship and contact is systematically sustained, the power of the internalized structure, which compulsively forces the person to break contact, diminishes and the person is then able to begin transforming his or her states so as to make fuller use of other interpersonal resources in the world, in order to grow and to live a richer, more flexible life.

Thus at all levels of developmental experience and personality structuring, transformation occurs in the wake of psychoanalytic breakdown of constricting, limiting psychic and physical structures. At each of the four levels, the analytic technique of interacting in order to bring the structure into focus for analysis is quite different, so that, other than the frame technique advocated by the classical analysts for the treatment of neurosis, we can now speak of three additional listening perspectives with variable techniques for transference and resistance analysis.

KOHUT'S VIEW OF THE ORGANIZING EXPERIENCE

In Kohut's posthumously published *How Does Analysis Cure?* (1984), he contrasts the analyzability of neurotic and narcissistic personality organizations with those of psychotic and borderline states.

In the psychoses, including those covertly psychotic personality organizations (central hollowness, but a well-developed peripheral layer of defensive structures) for which I reserve the term borderline states, a nuclear self has not been shaped in early development. . . . In these cases the psychoanalytic situation [as presently conceived] does not bring about the long-term activation of the central chaos of the self within a workable transference that is a precondition for setting in motion the processes that would lead to the creation, de novo, of a nuclear self. In order to lead to a causal cure, the therapeutic process would have to penetrate beneath the organized layers—the defensive structures—of the patient's self and permit the prolonged reexperience of oscillations between prepsychological chaos and the security provided by primitive merger with an archaic selfobject. It is certainly imaginable that, even in adult life, the repeated experience of optimal frustration in an archaic homeostatic selfobject environment brought about in the analytic situation would lead, as in earliest infancy, to the birth of a nuclear self. But I cannot imagine that an individual would submit himself to the dissolution of defensive structures that have protected him for a lifetime and voluntarily accept the unspeakable anxieties accompanying what must seem to him to be the task of facing a prepsychological state that had remained chaotic because the selfobject milieu in early life lacked the empathic responsiveness that would have organized the child's world and maintained his innate self confidence. [p. 8]

Kohut acknowledges that in expressing reservations about the analyzability of prepsychological states, he may be expressing his own personal limits as a psychoanalyst. As a diagnostic relativist, Kohut defines the categories of psychosis and borderline as states of prepsychological chaos, which the empathic instruments of the psychoanalytic observer are unable to comprehend. Kohut acknowledges that the basis for his conviction may be his fear that in following a person empathically into prepsychological territory he would not be able to hold the empathic bond when the basic transference emerges and the person for protracted periods of time would have to "borrow the analyst's personality in order to survive" (p. 9).

Kohut's words were issued before his death in 1981. The body of his work over thirty years has profoundly affected the paradigm shift that has occurred in psychoanalytic thought in the last two decades.

By now the limitations in empathic instruments about which Kohut speaks have been considerably altered so that sustained and reliable empathic immersion in psychotic and borderline states under many conditions is deemed possible. The present definitions of symbiotic and organizing experience and the technical considerations by which the symbiotic and organizing transferences and resistances can be framed for analysis do indeed follow along the lines Kohut envisioned. It turns out that the dread of reexperiencing the primordial fear and chaos, which Kohut could not imagine anyone being willing to do, can be satisfactorily accomplished. Furthermore, it can be accomplished in exactly the manner that Kohut foresees—through the person's willingness to permit a relaxation of defensive structures and then to allow painful and prolonged "oscillations between prepsychological chaos and the security provided by primitive merger with an archaic selfobject," the analyst.

THE LISTENING TOOLS FOR DIFFERENT DEVELOPMENTAL EXPERIENCES

As Freud engaged in a study of his dreams and the psychic symptoms he himself experienced (train phobias, migraine headaches, and impotence), he discovered his psychic themes to be already written about in *Hamlet* and *Oedipus Rex*. The literary elaboration of these mythic themes in turn provided Freud with crucial listening tools for tuning into himself, and subsequently to many of the people who came to him for analysis. All later psychotherapy has been built on Freud's first listening tools, the theories of the Oedipus complex. Freud's formulations of the Oedipus complex assumed that there were basic or fundamental instincts or drives of sexuality and aggression that the 3-through 7-year-old child found various ways to blind him- or herself to (repress). Freud came to believe that inhibited sexual and aggressive drives caused people psychological and physical problems. So Freud, the classical analysts, and later schools of psychotherapists have found it helpful to use "Mother, Father, and Me" themes as listening tools.

When Kohut (1971) began to teach how to listen to the narcissistic issues characteristic of 24- to 36-month-old children, he became
aware that the most salient concern at that age is "Who am I as a self?"
There are certainly precursors for self to selfother resonance. And
selfother functions continue throughout life. But Kohut isolated the
way a young child approaches and relates to others in order to use
them as parts of his or her developing self, as listening tools. Kohut
defined three ways in which the young child uses others to establish
self cohesion: looking for affirming through mirroring, looking for
confirming through twinning, and looking for inspiration in finding
others to idealize. The grandiose self of the child is thus experienced in
relationship to the mirroring and twinning functions of others. The
grandiose self is also projected onto idealized others. With these
listening tools it became possible to bring heretofore invisible aspects
of psychic functioning into view as narcissistic or selfother transference in the analytic relationship.

Mahler (1968) utilized a metaphor borrowed from biology, "symbiosis," to capture the *intrapsychic* aspects of the bonding dance that
develops between the mothering caregiver and the 4- to 24-month-old
child. There are endless variations in the dance that may occur in this
period until the child is finally able to say "no," to refuse mother's
preferred ways and to move on to more self-definition. The "no" may
need fostering. Mahler's formulation of an *intrapsychic* symbiosis
arising from a mother–child mutual cuing process from which toddlers
later separate and individuate provides a special way of listening to the
group of people called "borderline," or to the character part of
personality called "symbiotic" or "borderline." The dyadic bonding
dance that each person compulsively seeks out in significant relationships can be looked at, listened to, and scrutinized in the replicated
transference so that it can be relinquished and/or lose its power. The
notions of "symbiosis," "scenario" (Hedges 1983), and "separation-
individuation" provide valuable listening tools for these developmentally based structures.

Conceptualizing an organizing experience that characterizes the
developmental era of four months before birth to four months after
allows an entirely different way of listening to some of the deepest
human concerns, whether they be lived out pervasively or in more

limited pockets or enclaves. The analytic listening tool here involves encouraging contact and then learning about the organizing or psychotic transferences by watching the way a person avoids or breaks contact and ruptures the relating. The interpretive act entails finding ways of holding the analytic speaker—through various transference and resistance agonies—until the structure of the psychotic mother can be experienced as delusional and worked through.

When an individual comes to the analytic consulting room with concerns about marriage, children, or parents, or whether the reason for seeking analysis has to do with addictions, eating disorders, ritual abuse, multiple selves, abductions, or whatever, the therapist is now able to *listen to the self and other relatedness patterns* that are implicit in each concern as it is presented. How does this individual relate to the people around him or her? How does this individual re-create relatedness patterns and resist re-creating them in the psychoanalytic relationship? How can those relatedness patterns be conceptualized to make them optimally available for analysis?

Triadic patterns can be brought to life and understanding by Freud's listening perspective. Selfother patterns, using the other as a part of the self to confirm the self, stem from Kohut's listening perspective. The bonding dance between "Mommy and me," and the unique way that it appears in the scenarios of the analytic relationship can be listened to and relinquished. And now, there are at last ways to listen to the earliest search for connection and to determine narratively what happened when that search became thwarted by the environment in which the child lived. The organizing experience represents an additional listening perspective added to our armamentarium of clinical tools for being present and responding to the material of the clinical hour. The relationship that develops in the psychoanalytic encounter can be looked at with this particular lens so as to see what each person's fundamental orienting, organizing, extending, reaching concerns are, and, most importantly, to discover the ways in which the personal search for human contact is internally thwarted, aborted, and/or ruptured.

By conceptualizing our tools at different developmental levels as metaphors derived from our understanding of child development, we are able to understand that these tools are thought tools to help us grasp the nature of the interactions that happen between any two people, particularly the two people of the analytic couple.

THE ROLE OF THE ACTUAL PERSON OF THE ANALYST WHEN ANALYZING DIFFERENT DEVELOPMENTAL CONCERNS

Franz Alexander (1961) speaks of a "corrective emotional experience" arising as a result of psychoanalysis. There is no question that, as a result of an analytic experience, a corrective emotional experience indeed occurs. One experience of emotional life was developed during childhood and, in analysis, that experience becomes transformed, that is, undergoes corrections. But the difficulty with conceptualizing a corrective emotional experience is that the analyst then tends to believe that his or her task is to produce a corrective emotional experience. Sometimes this issue is spoken of as "reparenting." With the introduction of such an attitude into analytic relatedness, the door becomes opened for all manner of manipulations, treatment strategies, behavior modifications, moralizing, and a variety of techniques that, in fact, can thwart or even reproduce the very traumas that the child was subjected to when parents were highly focused on raising their children.

If either a parent or an analyst is focused upon doing something so as to produce a given result, the result is bound to be limited or warped in one way or another. Whereas by simply being with, being tuned into, and relating to a child or to an analytic speaker, the possibility of transformation spontaneously arises, which is likely to result in greater flexibility of personality functioning. Psychoanalytic transformation occurs in the wake of analysis of (breakdown of) previously overlearned psychic structures, and options more in keeping with the possibilities of an adult mind become available. Concepts such as *corrective emotional experience* or *reparenting* are superfluous to the task and to the result. By listening and interpreting differentially according to what kind of developmental relatedness issues are being presented for analysis, overlearned patterns from childhood break down and greater personality flexibility becomes possible.

In considering the techniques for use in analyzing different developmental issues, it is important to consider the role of the actual person of the therapist or analyst. In the analysis of neurosis, both parties understand that there is another complete and whole separate person in the room (i.e., self and other constancy exist). Both parties are assumed to have well-developed, intact ego structures. This means the analyst can remain relatively neutral, relatively blank, relatively frustrating, and relatively nongratifying — in short, a shadowy figure opaquely mirroring in the background. This classical role of the analyst permits transference objects from the Oedipus complex to be projected into the space of the room, into the analytic relationship, and onto the figure of the analyst with minimal interference from the actual person of the analyst.

However, when Kohut began teaching how to work at the selfother preoedipal relatedness level, he was quite clear that empathy and emotional resonance can only occur between two very real people. Human empathy is extended by the analyst in every way possible. The analyst then waits until, at some point, a break in empathy occurs. When it does, the possibility arises of seeing and analyzing the archaic selfobject need that empathic attunement failed to meet.

According to Kohut, the interpretive process follows the understanding process. Every few weeks, Kohut maintains, a session tends to occur that is characterized by "summarizing reflections." In a session of summarizing reflections, the self-to-selfother resonance that has been passing before the eyes of the couple for the past few weeks can now be summarized, put into words. The summary includes the ways in which the two had connected well, the ways in which there were breaches in empathy, and the ways in which those breaches were mended so that the sense of self could be restored. In this way, verbal interpretive activity follows the establishment and understanding of the actual selfother relatedness patterns that emerged as resistance and transference. This analytic technique requires more actual presence of the person of the analyst than the classical mirroring technique of Freud.

When bringing into focus relatedness issues of the 24- to 36-month-old level, the actual person of the analyst is much more involved in the interaction, resonating emotionally with the client. When considering the level of the intrapsychic symbiosis, the analyst must, in a variety of ways, be able to *actually engage in emotional relatedness* in order for the symbiotic material to emerge into view. The limits of the analyst's actual engagement at this level are generally defined by the personal and professional integrity of the analyst rather than by any *a priori* technical considerations. Whatever his or her ultimate personal or professional limits and boundaries are, the analyst will choose not to extend analytic relatedness into those areas. But there are many situation-dependent gray areas. And the relating issues around personal boundaries in these gray areas almost always become a central issue around which symbiotic analytic material revolves, since the flexing of "Mommy and me" boundaries is an essential feature of working out a symbiosis. Boundaries decided on in advance and rigidly adhered to are readily sensed as fraudulent by children and analytic speakers—and are regularly seen as stupid and abusive.

In most areas of work with symbiotic replications, much more flexibility in modes of relatedness is required from the analytic listener than with upper levels of relatedness development. Symbiotic scenarios become represented by replicated affective interactions between speaker and listener utilizing the gray areas of boundary definition. The preverbal affective interactions of the symbiosis are not recallable through ordinary forms of memory or verbalization; rather, they become available for analysis through "knee jerk" kinds of interpersonal affective interactions. Unless the analyst is affectively engaged and the interpersonal boundaries somewhat flexible, the material simply cannot emerge and therefore cannot be analyzed. The analyst unable or unwilling to engage in deeply personal interactions with analytic speakers is limited to cognitive, behavioral, and supportive techniques in working with borderline, character, and symbiotic issues.

When presenting organizing level issues and concerns for analysis, even less ego structure is available to the speaker at that moment. Winnicott (1949), when considering the earliest psychic structures, points out that the span of the ego is extremely limited in terms of what it can encompass at a given moment in time. In context, Winnicott is pointing out that, with an organizing structure, the person's memory, perception, movement, and judgment may completely omit considerations of what happened an hour ago, a day ago, or a week ago, and that reality testing may be very limited. When recalling by living an organizing experience, the ego is only able to function in concrete and/or bodily ways at a given moment in time, so other customary aspects of ego functioning will be temporarily unavailable.

Many implications for work with organizing experience stem from the spatial/temporal limitations of ego functioning, whether with a person living pervasive organizing experience, or whether the analytic focus at that moment is on a more circumscribed pocket of organizing experience. This means that analytic technique, in order to properly frame the organizing transference, requires not merely more emotional involvement from the analyst, but more actual presence and intervention. At this level, the analyst responds with his or her whole person in order to facilitate the experience of object permanence. The real person of the analyst must come to the experience in a variety of ways. At such times the analyst must attempt to remain fully present in sustained relatedness. Responses need to be realistic, temporally relevant, and concrete. Questions, comments, and interpretations that are appropriate when working on higher developmental issues can only be experienced as intrusive and/or traumatic during moments of living out organizing experiences.

The importance of the analyst's ability and willingness to respond concretely and specifically in the moment must be emphasized. Only later can the two look back to understand where ideas and transformations may have come from in their experience. To do this kind of work the analyst must be able and willing to be fully attuned by expressing personal concern and, at times, even caring and affection appropriate to the professional situation. The affection that exists between mother and infant can be observed in facial expression, in the smile, in the tone of voice, in the body rapport, and in their overall emotional connectedness.

On this level there arises a certain need for the concrete aspects of *interpretive* touch at certain critical times when the person breaking contact may be helped or encouraged to sustain it. This is because, for the unorganized person, everything is held and comprehended in a sensory manner, so that at moments of living organizing experiences out in analysis, the look, the sound, and actual touch are the only vehicles by which communication is receivable or acceptable. Not expressing ourselves through the sensory medium when an organizing experience is present is not only to be depriving and withholding, but replicates exactly what the "psychotic mother" did. She may have held the baby on occasion, but she did not really hold that infant with a sense of personal presence, enthusiasm, pleasure, and relatedness. Our speaking, gesturing, and occasional focused interpretive touching has to occur at particular moments when this individual cannot find or hold onto us in other ways. The auditory, visual, and tactile environments often play important roles for the organizing person as well as the sense of smell and taste. For example, those aware of the importance of smell to an infant encourage mothers not to wear perfume in the early months, so that the infant can identify mother by her body smell. Early in life the infant turns her head to the mother's smell or to the sound of her voice.

In summary, because of the concrete level of functioning that is exhibited when people are working on organizing experiences, it is incumbent upon the therapist not only to be fully emotionally involved, but to be extremely aware of all of the concrete sensory modalities and their potential for achieving or breaking contact. The critical aspect of work with organizing experience revolves around achieving and sustaining contact, and analyzing the ways in which the person compulsively breaks contact. It is through perceptual, motor, affective, and sensory aspects of experience that the ebb and flow of contact can be observed. It is not uncommon for smells, tastes, sights, sounds, and tactile sensations to be a part of organizing transference experiences.

A TECHNICAL DIFFICULTY: MAINTAINING FULL PRESENCE

The technical difficulty that arises in working the organizing experience occurs when the analyst is not able or willing to stay emotionally present at the concrete sensory level of connection and disconnection. This is particularly difficult for the analyst when the analytic speaker (1) displays very well-developed aspects of personality, (2) presents very complex and intriguing psychotic content, or (3) engages in highly complex verbalizations that are irrelevant to the task at hand. If the analyst fails to stay attuned to the moment and to the concrete, the mimical self continues or the person fragments, shatters, or disconnects again. What has then happened is that the original traumatic experience, caused by failure of parental empathy, has been repeated by the failure of analytic empathy. And, more than likely, the analyst and parent both somehow blame the failure on the infant or analytic speaker. But the response from the speaker suggests, "You are now taking the focus away from me and onto you with your search for themes, symbols, ideas, and words. In doing so, it seems you expect me now to move into an ego state so that I can hear you and think with you. You're asking me to be where I'm not, and to meet your needs." Such implicit demands from the analyst inadvertently replicate the psychotic mother experience for the client and make analysis of organizing experience impossible.

An analyst is in the habit of considering interactions of the moment or transference aspects of the moment within the overall thematic context of activities that have occurred within the last few days, months, or even years. But by trying to contextualize the immediate, concrete organizing experience in a broader framework, the analyst *de facto* has left the immediate interpersonal situation, and the client is likely to experience the analyst's preoccupation as the psychotic mother once again intruding to destroy. The contextualizing is an intellectualizing activity of the analyst, just as mother is constantly thinking about what is going on with her baby and what she is going to do next. But for the moment that contextualizing activity can only be known to the person in an organizing experience by the way the analyst remains present. There will be plenty of time later for talking about the experience.

The analyst's mental activities in following such things as the flow of the themes in a session, the meaning of the ending of the session, and administrative issues such as ending on time and the collection of fees are likely ways in which the analyst withdraws actual physical and emotional presence for the moment. Only concrete sensory contact or rudimentary thoughts can be actualized in the client's experience at that moment. Any greater offering from the analyst is bound to be experienced as the psychotic mother cropping up to block contact. The trauma of infancy is once again repeated, but this time by a real failure of the analyst. It seems inevitable that this will happen again and again, and that the analyst must be sensitive to the ways in which he or she is constantly leaving the interpersonal space, thereby providing a reenactment of the traumatogenic experience. It becomes clear that the two people are working against the flow of the therapeutic process! The analyst resists empathy with the primitive agonies and fragmentations that the analytic speaker resists re-experiencing.

THE CLINICAL ADVANTAGE OF
LISTENING PERSPECTIVES

The history of psychoanalysis has witnessed an inclination that is common to various types of human inquiry—an attempt to objectify, in analysis, various aspects of the mind. This trend began with Archimedes and was articulated most clearly and put to use by Newton. Newton's objective approach enabled him to define the invisible force of gravity and other invisible forces operating in the universe. The march of science has been based upon a belief that if we just knew enough we would be able to see objectively the true nature of the world (e.g., Newton), or the true nature of human beings (e.g., Descartes), or the true nature of the human mind (e.g., Freud). Einstein questioned this simplifying assumption, and the quantum physicists and chaos theorists who follow Einstein (e.g., Heisenberg) have developed an entirely different way of thinking, realizing that we observe only what we are prepared to observe and that certain events are destined to remain forever unobservable. We research what we want to research. The observer is now understood to be an integral part of whatever it is that he or she chooses to observe, so that objectivity as a scientific attitude has diminished considerably in favor of understandings based on various forms of systematic subjectivity.

In attempting to observe and to understand the psychoanalytic experience, there has been a tendency to reify, that is, to make real, such concepts as instincts, drives, ids, egos, splitting, separation-individuation, rapprochement, psychotic objects, selfobjects, internal objects, and a host of other concepts that have served to define various "ghosts" in the human machine. It is now clear that we are in a better position to work clinically if we understand that what we are looking for is the way in which each person comes to understand and represent his or her experience in human interactions. The developmental metaphors give us listening tools that help us hear the ways in which a person is choosing to relate to the people in his or her environment, including the analyst.

The reason this accent on listening tools, as opposed to objective findings about the nature of the mind, is so crucial is that when one works with finite discoveries one is constantly comparing past models to novel present realities and drawing laws that then govern the way one sees the present. Whereas, after grasping the infinitely complex and ever-interactive aspects of the universe and of human realities, one realizes that, at best, we can define what we observe at present. But we must always be ready for the new, the unexpected, the surprising. By reorganizing clinical findings over the last century that have been thought to reveal the true nature of humans into a dimension of relatedness, which is to be used as a listening tool with the infinite in mind, the clinician remains ready for the new and the unexpected. The listening perspectives approach first advocated by Hedges (1983) allows a more fine-tuned approach to the uniqueness and individuality of each person that we work with.

The listening perspective approach highlighting systematic subjectivity in inquiry is a critically different stance from the scientific objective stance in which we search for the truth of how human beings are made. Objective science attempts to know the true nature of the mind and the nature of the psychoanalytic process. This particular thought mode is very limiting. Newton's view is that the universe is a giant clockwork set in motion by the hands of God, and that it is our task to discover the true nature of God's universe. At the present time, our epistemology is considerably different. We now realize that there are infinite complexities, many of which are, in principle, forever unknowable. But there are many ways in which we can organize observations and interact with the universe and there are many ways in which we can organize observations and organize our minds in order to enhance our understanding. But our understanding is always tentative and needs to be formulated in tentative ways aimed at enhancing our listening possibilities rather than being oriented in positivistic ways of finding and knowing. To some people this may seem like a small point, but *grasping the importance of how we formulate, and being explicit for what purposes we formulate, changes entirely our world view and the way we conduct our work.*

The critical point regarding contemporary epistemology has to do with the extent to which one believes in the theories one constructs. As infants and children we learn to turn things over, to put things in our mouths, to test out reality to find out how things "really" are. Throughout our growing up, we attempt to gain knowledge through testing hypotheses and forming theories about things. We come to believe that if we have a theory about something—say a chair, or a table, or a character structure—then we know its nature. We believe we have discovered some sort of profound truth and we are narcissistically pleased that our personal experience has given us the truth of the universe!

Until the last few decades, humans have universally applied the same ways we learned as infants to discover the nature of the world to discover the nature of other people. But when we look at the complexity of the universe and the complexity of humans and of human relationships, we can now realize that other people and relationships are far too complex for this method of knowledge to work. We fool ourselves when we have a theory about something and have organized our ideas in a way so we are now certain we have the truth about the way the universe is and people in it operate. Uncertainty, awe, surprise, and disbelief are more fitting attitudes for clinical discovery. To remain alive and fresh we have to change the fundamental way we approach the world, the way we think about ourselves and others, and the very way we conduct relationships and relatedness in our clinical work.

16

Common Subjective Concerns and Empathic Considerations

This chapter addresses common issues that arise within the subjective experience of people working on organizing issues. I make suggestions here, based on my experience, on how listeners may empathically position themselves to promote transformation of organizing experiences.[1]

"I FEEL VERY CRAZY"

Clinicians working with persons with significant organizing experience often discover that the speaker has been to a number of therapists prior to coming to treatment. A relative lack of sophistication in the therapeutic community of how to isolate, identify, and

---

[1]Special acknowledgment is expressed to Joyce Hulgus, Ph. D., for her significant theoretical and clinical contributions in thinking out the issues in this chapter.

interpretively respond to the organizing disconnection means that most therapists practicing today are not sensitive to the basic disconnecting transference that the person is bringing for treatment and its seriousness. The speaker has no way of telling the therapist directly about the deep nature of the primitive somatopsychic dissociation that continues to produce ruptured relationships. There is no way of simply putting the experience into words. The therapist not attuned to organizing experiences provides therapeutic approaches more appropriate for neurotic, narcissistic, or borderline states than for organizing states. After a while, the client will sense that the listener does not know how to reach with him or her the depth that is required. The speaker moves on to another therapist, much as an infant routing for a breast may spend some time trying to find what is needed.

Little (1990), in her account of her own analysis with Winnicott, indicates that she had several previous therapeutic experiences, as well as her own training analysis in the British Psycho-Analytic Institute before she found Winnicott. When Winnicott told her that she was really quite ill, she reports feeling a tremendous sense of relief that at last he saw the part of her that was very primitively developed, that was unorganized. He was a pediatrician/psychoanalyst and spoke of her organizing experience in terms of illness, letting her know in his language that he saw the depth of her distress. Many therapists fear labeling or speaking to the client about the extent or the depth of the problem, preferring instead to "normalize" things that the client knows full well are quite mad. In failing to acknowledge the depth of the client's concerns, listeners may be failing to reassure the speaker that they see, that they understand, and that "we have some very difficult and perhaps frightening work to do."

As therapeutic experience expands with organizing experiences it becomes increasingly clear that pockets of unorganized development are universal. The more awareness we have of how to discern organizing experiences embedded in otherwise well-developed personalities, the more we have also become aware of how pervasive organizing experiences are in a great many people who have somehow found ways of functioning in the world and of "passing" as relatively normal. Many of these clients are quite persistent in searching for a therapist; in searching for a place to do their work, they show remarkable capacities, skills, intelligence, and perseverance. I have come to believe that in many community clinics and in many socioeconomically depressed communities there are large numbers of organizing people who simply have not been able to find the resource to begin to develop themselves. What seems to be common to all people with pervasive organizing experiences is that whatever capacities they might have as human beings, they have been remarkably unstimulated and undeveloped—given whatever potentials seem to be native to their nature. The cost to our society of not treating these people is staggering in terms of the social burden they become due to unemployment and disability benefits, lawsuits, Social Security, crime, and medical expenses—which could be drastically reduced if these people were offered treatment.

"I FEEL LIKE I'M FALLING APART OR DYING"

As therapy progresses and the client has begun to work on the problem of connection and disconnection and the client is beginning to develop the capacity to sustain connections with the analyst, the fear may begin to emerge that "I'm going to fall apart and go crazy" or "I'm going to die."

Winnicott (1974) came to understand such fears as memories. That is, the dreaded breakdown or death *has already happened* in the primordial past and is being recalled or relived as a fear that the experience is going to happen. Further, fears of fragmentation, breakdown, insanity, debilitation, disease, and death may emerge as resistances to the emergence of organizing transference terrors. That is, in keeping with Freud's formulation that resistance in psychoanalysis is a memory of the dreaded transference configuration and emerges to forestall the establishment of the transference attitude within the analytic relationship, we have come to think of the fear of breakdown, illness, and death as a representation of the nature of the experience of infantile trauma. The trauma from the organizing level is retained in contemporary personality functioning as transference from the psychotic mother. The psychoanalytic vision has always been that freedom from overlearned childhood patterns of emotional relatedness can be obtained by allowing the experience to emerge into the full light of day in a transference experience with the analyst. Resistance to transferential reexperiencing takes different forms for different developmental issues. At the organizing level the transference is warded off by the fear of breakdown and death because that was the infant's subjective experience, and that experience must recur in transference for its power over the personality to be transformed.

These fears of breakdown and death that mark progress in analyzing the organizing experience need to be distinguished from fears of death, fears of mother dying, and fantasies of suicide that emerge in work with borderline or symbiotic level issues. In analytic work, after the symbiotic bonding experience or dyadic dance has been brought to light and is beginning to be given up, the client may begin to talk about death (her own or her mother's) or suicide. Such ruminations seem to the listener to come "out of the blue just when we were doing so well." But from the speaker's standpoint, "doing well" means "I am losing the sense of the mother I once knew who has sustained me so far in life. I'm losing the self that once loved my mother in special ways and that expects love in certain ways." The death thoughts and suicidal preoccupations that occur as transformational progress begins are representations of what is, in fact, happening. The mother of the past is dying. The self that sustained those patterns and modes of relating is likewise dying. The suicide ideation and death thoughts can be interpreted as representations of the loss of an entire way of being based upon the person's earliest love bond. This progress in the context of symbiotic structures anticipates that confusion and/or grieving is not far away as the actual loss is already being represented in the fantasies.

In contrast, when a person is experiencing internal loss when seeking to transform organizing experience, the results and expectations are quite different. The giving up of the internalized experience of the traumatizing (psychotic) mother means that lifelong body constrictions that prevent emotional experiencing of others are crumbling. Intense pain, panic, and confusion are to be expected as the protective barrier that was once erected to prevent bonding begins to disintegrate and movement begins toward sustained relating. This somatopsychic barrier is the relational self developed during that period and it relates to others by walling out interpersonal experiencing in endless forms.

The disintegration of the body barrier is the death of the self as knowing, the fragmentation of the early secure psychic structure. It becomes a critical time for the therapist to be available in all ways possible. This is a delicate juncture at which the person is losing the internalized psychotic mother, feeling greatly overstimulated, and beginning to build emotional connections with the listener. If the listener is not reliably and readily available in known, specific, and concrete ways, that absence can feel like a frightening death moment as well—a replication of the original trauma of an emotionally unavailable mother. That is, at the critical time period in which the organizing transference is breaking down, the person experiences panic, overstimulation, precarious vulnerability, and psychic fragmentation not unlike he or she did in infancy. More differentiated and abstract forms of living and remembering have been set aside by the speaker so that the therapeutic appreciation of the organizing experience can occur. The only time that is sensed in such states is *now*, the present. The only location that is sensed is *here*. Life itself without assured contact with the mothering other (now the therapist) feels threatened.

I have the impression that many of these people in infancy or in utero did subjectively experience terrifying threats of actual death such that some form of survival instinct was mobilized in order to cling to the only known source of life, the maternal body. For these deep threats of death to be reexperienced in the therapeutic transference regression, the state of mind that must be achieved is that of a helpless, dependent infant who cannot find its desperately needed mother. The reemergence of organizing states cannot be totally contained within the scheduled analytic sessions all the time, even when the person has an otherwise well-developed, intact ego. Winnicott's many papers and Little's (1990) lucid discussions of psychotic anxieties and their containment illustrate richly the kind of terror, panic, and desperate search for contact with the person of the analyst that can be expected in this kind of work.

"I FEAR I WON'T BE ABLE TO FIND YOU WHEN I NEED YOU"

The present work on the organizing experience expands on previous discussions in the area of the critical importance of therapist availability during times of deep therapeutic regression (Hedges 1983, Chapter 10). This may mean temporarily increasing the frequency of sessions or adding brief daily telephone contacts. Whatever sense of continuity with life, with others, or with the self the person feels is being obliterated by the analytic work, some kind of new or fresh possibility for connection needs to be available to the person at that time. The person cannot work through the barriers to contact and the terrors they entail unless the possibility of contact with a human being is *real*. This availability, in whatever forms it may be offered, is not gratification in any sense of the word. Rather, real emotional availability constitutes the very *frame* through which the terrorizing organizing transference may be secured for analysis. Many therapists, perhaps somewhat reluctantly, have had to give up weekend time or vacation time in order to stay in contact by phone, or some other way, so that the fragile tendrils of connection that have begun to extend can be sustained through being met. *If increased therapist availability at first seems like a departure from traditional psychoanalysis, more careful consideration reveals this availability to be what frustrates the person's overlearned patterns of contact rupture from the organizing period.*

By way of contrast with the borderline or symbiotic experience, when the death thoughts or suicide thoughts emerge, we would expect grieving, but what the grieving process tells us at this developmental level is that a different mother has been found, a different connection has been found; the old connection has been lost, relinquished, given up. The person may feel quite shaky and extra time and contact may be requested and needed. With symbiotic scenarios the listener need not feel obligated to set aside temporarily his or her ordinary professional boundaries in order to meet the person because a much more advanced state of ego is present in the speaker. With symbiotic scenarios the progress that is being heralded by death and fragmentation fears is the progress that new connections *have already been made*. This cannot be assumed with the organizing experience. Progress from the organizing experience is like a baby ready to take its first steps; it needs someone to go toward, some concrete person who is holding out his or her hand waiting encouragingly.

If the technique seems different it is only because the listener must respond to different developmental issues differentially in order to achieve the same analytic result—the breakdown of the limiting mode or pattern of relatedness.

A further point of contrast that clarifies the distinction between symbiotic experiences and organizing experiences is that the hallmark of the symbiotic experience is the fear of abandonment. The hallmark of the organizing experience is the fear of emotional contact, of interpersonal connection. When the person presenting symbiotic issues has learned to let abandonment and separation occur, that's when the loss of the old internal mother and self sense occurs. With the organizing experience, when the person has begun to see the importance of making contact, a terrifying thing occurs at the moment of connection—the memory of the primordial trauma of past connections suddenly appears in a myriad of forms to ward off, to resist the possibility of a real connection that is also feared to be traumatic. The resistance is embedded in somatic reflex so tightly that it completely evades consciousness. The experience is that "something happens," the personality simply "switches" to another, a hallucination or delusion appears, the affect suddenly changes, the demand for something from the other increases, or the topic of conversation or nature of the interaction becomes shifted.

The deceptive thing to the listener is that often people living the organizing experiences express the fear, "I won't be able to have you" or "You're going to leave me," when in fact the fear is that "We're going to connect." That is, fears of abandonment, dependency, or helplessness are so universal that anyone expressing them can feel somehow understood. But to an organizing experience these fears are resistance. A clamoring fear of abandonment expressed by a person working an organizing transference is more likely *another way to disconnect or not be fully present and engaged in the moment* so that the abandonment content per se can be disregarded and/or interpreted as resistance to sustaining connection. It is important for the analyst to differentiate the fear of abandonment from the fear of connection, which is terrifying and marks the appearance of the traumatizing psychotic mother. In organizing experiences it is always the connection that is feared. And without the assured presence of the other, the fear can lead to a negative therapeutic experience.

The delicate sense of working or learning to be together that may have been nurtured for a long period of time in therapy can be obliterated if it is allowed to go unattended to for very long. The important thing is that availability be possible during delicate working-through phases so the resistance to reexperiencing the abandoning, traumatizing mother transference can be shown to be delusional. "I am here, I am available. Can you find a way to push past your fears and connect with me? I am here." But the therapist must in reality be present, available, ready, and desirous of authentic interpersonal contact or the transference cannot be framed for analysis against a backdrop of reality.

"IF I CANNOT HOLD ON TO MOTHER, I'LL DIE"

Throughout time and in various cultures, as madness has been defined and people have been labeled "psychotic" or "insane," not only do they display a variety of psychological preoccupations about their body parts, but in fact they are often in very poor health and concerned about staying alive. Babies who fail to make a psychological connection die of marasmus. People at different phases of life who are unable to benefit from interpersonal connectedness to others often develop organic diseases that threaten their health and their life.

One way in which concerns about safety, health, and survival appear in clinical work with organizing experience is that at various times when the client is aware of the loss of connection, terrors emerge. The reaction seems to be the re-creation of the infantile and perhaps instinctual terror, that "If I cannot hold on to the warm and safe maternal body, if I cannot hold on to the connectedness to my mother and to the human race, I will die." Many babies who have difficulties during this organizing period have internalized that fear at some basic body level, and, as adults, reexperience that fear when they cannot connect to the analyst in ways they feel they must in order to survive.

Concerns about survival and the terror of death are often much more than a mere analytic metaphor. Many of these people, at certain points in their therapy, are in danger of dying either for health reasons or from actually killing themselves. The therapist not sensitized to the extreme danger of these fears and of acting out these early internalized disconnect modes may find he or she has a seriously ill or a dead client. More subtle forms of dying include losing extreme amounts of weight, dissociating, becoming dangerously disoriented, not being alert while driving, and actual physical problems. There is ample evidence to suggest that organizing experiences may make a person more vulnerable to many kinds of diseases including metastases, bacterial infections, and viruses.

One client in intensive psychotherapy over a period of time developed a variety of disabling and debilitating physical problems that could never be diagnosed by many specialists. He became weaker and weaker and was hospitalized on various occasions for extensive diagnostic studies, until finally his therapist was able to voice to her colleagues in a case conference her fear that her client was actually going to die. The group encouraged her to speak her countertransference fear to the client in hopes of gaining some clue as what was going on. When she told him how worried she was about him, that he was not letting himself be fully alive, he said suddenly, and almost glibly, "Oh, well I told you that I was born dead, didn't I?" In ensuing sessions it was revealed that the infant's heart had stopped during delivery. The infant was resuscitated, but he was essentially born dead. The client apparently needed to reexperience in the analytic situation the many somatic memories of complications of this death experience. His various organs had been deteriorating and his doctors believed he was indeed in danger of dying. Once this experience that was being reawakened for analytic study could be talked about, interpreted, and understood as a memory that was being relived, his health improved dramatically.

A person living in an organizing state, whether it is part of a pervasive picture or a pocket that has been opened up as a result of a therapeutic regression, will feel moments of extreme panic and will reach out to make contact with the therapist. In light of the therapist's own needs for weekends, vacations, privacy, boundaries, and protection of his or her own space, this organizing panic creates difficulties at times. If the therapist is not prepared to make him- or herself briefly available at times other than regularly scheduled sessions, this kind of work should not be undertaken.

Therapists often fear the manipulative client, or the client in deep regression who may feel exceedingly dependent or overly needy and, in such states, use or misuse the therapist's time, taking advantage by calling, wanting to talk, or wanting to do therapy over the phone. But people living out organizing states generally do not need to abuse the therapist. Rather they need to know where the therapist is and how they can reach him or her if they become lost, or frightened, or fragmented.

This single and straightforward need to know in concrete terms where the mother/therapist is and how she/he can be reached—the need for availability and for potential contact—contrasts strongly with higher-level borderline or symbiotic replicated transference experience. When working with clients expressing symbiotic or borderline states, untoward reactions on the part of therapists are often justified in terms of the "Mommy and me" scenario that is being replicated in the analysis at the time. Symbiotic transferences arise from well-established mutual cuing interactions that were formed by a strong, firm (even if intrusive or abusive) connection between the infant or toddler and the mother. The particular *psychological quality* of that internalized interaction may be one of mutual manipulation, abuse, neglect, taking advantage of, or any other interaction that intrudes on the therapist's space. Such a scenario will need to be somehow replicated for the purpose of communicating the nature of its abusiveness and/or intrusiveness. But with symbiotic or borderline scenarios, there is also a considerable amount of ego operating within the scenario, within the demand, and within whatever manipulation may be a part of the communication of that demand. As such, the ego state usually does not require immediate or urgent response, and may be attended to more easily within a time frame more convenient to the therapist and amidst transference fears and complaints of abandonment.

In sharp contrast to these very difficult replicated transference formations that arise from the symbiotic period, the urgent need for contact that arises out of organizing experiences is quite different. It is generally an error on the part of the therapist to consider these urgent pleas for contact as manipulations, or gratifications, or any other kinds of attempts to use and/or misuse the therapist's person and time. In an organizing state, the infant is attempting to find mother so that safety, comfort, or survival can be assured. In a panicked organizing state, the infant is attempting to find mother so that safety, comfort, and/or survival can be assured. When a person is living out an organized transference and cannot find his or her therapist, he or she experiences the therapist in concrete terms much as an infant might— as gone, absent, missing, dead, or nonexistent. The transference experience, or the real experience of the therapist, may even go so far as the client feeling abused or sadistically treated by the therapist; the therapist has indicated an availability by agreeing to work with the client and then, at a moment of critical need for contact, the therapist has not been able to meet the need, or has withdrawn in a way that the infant, or the person in therapy, can only experience as cruel.

If what is being experienced in the client's quest for contact on weekends or vacations is true organizing transference, then the panic that the person is experiencing must be understood by the therapist as the reliving of a panic of life and death proportions that must be responded to as rapidly and as efficiently as possible. *Without such therapist availability the organizing transference will not be allowed to come into view, and the person cannot safely reach past overconditioned fear responses and find that connection can indeed be safely and reliably made.*

Many clients in therapy may get stuck in prolonged manipulating borderline scenarios, causing considerable difficulty and harassment to their therapist, simply because the therapist is failing to recognize the existence of more primitive needs that require prompt and cheerful response in order to be made known. That is, in denying availability, the therapist unwittingly prevents the therapeutic regression from reaching the organizing depth it needs to.

One way misunderstanding might occur is that, early in therapy, a borderline scenario of somewhat abusive proportions is being worked on. The therapist rightly draws some limits, makes rules, and withdraws somewhat, so as not to receive the abuse. As the abusive scenario begins to get worked through, the more urgent organizing panic may begin to emerge. The therapist may fail to follow the switch from the more manipulative ego state, which may not necessarily require urgent response, to the deeper, more primitive organizing panic, which does require availability and response. One client described her attempt to get the therapist to recognize the underlying primitive state by borrowing or feigning a variety of pathologies, to try to get the therapist on track with her, back to that very young level of need. It took a number of months for the therapist to recognize that the particular "pathology of the moment" was really not what was going on, but that there was a younger level of need to which the client was trying (preverbally) to direct the therapist's attention.

Such manipulations may be designed to get the therapist to begin to recognize the younger-level need and the crucial importance of therapist availability at certain critical times. Winnicott has pointed to the enormous difference between gratifying a wish and being responsive to a need. And, at the organizing level, once the disconnection is being worked, the need is for availability and potential contact. We can watch infants relax and melt out of whatever storm they might be in, at the mere sight, sound, or touch of their mothers. Such is the case with these urgent requests for organizing contact. The therapist's conscious or unconscious fantasies may have something to do with being manipulated, used, or misused; but the client's need is simply "to hear your voice and to know that you're there, that I can find you, and that we're connected so I can go on with my life."

The client's reaching the therapist is not unlike the demand feeding of an infant, when *the act of finding mother organizes out of mother's response to the demand.* Without mother's understanding and willing response, the panic, the agitation, and the anxiety only intensify and create multiple problems. When one's body is organized in the context of the mother/other, there is a sense of safety, and one's perceptual and motor apparatus can remain intact. When an infant is in contact with mother, his or her entire body and mind become immediately organized. When the child is out of contact and panicked, the child's body is out of control. The child's memory, judgment, perception—all fundamental ego processes are in danger of becoming chaotic and the child becomes endangered even to the point of feeling that survival itself is threatened.

Most organizing experiences revolve around the question in the infant's psychological, biological, and genetic structure: "How will I be able to survive and thrive?" Whatever instinct for survival a child might experience bodily or psychically in the organizing period is easily aroused by neglect or abuse so that the child's mind becomes precociously activated in an attempt to find ways of feeling safe. When survival is an issue the body tightens, the voice grows tense, and the entire body either freezes or begins to flail and convulse. The moment appropriate contact with another, particularly with the mothering person, can be achieved, the panic, pain, and somatic rigidity subside. Therapists who understand this have less difficulty with brief evening and weekend phone calls.

Using this understanding of the client's (organizing level) urgency for contact with the therapist, the two can discuss in advance what kind of contact is workable outside of the regular therapeutic session. It can be agreed that these contacts are to be brief, and that the purpose is basically to achieve momentary connection, not for lengthy processing of material that can be done in sessions. "We will know that our voices are meeting, that we are contacting and thinking about each other, and that we can share a few words about the day, the weather, or what's happening at the moment." This agreement relieves the client of having to invent a complex set of reasons about why he or she had to call, so as to justify it. Nor does the therapist need to feel obligated to go through any complex interpretive or understanding activities. He or she can feel free to terminate the call fairly rapidly. Interpretations, long accounts of events, or complex reflections introduce ego states into the conversation when this is not what these phone calls are about. With clients working at the borderline or symbiotic level, should the therapist choose to be receiving telephone calls outside the session, more ego is involved. In the symbiotic context outside contacts can be more limited, more controlled, more delayed, and perhaps at times not even responded to. Not so with the urgency for organizing contact. The therapist's fearful fantasies about the length, the complexity, or the difficulty of such contacts are generally unjustified, but the extra contacts do require efficient management.

One client who did need to make contact at various times during the day and night would call her therapist. When her therapist answered, she would say, very briefly, "I felt like I was going to disintegrate. I needed to find you. I needed to hear your voice. I know I'm disturbing you, but thank you for letting me hear your voice. I think I can now make it through the night." The interaction was always very brief, and it was almost identical each occasion that occurred. This seems to be the nature of the organizing need for contacting the therapist.

Practically speaking, trying to respond to these urgent requests in the past has been very difficult. But with modern telephone communication, the burden is considerably eased. There are many ways contact can be arranged by different therapists, so that reasonably prompt response can be made. I have found that a telephone recording whereby the client can make contact with the therapist's voice is often all the person needs. Sometimes people actually want to leave a message on the voice mail, knowing that in a few hours the therapist is likely to hear it. But if there's also a provision on the voice mail for an emergency beeper, or for an emergency response system through an answering service, then the instruction to the client can be, "I will be back to you within an hour if you put an emergency call through to me. And if there are unusual circumstances where I simply cannot get to a phone, it will be within a matter of three hours."

But however the details are arranged to fit comfortably into the therapist's life, it is important that there be a clear and concrete definition of exactly what the ongoing availability of the therapist will be, and exactly what the time frame for response will be, because when a person is in an organizing state there is no room for ego functioning to figure out "What is this? What is that? What did he say?" The person needs to know simply and exactly "How I can find my therapist/ mother."

In working through complex scenarios with a borderline client, the ego states, needs, and demands, as well as the limits of both parties, often become discussed extensively. Interpretive therapist disclosures are often required in order to bring to light exactly the nature of the demand, the manipulation, or the exchange that is being revived in transference. Often countertransference protests must be made with a borderline client, explaining what I, as the therapist, do not like, and why. Because in the projective identifications that the symbiotic client engages in, it is often in the countertransference that the client's infant voice appears rather than in the transference. That is, in interpreting the countertransference (Hedges 1992) we see that the protest that the infant was unable to make about "the way I'm being treated," comes to reside in the emotional experience of the therapist. Since the client cannot speak the preverbal symbiotic structure, it is often the therapist who must do the speaking for the infant need. But these are needs that are comparatively highly struc-tured within early ego states.

In contrast, organizing states contain very little ego, and when a person is living in an organizing state, the body may be out of control, the mind may be out of control, and a severe panic ensues that can only be responded to through actual (mothering) contact. Any elab-oration by the therapist of the reasons for the contact being achievable in one way and not another, or the states of mind that the therapist might or might not be in, or the ways in which the therapist can and cannot receive such calls, simply gets in the way. In advanced ego states, explanations are appropriate. In primitive states, only the facts need to be conveyed: "If you feel frightened or in an urgent state, you may reach me this way. I will respond to you in such and such a time frame. We can talk five minutes or so. The purpose is simply for us to have contact." Nothing more need be stated. Anything else intrudes, is burdensome, and creates problems, dilemmas, and debates within the client at a time when the client is really not prepared to think about such things.

When all of these issues are taken into consideration, it can be seen that not only is it important for the therapist to have a way of being contacted, but that there is a need to have a "Plan B," in which, at the times the therapist cannot be available, someone else with whom the client has some rudimentary relationship will be on call and will be available. With an infant, concerned parents try to leave the child with a relative, a family friend, or a familiar babysitter, so that when the mother cannot respond, there is someone familiar who can.

Therapists and analysts trained in traditional approaches to psychotherapy not only find these considerations difficult to imagine responding to, but they find rationalizations for why they are not necessary or appropriate. But each rationalization, such as "the pa-thology or dependency should not be reinforced," "the patient must learn to delay gratification," "the client must learn to develop ego skills," and so forth, are constructed for the convenience of the therapist and for use with clients with better ego development. They show a total lack of understanding of the acute and serious nature of the organizing experience when a client has allowed it to come forward for analysis. A therapist's beliefs that primitive demands will go forever, that pathology must not be reinforced, that wishes must not be gratified but analyzed, all represent a treatment approach appropriate to neurosis or rationalized fears of the therapist. True, there are periods when the organizing state has been brought forward for analysis, and for several days, weeks or even longer periods, there may be a need to be able to find the therapist on a moment's notice. But these do not go on forever, nor is there any reason why anything more than brief contact be provided or that it should be considered as gratifying or reinforcing of pathology.

Such arrangements may require the therapist to adjust the way he practices and responds to telephone calls. But *if a therapist or analyst is not prepared to meet the client when he or she is extending in organizing states, the therapist should not attempt this work.* The therapist will only be bothered, disturbed, and perturbed by what he experiences as endless demands, manipulations, and frantic attempts to manipulate or abuse the therapist when, in fact, something entirely different is being sought. In the end the client will become discouraged and end treatment. It is also true that if the therapist proves unresponsive to contact when needed, that the emergence of the organizing transference will be obscured and/or not permitted to emerge due to the realistic difficulties the client is having getting the therapist to understand his or her material. Unresponsiveness on the part of the therapist promotes mimical and false self adjustment to the therapist's personality—not analysis of the organizing transference, which requires a different frame to secure.

One client, who was very well developed, but who occasionally would fall into an organizing state as he was trying to reconstruct some fundamental pattern of his neonate period was finally able to express his private pattern of experience. As an infant he experienced needs. Mother felt overwhelmed by the baby's needs. As a child he came to know his mother's reluctance to respond, and began to develop strategies of persuasion in order to have his fundamental needs responded to. His strategies completed a self-perpetuating circle in which the mother turned her back, refusing, or abandoning the child. This vicious cycle led to the formation of chronic rage in the child, because the child had internalized the expectation that his needs were not going to be responded to on a regular basis. The child then took on a self-concept of being a needy, manipulative, naughty child, who was always trying to coerce everyone to do what he wanted.

A person may move into a place where an organizing experience of transference is activated. The person then reaches out in an attempt to make the required contact so that calm and safety can be experienced. If that urgent need for contact is not met, states of confusion and fear arise, leading to self-destructive acts, mutilation, drunkenness, drugs, sexual acts, and even more frank suicide attempts.

"I AM OVERWHELMED BY WHAT SEEMS EASY TO YOU"

Another concern of people who live dominantly in the organizing experience is the amount of strain and energy that it requires to get through an ordinary day. True, they may have developed a variety of coping mechanisms of a false or mimical self variety, so as to appear normal, to function adequately, or to "pass" in a complex social world. But the adaptation is extremely taxing. It is difficult for therapists to remember that sometimes even to get out of bed in the morning, to put on one's clothes, or to walk through the ordinary, seemingly simple, aspects of the day is a great deal of strain when one is living in organizing experiences. Therapists may mistakenly give these people complex interpretations or difficult assignments or expect them to be able to function in certain ways that they simply cannot at the time. For example, therapists might put these clients into group therapy, or expect them to hold down a job, leave an unsatisfying relationship, or handle family or financial matters without support, when in fact these people do not have the energy to engage in ordinary social activities at the level the therapist expects.

Another clinical implication of a person functioning at a very concrete level during periods of analysis is that what may seem to be very simple things to the therapist require an impossible amount of concentration and energy for the speaker in analysis. How easily overwhelmed a speaker can be by demands such as having to deal with too many thoughts and interpretations, trying to remember things from previous hours or days, or simply coping with ordinary realities.

At the end of the session it is essential for a person to transition out of the unorganized state to more organization so that he or she will be able to move into and function in the world outside. Some time or assistance may be necessary to accomplish this smoothly. Likewise, if mother/therapist brings too many of her needs, her emotional states, and her thoughts to the experience with the infant, there will be no room for the infant to connect. If the therapist uses too many words, or discloses too much personal experience, the person in the organizing state will not be able to connect. In all probability he or she will end up trying to adapt to the therapist, just as the child tried to adapt to the psychotic mother, but the effect is burdensome and the results false.

"I NEED NOT TO BE PRESSURED OR RUSHED"

In work with unorganized states, it is not uncommon for the therapist to feel that he or she is being manipulated, cajoled, forced, tricked, duped, and made to do various things against one's wishes. In looking carefully at the organizing experience, these countertransference feelings are generally inappropriate to what is actually going on, although they may register something important about the analyst's experience in the transference role of the psychotic mother or the traumatized infant. That is, infants have a great many needs such as (1) to be held, (2) to be held longer after the feeding so that perception can gel, (3) to be talked to for extended periods of time so that sounds can be enjoyed and so that the mind can organize auditory stimulation, (4) to feel and to smell, (5) to be able to take time, (6) to feel in possession of the maternal body and mind, and (7) to have smooth transitions into and out of contact. These are all necessary for the infant's mind to organize time and space with the body and mind of the maternal person. Since many of these needs are thwarted in infancy by various factors in the mother's life, organizing pockets or more pervasive organizing experiences may occur. When these organizing experiences are reactivated in therapy, the need for such things as continued time, sound, space, satisfaction, comfort, and the need not to have these things abruptly taken away or interrupted prematurely may be very intense and experienced with a great deal of vehemence and perhaps even aggression by the client. For the therapist to feel persecuted or manipulated by these reactions is indicative that the therapist is not in empathic attunement with the nature of these needs. Therapists' narcissism often demands that they be treated rationally and with respect. But such reactions are not in tune with irrational infantile demands.

Yes, the therapist, like the early mother, has other duties in life. But the demands of these other duties must be weighed against trying to provide continuity of experience and trying to make provision for slow withdrawal from, rather than traumatic disruption of, critical linking experiences. It may take much time and learning, and require thoughtful preparation on the part of the analyst to provide these. At times there may be no way that, practically speaking, the client's sense of loss of continuity can be experienced as anything other than traumatic transference from the withdrawing psychotic mother. But once again, *although the trauma may not be avoidable by the therapist, what the therapist can anticipate is the nature of the trauma, and to allow time and space to focus on the understanding of the nature of the break in the contact.* It can be understood how anticipation of faulty experience is carried on inside the speaker, and inevitably experienced whenever unsatisfactory experiences occur in the outside world. Such understanding may or may not be possible at every given traumatic moment. But over time, and with sensitive handling, the therapist can find ways of being in a position to go in one of two ways: either to foster linking and continuity through gradual withdrawal, or if that experience is not going to be possible because of the client's transference, to allow the time and space to focus on what the nature of the traumatizing transference experience is at the moment.

Difficulties may arise in a therapist's learning how to provide empathic contact with such experiences of desperation. Finding ways of maintaining a satisfactory sense of continuity may be particularly difficult when a client has had previous therapy and now fairly suddenly presents a regressed experience to a therapist who has not yet had sufficient experience with this particular person to know the nature of the deprivations being studied, or to have sufficient knowledge or means of making contact with these traumatized areas, or to show the person how transference is being projected upon something that is really happening.

"THERE MUST BE TIME AND SPACE FOR MY SPONTANEOUS GESTURES TO BE MET"

Winnicott (1971) has emphasized the importance of "the space between" the mother and child. He says we do not ask the child whether the child created the breast/mother, or whether the child discovered the breast/mother. The mother or the analyst often has no way of knowing whether creativity or discovery is being experienced at a given moment. But if the mother/therapist fills that space with herself, neither creativity nor discovery will occur. Winnicott emphasizes the necessity for waiting until the spontaneous gesture occurs, and when it does, meeting it in a timely fashion.

The importance of time and space for the spontaneous gesture has many implications for child rearing and working mothers. The longer the organizing experience is studied, the clearer it becomes how absolutely important it is for the primary mothering persons, preferably the biological mother, to be as available as possible during the first three to four months of life, so that as many as possible of the spontaneous gestures and creative acts of the child can be seen and responded to.

It is very difficult for someone other than the mother with her primary maternal preoccupation to be able to fully meet the child in optimal ways. Without such maternal preoccupation the child will mature in most ways. Many ego functions will evolve. But all of the failed times that the child reached out needing to be met, needing to be responded to, needing to be cared for, held, and stimulated by the mother will be recorded in (withdrawal, disconnecting) memories that will permanently stifle the person's full capacity for relating to people. Such unmet experiences cause withering and withdrawal, which leave whole aspects of the person undeveloped. Once the child has begun to form a bonding relationship, once delay, frustration, and a rudimentary sense of object permanence become available, the child can know when mother is leaving and can recognize mother once she returns. But prior to this time, during the earliest months, the child's experiences simply wither, leaving undeveloped aspects. Creativity and spontaneity suffer when infantile desire goes unmet.

"I MUST BE ALLOWED TO ESTABLISH A CONTINUITY OF BEING AND RHYTHM OF SAFETY"

Tustin (1986) has spoken of the "rhythm of safety." In reading this paper to a group of American analysts in Paris in 1985, she said that she was inspired by watching a young relative nurse her infant. Mrs. Tustin said she had forgotten how active the nipple is in relation to the mouth. It is not simply a mouth seeking a nipple, but also a nipple seeking a mouth. She observed the nursing couple adjusting first this way with a little bit of sucking, and then another way, and another. At last the two found each other, satisfactorily connected, and the rhythmical sucking begins. Then the two bodies relax into a sense of safety. In the analytic encounter this metaphor helps us understand the unrest that a person in an organizing state brings to sessions. The analyst feels the unrest not quite knowing what is required, or how to respond, or how exactly to position one's self, until at last some kind of safety can be achieved when the two have found a synchronized mode of being together, of connecting. What often happens is the analyst is satisfied that a connection is occurring as the analytic speaker settles down to the rules and rituals of analytic practice. What this may instead tell us is that mimicry and falseness are operating. The organizing transference will never become available under such circumstances. The unrest of the internalized psychotic mother transference must be allowed as well.

Another subtle area of content that frequently appears as people are recalling and bringing to life in the analytic situation their internalized organizing experiences has to do with the sense of failed continuity. Winnicott, in his work with children, regularly interprets snake images not as the expectable paternal phallus, but as the child representing movement down the birth canal. Wriggling or crawling is a primordial archetype of movement that allows a baby to find continuity with life outside mother's body. Further, midwifery teaches that if the child is placed on the mother's abdomen immediately after birth the child will wriggle or crawl upward until the child finds the mother's breast with a rudimentary kind of grasping activity. Many children have been deprived of satisfying wriggling experiences due to a caesarean section or a traumatic birth. Other children are removed from contact with mother's body while being put in incubators or other lifesaving devices. Many mothers are so preoccupied with their own needs that continuity for the newborn is lost. As a result they may remain stuck in some way, still trying to find the early mother.

Today hospitals and nurseries are much more aware of the importance of immediate contact with mother's body after birth. But many people in analytic settings were deprived of appropriate contact through the mother's not being emotionally or physically available after birth to receive the child so as to bridge the gap between intrauterine life and extrauterine life. Adopted babies, even with favorable adoption arrangements at birth, seem to have lost this sense of continuity. And in analysis this difficulty shows up in various forms of transference fear.

"I NEED TO HEAR, SEE, SMELL, AND FEEL YOU"

Many infant researchers such as Stern (1985) have been successful in demonstrating the extreme importance of the total sensorium in the organizing period before and after birth. In analyzing organizing experiences, people frequently communicate a need for either a cessation of sensory experience into calm, soothing, or safety, or an activation of sensory experience into liveliness and stimulation. It is incumbent upon the therapist working with organizing experiences to be attuned to and responsive to such sensory experience.

Numerous clients, while needing silence for a period of time, also come to the point where they need to hear mother/analyst's voice. It is not the words per se but the fact that she is speaking, her tone, her gentleness, the serenity, or interest that can make possible organizing around mother's voice. Many clients simply ask, "Please speak to me."

Likewise, the olfactory sense is very active in infants who are able to find mother through smells. People living organizing experiences are often extremely sensitive to the smells in the analytic room and to the smells of the person of the analyst. They make reference to familiar smells that may make contact possible. One therapist who works with many organizing clients regularly puts a small drop of her perfume, which she wears every day without fail, on her business cards for these people to carry with them. If they need to remember or to orient, they can orient to her through smell. A photograph of the analyst, or a tape recording with the sound of the analyst's voice speaking or perhaps even reading poetry or a story helps people maintain continuity of contact through familiar auditory stimulation.

At various moments it may be critical for people living organizing experiences to establish some kind of actual physical contact, perhaps with vision or even by holding hands or sitting near the analyst. The senses, in a very realistic and concrete way, must be acknowledged when trying to re-create early developmental experiences. The re-creations will involve searching for contact in order to find safety, but may also provide entrée into framing some transferential disruption of contact that represents the ways mother abandoned or disrupted the contact with the child. It is often only through sensory modalities that the connection and the disconnection can become known and can be worked with transformationally. (See Appendix for a sample informed consent form for physical contact.)

One woman therapist was initially somewhat alarmed by what appeared to be intrusiveness and possibly seductiveness on the part of her male client. His sessions were held shortly after dark. He would move his chair up to where his knees were practically touching hers and would readjust a nearby light so it shone brightly on her face. She was extremely uncomfortable, feeling perhaps the man was attempting to be assaultive, seductive, or intrusive, until he was able to say, "I can only know you by watching your face." The man's employment, it turns out, involved making decisions on large-scale dollar loans. He was a genius at paperwork and numbers. When a loan application would be presented to him, he could quickly mentally compute and ascertain the paper qualifications. But in his interviews with clients, it was discovered that he would invite the potential customers in, and for a long period of time, thumb silently through papers, but continue to watch people's faces until he believed whether or not they were going to be reliable customers. He had no idea how he made his decision, but his track record for placing reliable loans put him at the top of the bank's loan executives. He had developed a keen sense of knowing how to judge people's reliability through studying the lines in their faces and the movements of their eyes, mouths, and noses. It was the mapping of the face that allowed him to develop this highly specialized skill into a refined art!

Another client arranged four hours, Monday through Thursday, of absolute silence in an advanced phase of her psychoanalytic work. Toward the end of the fourth hour, in a very quiet voice, she explained to her analyst that this was exactly what she needed, that she had never before in her life had an opportunity to feel that her thoughts and her mind could come together in a way that was real, and that she felt to be her own. In her very busy, active, and competent life, and in the activity of the ordinary analytic exchange, she could function based upon false self or mimical self aspects quite well, but she never felt quite real. In the silence the sensory overload could be quieted and she could begin to know that she existed. She said, "I need you being here and being quiet – not doing anything, not thinking anything else, and not eating grapes like you were yesterday, but simply being here quietly with me. If I can't have that, I can't do what I have to do."

Another client, for some years with his analyst, always came to sessions with tinted glasses on. It was not until the participants of a case conference group asked about the sunglasses that it occurred to the therapist that they were not prescription. This was his way of avoiding making contact with the therapist. Following that, the therapist was able to begin asking the client, when possible, to remove the sunglasses so that visual contact could be made. The most fascinating saga followed, which revolved around when the glasses had to be worn, and when they could be taken off. It had to do with the tolerance of connection, the terror of connection, and the need to disconnect visually.

"I NEED TO HAVE A TOTAL BODY EXPERIENCE"

When thinking about the organizing experience, one is on shaky ground if one attempts to distinguish too sharply between psyche and soma. Freud (1911) commented that no theory of psychosis is complete without a discussion of hypochondriasis. This comment registers Freud's understanding that concerns about body experience were an integral part of primitive psychic experience. Subsequent writers on the subject of psychosis have talked about the centrality of somatic experiencing. Our typical stereotype of a schizophrenic in a state hospital is a person whose body is rigid and who walks like a board. The manic-psychotic person is one whose body is wildly agitated. The psychotically depressed individual is one whose body is morosely depleted and depressed. The autistic child walks as if on air, as if he/she has no ground to walk on.

The body is grossly expressive in the organizing experience. But up to now the emphasis has been primarily on making a symptomatic description of body experiences. In a classic case by Tausk (1919), "The Influencing Machine," he writes about a woman in a hospital who was hopelessly paranoid, and talking to everyone about a dreadful "influencing machine" that was running her life. In a flash of insight, Tausk asked her to draw the machine. She drew a picture of a body. Bioenergetics therapists (Lowen 1971, 1975, 1982, 1988) who have studied extensively the necessarily inseparable aspects of psyche and soma, have much to say about the somatic involvement in all psychic structures at all developmental levels, but are especially tuned in to basic body constrictions and distortions that occur in relation to the earliest other.

At the level of earliest organizing experience it is clear that the infant is organizing the perceptual/motor system to find or to refind, mother's body. In utero there was a certain sense of where the infant's body was in relation to the maternal body. Self and other were not conceptually separated, but movement against the intrauterine wall or by the intrauterine wall could immediately create sensation. Intrauterine movement would be responded to instantaneously with counter-movement.

Outside the uterus, the child is constantly reaching and stretching with all of his or her faculties to achieve nurturance, comfort, and stimulation. Young babies can be observed noticing their hands pass in front of their eyes, or occasionally noticing a foot within the visual field. In earliest phases of learning to coordinate movements there appears a more or less spastic quality that represents an aspect of infancy, that is, that bodies are at first uncoordinated. Slowly, meaningful reaching, meaningful coordination, meaningful self and other touching, meaningful eye–hand coordination come into play.

In advanced stages of therapeutic work with organizing experiences, when making and sustaining contact get under way, the mental and emotional contact that the therapist has been encouraging cannot be separated from various bodily experiences that the client is having. Sometimes a client experiences needing to be touched, or wishing to be soothed. The client feels safe in the presence of the therapist, safe in the consulting room, safe listening to the therapist's voice. All of the sensory modalities and the motor modalities of going to the same place, hearing the same sounds, smelling familiar smells, seeing the same figure, can be soothing. And yet, on the other hand, if the person at a moment in time is experiencing the resurgence of the psychotic mother transference, these same experiences can be terrifying and can produce pronounced body movements with uncoordinated shaking, compulsive rocking, and other "autosensuous" (Tustin 1981) activities that bespeak the momentary sense of total absence of the other and being lost in a terrifying void. But once the reaching process begins, vibratory movements in various parts of the body, sometimes in the arms, sometimes in the legs, eyes, face, head, neck, mouth, or any other parts of the body, begin. Sensations and movements in the gastrointestinal tract, the lungs, heart, or the pelvis may occur during the revival of organizing experiences. The person may fix attention on any and all body parts, feeling that they are malfunctioning in some way when primitive somatic responses are being revived for analysis. All aspects of somatic functioning are subject to reinstatement during the therapeutic regression to refind the mind–body experience that was unable to connect with mother. Clients, and perhaps therapists, may at first be frightened by the sudden appearance of spasms, or vibrations, but these should be encouraged and the emotional experiences that come along with the body movements encouraged as well. Vocalization and/or verbal expression may be gently encouraged during or following such moments as additional ways of reaching.

One example is a woman who, on the couch, when feeling the terror of contact would begin to go into violent spasms. She learned at that point to reach her hand toward the analyst, sometimes out from under a blanket she covered herself up with, to know that he was there. Holding her hand during these violent periods gave her a sense of containment. Occasionally there were the therapist's two hands holding her two hands while her body writhed violently on the couch as she reexperienced infant battering. At times she issued soul-piercing screams until at last she felt safe to be in contact. Her resistance to contact had to be reenacted at a physical level until she could feel safe being physically present in the room.

Complications in such procedures may exist when therapists themselves are uncertain about or frightened by the nature of the experience, or if the needed experiencing stimulates too much in the therapists, or if they themselves have serious inhibitions about physical experiences. It may possibly be even more complex when the particular nature of the physical experience that the client wants is simply not feasible within the legal-ethical bounds of psychotherapy. For example, in California the business and professions code specifies that unlawful sexual touching includes not only breast and groin contact, but also buttocks contact. The patient may wish to sit on the therapist's lap, but according to law this is a sexual violation. Voice contact, eye contact, finger touching, hand holding, and feet touching are all legally permissible when the course of therapy justifies it. All physical contact needs to be constantly evaluated in terms of potential misunderstandings, and needs to be justified in terms of essential transference and/or transference interpretation reexperiencing. Therapists who have misgivings about physical contact or are themselves overstimulated by it should not undertake this kind of work.

A therapist wishing more ethical or legal protection may have a third party involved to monitor the effects of all such procedures. I emphasize that any physical contact (other than formal body work) needs to be thoroughly discussed in advance and fully informed consent be obtained. Further, I believe that in ordinary analytically oriented psychotherapy *physical contact that is therapeutic is only done interpretively*, that is, in the service of saying concretely, "You have been taught that to have contact is traumatic. It is possible for you to have contact with me that is safe." (See earlier discussions in previous chapters on interpretive touching for its uses, abuses, and limitations.)

Therapists specializing in body work have developed a variety of forms of physical contact. If the therapist is in doubt, a consultation can be made with someone who practices body therapy about the kinds of contact that might be useful, the kinds of physical containment that might be appropriate and safe. Arranging for parallel body work with a professional trained in body work may be the most viable way to go. But there needs to be a collaborative relationship between the professionals involved. "Split transference" implies that a higher developmental level is in focus and is not at issue at the organizing level. But what is missing is the split between experiencing and observing ego. A case monitor can function temporarily as an auxiliary ego. And the client needs to be able to see the body work as integral to the psychotherapy work.

My standard caution if the therapist is going to consider physical touching or physical contact in more than a token, interpretive way is that the therapist seek consultation, so that the therapist is at all times keeping the contact and the relationship safe legally and ethically and well monitored by a third party for transference and countertransference features. The total lack of distinction between psyche and soma during the organizing developmental period means that the analyst who believes that all containing and interpreting can or should be done verbally sadly misunderstands the nature of the analytic issues at stake in the organizing experience or is badly self-deceived.

"I NEED YOU TO BE ALIVE TO ME"

Green (1986) has written about the "dead mother." The infant's experience of a mother who, in any one of a variety of ways, cannot or will not respond, may be revived many ways in a psychoanalytic experience. The message that seems to be represented in a variety of ways by the experience of a dead, crazy mother, is "I don't want you to exist. I wish you had not been born. Please go away." In the necessities of clinical practice, the analyst may, at many junctures, need to state various personal or professional limits of things that are not feasible, not convenient, or not desirable for the analyst. For the therapist simply to justify such limitation or refusals as part of the "ordinary boundary or limit setting of psychotherapy" means the therapist tunes out completely some of the devastating messages that such actions seem to spell out for clients. In transference from the psychotic or dead mother, the client may experience such refusals or limits not as simple requirements to enable two people to continue relating analytically, but rather as reaffirming statements of the mother such as, "I don't want you." "You should be dead." "You should not have needs." "This is your fault." "I'm going crazy because of you." "Get out of my life." "Don't you see I have more important considerations?" The therapist is faced with the tricky technical task of feeling it necessary to provide some kind of limitation without communicating, "You don't have a right to exist," or "I don't want you to exist."

A subtle variation on this dead mother theme has been provided by Winnicott (1975) when he discusses the problem of reparation in relation to mother's depression. Winnicott formulates that reparation, that is, doing something to make up for having injured another, ordinarily occurs within the context of a child being aware that he or she has done something painful that has caused mother to withdraw.

The child, then, can go into reparative activities to bring mother back. But when mother is chronically unavailable through depression or other preoccupations, the child develops a state of chronic reparation as an effort to bring mother back to life, when in fact the child is not guilty of doing anything wrong. A failure in development that occurs under these circumstances is that the child never has a sense of when he or she did or did not do something to make the other go away. The retained scenario involves a continuous sense of guilt and continuous reparation. Searles (1979) speaks of psychotic guilt in a special way as though the person were saying, "I feel guilty for not being a good enough baby to give my mother what she needed to make her whole so she could mother me in the way I needed."

"PLEASE BE AVAILABLE OR
DON'T TANTALIZE ME"

One way in which infants experience breaking of contact is when they are exposed to a chronically tantalizing mother. A mother may offer herself in various ways, arousing the child, and at the point of excitement pull away, breaking off contact. This leaves the person, in a later transference situation, desperately working, reaching out, struggling, always experiencing the analyst as breaking the contact. Upon more careful examination, we may find that it is the client re-creating, through transference projections, the problem of the tantalizing mother in which the analyst may or may not in any real way be personally withdrawing.

One man, late in the analysis of his organizing experiences, recovered enough information to piece together the following story. "My mother grew up on a farm erotically idealizing her own father. There may have been actual incest. I don't know. But it doesn't matter because the emotionally exciting and dangerous aspects of incest were certainly operating. Her heart was broken when he suddenly left when she was eleven, shortly after her menses began. She had emotionally sought a re-creation of this wildly erotic idealizing love and finally found it in the man I believe to have been my biological father. She became pregnant with me and shortly thereafter he was suddenly killed in a motorcycle accident. Under hypnosis I once saw his head being crushed under the wheel of a large truck. This was the early 1940s and the man whom I grew up believing was my father married her to save her from shame. It took me years to realize that in a whole family of photographers there were no pictures of their wedding. They got married quietly so as to obscure the date. She was dutiful and remained loyal to him until her death more than fifty years later, though, so far as I could tell, the relationship contained much resentment and little excitement or enjoyment.

"So I was born, the living embodiment of that erotic, incestuous, idealized love. I learned to become excited in order to excite her interest in me. The pitch of interaction would build with my taking her higher and higher until she reached her threshold of titillated, incestual excitement when she would abruptly turn away. When she turned her back I knew I had touched her deepest love for me – but it left me agonizing. Though they didn't use the term *hyperactive* in those days, I'm sure I would have qualified. I did get an unsatisfactory mark for interrupting in first grade. By 11 I had developed a caffeine addiction which brought the excitement of mother in a cup.

"My relationships have always been characterized by people seeing me as generous, giving, active, and helpful, which has been for me a style of exciting the other, of bringing 'mother' toward me. The people I have chosen to relate to all my life in one way or another have always disappointed me by turning away at some peak moment of mutually excited involvement. It is interesting to think how each important friend or lover has accomplished this differently according to their personality makeup. But the emotionally identical factor has been the mutually seductive build-up until at a moment of peak excitement for both, the other (my mother) turns away because of fear (incestual) of overstimulation, overexcitement, in the interaction. I feel after all these years of analysis I have finally 'hit bottom,' finally seen the foundational emotional basis which has organized my entire life."

After these realizations in the working-through period he reported the following dream. "I was a whaler holding fiercely and tenaciously onto the whale line, determined no matter what never to let go. I get the great whale but somehow in the process my vessel is lost. I feel the tragedy of the loss but know I have done what was right. I see a slight, frail Eskimo girl (one of many I sensed) cautiously approaching my whale for some blubber to eat. Suddenly my catch seems to have shrunken considerably in size but I generously help her slice off a piece and go on her way. There are many shadowy others also having a feast. I have fed the multitudes (like Jesus) but I am left alone, saddened by the loss of my vessel and not feeling compensated by the results of my heroism—either with the size of the catch, which does me little good or with any joy about giving it all away to others. As I awoke I thought of Captain Ahab and his monomania to land the great white whale at any cost, any sacrifice. The Eskimo waif was anyone and everyone who has shared the spoils of my personality success and my sadness at having sacrificed body and soul (vessel) to hang onto that evasive witch!" While this description indicates the mother and child connection to have evolved through the symbiosis, when the theme and dream finally arose in an extended transference relationship they clearly had the hallmarks of representing the deepest organizing themes of this man desperately clinging to mother even when she had lost her value and had to be given away.

Six months later he reported the following story. "Friday night I went to drop by some housewarming champagne at the new apartment of an acquaintance whom I don't know well but would like to know better. His new lover was there and they were celebrating the excitement of two people having made a commitment to live together. It was refreshing and lovely to feel—two people excited about their new place, their many new things, and their new life together. His friend needed to get up early to work and so he retired early. Bill was still going on about how wonderful the relationship was, and how great it is to be in love—you know, we've all heard the infatuation story many times. Suddenly I felt a wave of grief pass through him. I'm not sure what I saw, perhaps a shudder of sadness. I responded with, 'Bill, I see how happy you are and how wonderful the relationship is. But I am also experiencing something else. Is there some kind of sadness here, too?' He hesitated a second and then burst into tears, sobbing, 'My last lover, Mark, was shot in front of a gay bar at 2:00 a.m. and died at my feet a little over a year ago.'

"The next several hours were spent doing grief work with Bill. I never do therapy with my friends, but some invisible force pulled me along and I helped Bill grieve his loss of Mark, which I soon saw was quite incomplete. [The man is a therapist by profession.] I realized that he was deeply involved emotionally with his new lover. He had come to the point in the relationship where to continue loving more deeply would be to betray the previous love he had for Mark, whose death he had not completed mourning. As I worked with Bill around unfinished business he had with Mark, I continued to note how unusual it was for me to foster this kind of engagement in a social setting. I began to suspect that there was something in this for me and I told Bill so. He invited me to experience my own sadness and in short order I found some deep tears for a friend I am losing to AIDS.

"But soon I reached my long forgotten grief over my mother so often turning away from me. I then realized that my former understanding that she would turn away when the incestuous stimulation was too intense for her was a later edition superimposed upon something more basic. Being born as heir to her oedipal incestuous love for her father, and being the product of a passionate liaison with a man she was deeply excited by, my mother deeply loved me and shared wonderful excitement with me. But the moment she was in danger of replacing her love for an incompletely grieved father and lover with love for me, she abruptly withdrew. Here I was helping Bill mourn his loss of Mark so he could love in the present. It was clearly an attempt to cure my mother of what kept her from sustaining her loving, excited connection with me. This feels deeper and more accurate than the incest interpretation in terms of how throughout my life I have sought in various ways to bring people to me and then to help them work through some lost love."

Six months later he reported another dream. "This was a two-hour body dream. I don't know how else to describe it. I worked through a physically painful sequence many times over a two-hour period of waking and sleeping. What would happen was that I would feel some intense pain in some muscle or muscle group, like my calf or my foot. Al Lowen would then appear in the dream, moving into the pained, constricted area with one of his bioenergetic techniques for resolving muscular constriction. [The man is familiar with Alexander

Lowen's bioenergetic work and has had some personal therapeutic experiences with Lowen.] As he would touch me, moving into the constricted area, that muscle or body part would begin to twitch and then slowly and painfully to vibrate until the painful kink was vibrated out and I could relax into sleep again. Shortly, I would experience pain in another part of my body with the sensation of being roused again. Al would then begin bioenergetic work on that body part. Finally, every part of my body had been loosened until my entire body was vibrating—energetic waves emanating upwards and downwards from the now unfrozen pelvic muscles. With the vibration came body flexibility and looseness. I then melted into calm, soft sobbing. What came to mind was, 'But you didn't have to turn away (to my mother). You didn't have to leave me.' I feel now that the spell has been broken—and at a body level. The total pattern of somatic constrictions that have been organized around being 'up' in order to reach out to her, to hold her present—the entire set of coordinated constrictions has now melted into grief. All my life I have been working to bring her back in a myriad of forms. What relief there was when I could simply cry that she turned away, and somehow know that it was so unnecessary. A mother's turning away when her baby is extended toward her doesn't qualify under most definitions as child abuse. But from the child's standpoint it is abusive and it does leave its mark on all subsequent physical and psychological development. It has taken me years of self study to finally see the nature of my agitated desperation, of my frantic reaching to feel connected, of my agony at the other's preoccupations that replicate my deepest crazy dread that she would once again become preoccupied with her grief and turn away."

Four months later he reported, "As you know, my daughter, whom I have lived with for many years, left for college recently. We spent months in preparation for the change, reviewing our lives together, remembering things we hadn't thought of for years, crying, feeling sad at our separation, at her growing up, and happy for a number of wonderful changes in her life. But I've been alone and feeling it for a month. We were so close and took care of each other so well for so long. I miss her a lot. I guess I have to say it was sort of like losing a mother, a deeply caring person, all over again.

"And then came the anniversary of my mother's death. When she died last year I felt a slight sense of relief because of the circumstances. I had grieved her loss long ago but for months after she actually died little memories from the past would crop up to haunt me, to remind me of her and the love we had for each other.

"Retrospectively, I now realize that my physical reaction began several days before the anniversary though I was busy and didn't think much of it. I became a little hyperactive and a sinus infection began. As you know, my lifelong sinus problem has never been solved through years of physical and psychological treatment, though years ago I linked the flaring up of symptoms with my mother, as though I were allergic to her somehow. My body focus after working with Al Lowen permitted a cessation of the infection aspect of the sinuses, though congestion has continued sporadically. He said that sinuses are congested because tears are blocked, but I never could determine what tears might be blocked because I have never experienced any particular difficulty crying. But his idea intrigued me and the progress I did make was encouraging.

"On the morning of the anniversary of my mother's death my head was pounding with the worst sinus headache and infection I have had for years when it suddenly dawned on me what day it was. I began to feel weak all over, sick and feverish, and by night my entire body was in physical agony and practically paralyzed. I could barely climb the stairs to drop into bed.

"For two weeks I then had the most horrible experience of my life—or I should say that my body was recalling the most horrible experience of my life. I could barely walk to the bathroom. I only moved from my bed to roll around on the floor and cling to the legs of furniture, all the while in the most unbelievable total body and soul pain. One minute I would be freezing with nine blankets on top of me, literally. And the next I would begin peeling off the blankets until I was naked and pouring with sweat. I was hallucinating all manner of incomprehensible things as though in a fever delirium. I was having somatic delusions with body parts leaving my body and drifting around the room. I couldn't eat for ten days because none of my internal organs, the sphincters especially, would seem to coordinate enough to take food down, though I drank lots of water. My sinuses were impacted and hurting and I was frantic all over but physically in a state of extreme pain and quasi-paralysis. I dreamed, I slept, I awoke, I lost track of time, of days, of nights. At times I wasn't sure where I was. My friends were wonderful—calling, dropping by bringing fruit and juices, staying over to be with me. Of course everyone offered to take me to the doctor but I knew it wasn't illness I was going through. Later several asked, 'Weren't you afraid with all of that craziness and sickness going on?' I really wasn't, though part of the delusions and memories occasionally contained severe fright. I knew exactly what was happening. I've spent years coaching other people through regressive episodes and so I had perfect confidence that what was happening was of crucial importance, no matter how painful it might be. My body was remembering something and a bit at a time images, thoughts, and flashbacks began to coalesce as what was being remembered in my body slowly clarified in my mind.

"I pieced together from memories, family lore, and remembered photographs that my parents took a three-week vacation when I was 14 months old and that they had probably taken a number of weekend trips camping before that. I was left with my mother's sister, Aunt Stephanie, and my cousin who was a few months older than me. It was a familiar, ideal place to leave a baby but three weeks at that critical age—I shudder even to think of it.

"The meaning of the body experience began in my left hand. It began twitching or itching and I began rubbing my fingers together realizing that I was having a memory of clutching something. And then I began to chew on it—a quilt I realized. In a flash I realized what quilt—the one that belonged to Aunt Stephanie that I was feverishly clutching and chewing when my mother returned. A vivid picture emerged (from 14 months?) of my mother trying to take the quilt away from me to give back to my aunt and my refusing to let go. Family lore I recalled said that I wouldn't speak or at least not spontaneously with my mother for days or maybe weeks after her return. Many of the primitive body experiences I was having—excessive sweating and salivation, loss of bowel and bladder control, loss of temperature control, disorientation in time and space and no appetite—suggested a composite body memory, perhaps some of it dating from much earlier, or at least suggesting a regression occasioned by the abandonment trauma.

"Another left-hand memory found me feverishly grasping at something cold—glass I realized. As I stayed with the sensation I pressed the cold glass to my cheek to get relief from the feverishness. I realized I was clutching the foot of a table (from out of the 1930s) that had a cast-iron claw around a glass ball. I have since wondered if I was left handed and they later forced me to change.

"By the end of the first week my body was stiff and in pain. I called my dear friend John, who is a bioenergetics therapist. I knew that he knew of an unusually sensitive masseur and I felt I needed one. On the phone I explained I was ten days into the worst nightmare of my life, bodily remembering an abandonment from early childhood, and how much I was hurting. I felt 14 months old as I talked to him. He said it was Saturday night and he doubted he could reach his friend, but it sounded like he needed to be there and asked if he could come. I assented but before he hung up he asked, 'Have you tried surrendering to the pain? That often helps.' I said I had not and he urged me to try. In the hour it took for John to arrive I succeeded in locating a series of discrete pains and somehow (don't ask me how) surrendered to them and they melted. I now realize that I was experiencing a total body agony. By having to think where the pain was coming from, locating specific places and surrendering, giving in rather than fighting the pain, the muscle constrictions that were causing the pain relaxed.

"John stayed for a while, holding my hand, cooling my burning eyes with a damp cloth, stroking my forehead and talking softly. I was so dazed I don't remember what we talked about, except that he went to great pains to get two things through to me. First he said, 'I wanted to come because I heard a whimper in your voice.' In context, he was saying that he understood I was in a living body memory of infancy and from that place I had cried out in pain to him for help. As he emphasized that, he made clear that I had never cried out in pain from this place. I began soft, deep sobbing, knowing my tears were expressing what had always been blocked, that I cannot find my mother, that she is dead. As I spoke this and pronounced her dead, the sobbing increased until my entire body was shaking with release from the imprisonment of the tightness, the pain, and the refusal to admit that I had lost her. John's other point was implicit: that I reached out to someone, to him, for help from this place of utter helplessness. A young child cannot recover from such a loss without help and I had cried out to him in pain and asked for help—again, something I had never done from this place of helplessness. Everything collapsed, all my frenzy, all my uptightness, all the pain, until I was relaxed and calm. I don't remember John's leaving. I must have dozed off and he knew I was okay.

"More memories ensued for several days until I felt I had experienced it out, but the churning state was continuing, now almost pointlessly as if it had somehow taken on a life of its own. I called a psychiatrist friend, explained what I had been experiencing and that it was time for it to end now, and did he have a good pill for that? I also know that I had not been afraid of going into a completely psychotic body state because I know that it can be stopped easily with medication. He understood immediately and prescribed some Stelazine, which ended the experience in twenty-four hours.

"That was two weeks ago. I was totally spent, exhausted mentally and physically, but slowly got back into the real world for the weekend and back to work on Monday. What an experience! My body speaking so loud and clear of the early trauma.

"The experiences of the past year had prepared me to relive the trauma and to experience the maternal loss through connection to John, like a part of my mind that had been lost in frenzy and blocked sinuses had somehow broken down and was reorganizing. Both lifelong symptoms are clearing and somehow I feel I will never be the same. Breaking through the body disconnection and finding my friend there to meet me, to hold my hand, to cool my eyes, to hear my cry, to be there with me as I reached out to him in all my helplessness. What a victory! But I think I will be wasted for a while. She tantalized me. She was there. She loved me. Then without knowing how awful it would be for me, she left me. Or was it part of her disconnecting pattern she had lived all of her life and that I suffered so from? My mother didn't die last year, she died when I was 14 months old."

The episodes reported above occurred during an eighteen-month period following the abrupt cessation of a six-year intense analytic relationship. In the early phases, oedipal triangulations, narcissistic selfother tensions, and symbiotic scenarios had been systematically defined and worked through as they arose in the transference and resistance of the relationship. Then the analytic listener acted in such a way that the speaker felt brutally abandoned and betrayed. The empathic breach was sudden and unexpected and led to an immediate and angry negative therapeutic reaction in which the relationship was ended abruptly.

The whale dream leading to the incest interpretation and later to the grief interpretation indicated the gradual definition of the organizing transference. Immediately after the grief work he found himself saying, "Oh, now I can speak with Patrick again" (the analytic partner). In context this meant that the internalized personal dynamic that had led to the sense of disappointment, disillusionment, and betrayal could not be separated from whatever had actually happened. The relationship was slowly restored, but with caution and a still unforgiving spirit. The body dream ensued, being also interpreted as "I didn't have to do it (abandon him)." This interpretation marked the realization that the abandoning psychotic mother who had been identified with and acted out in the interpretation of the breach was now being experienced as internalized on a body level. There was now arising a desire to free the somatic constrictions that held this primordial transference structure in place. This wish was partially enacted in the body dream in which Al Lowen interceded to relieve constrictions throughout the body.

During the ensuing two months, greater safety, commitment, and openness were experienced in the restored relationship, with a wish to "forgive" the actions that precipitated the breach. But forgiveness as a concept implied that the cause of the rupture was external and this belief could no longer be sustained. Finally a full, open recommitment to the partner could be made without forgiveness being necessary. True, the analytic listener had acknowledged his failure of empathy in the events leading to the breach. But what was now emerging into conscious experience was more than an issue in empathy. It clearly came from an early internalized relatedness structure.

The final two-week episode in which body memories of early abandonment and betrayal could be restored immediately followed this full emotional reopening to the analytic partner. In the wake of the deep emotional reconnection, the horrible memories of abandonment in infancy, which had led to a turning away from the mother, were recalled in painful somatic experiencing. That is, in the context of the restoration of a deep and trusting connection, the internal cause of the contact rupture—the experience of a psychotic mother who abandoned him, thereby betraying his trust—could be brought from the chronic constrictions of the body tissues that held the memory into a conscious awareness that could be dealt with in contemporary life. The man affirmed a powerful sense that a core issue had finally been reached at the body level. He anticipated relief from the lifelong sinus and bronchial infections as well as relief from a certain frantic, manic, somatic edge that ran throughout his personality.

Clients living organizing experiences fret about withdrawal, worry about vacation abandonments, complain that they do not have enough, and beg or demand more. But we discover that it is not the "more" that is wanted. Rather the crying, the complaining, the demanding, the whining function as the person's way of breaking contact. Every minute spent fretting about what one cannot get from a relationship is a moment spent not enjoying what is available and breaking whatever contact might be established. Every person's organizing history is different. Therefore, the idiom of mother–infant transference is unique to whatever links could and could not be formed with mother. There is an infinite variety of ways these searches and breaks can be subtly carried out in adult life.

"I NEED YOU TO RELATE TO MY SENSE OF TIME AND SPACE"

Timelessness, according to Freud (1900) is an aspect of the unconscious as well as of infancy. When organizing experiences are activated during an analytic hour the ordinary ego-determined sense of time may be completely lost. Although the analyst has a regular schedule that is well known to the client in other states of mind, and although the forty-five minutes can be kept track of by the unconscious ego in other states of mind, while living in an organizing state the ordinary sense of time is lost. It is quite possible in organizing experiences that even with five minutes notice before the end of the hour, the transition out of the timeless space of the organizing experience will be entirely too abrupt and traumatizing. Given the critical aspect of timing in early maternal care, it is quite likely that a great many people bringing organizing experiences to the analytic consulting room will have issues around time: timeliness, premature timing, faulty timing, slow timing, intrusions into private time, personal use of time, and rest time. Time for beginning or ending a session or other questions of time may be experienced by the client in transference as the therapist acting out the role of the psychotic mother. There is little or no capacity in such states of time to tolerate or negotiate personal variations in the sense of time—"only my time is right."

The same kinds of considerations may apply to the use of space in the analytic consulting room. For example, a therapist who has a somewhat rigid idea of how the space of the consulting room is to be used, or who feels that under all conditions the client ought to be lying down on the couch or sitting in a chair, may miss completely the need to hide under a blanket, to curl up in a corner, to hide from the view of the therapist, or any other creative uses of space that re-create the sense of infancy implicit in the organizing experience being recalled. Likewise, the client may need the analyst to do more moving around the room, to perhaps be sitting on the floor, turning his or her back so as not to be watching all the time, or other alterations of the analyst's usual use of the consulting room space.

When the spatial constraints, as provided by the analyst, are experienced as too tight or too loose, various experiences of fright or desperation may occur. Similarly if the temporal availability of the analyst is experienced as too restricted, too long, or too short, desperation may occur. Because, in either case, the longing for and achievement of the contact, which has the power to sustain psychic functions, do not simply vary with time and space as seen in the ordinary consensual world and projected onto the consulting room time and space by the analyst.

When the analyst is announcing his or her needs, restrictions, limitation, or movements regarding time and space, the speaker may experience these as a total devaluation or rejection of him or her as a person. In transference, it becomes the psychotic mother saying, "I have other needs. I don't want you now. Please die. Hurry up, and get this over with. Finish feeding. Take care of yourself now." One client reported on this experience by saying that she actually had the feeling of being startled at the breast and feeling like "I am being pulled off the breast, and now I have to gather myself up and go in a state of confusion. My sense of existence has been intruded upon."

While there are objective aspects of the consulting room experience that the analyst feels a need to pay attention to, interpreting the potentially traumatizing aspects of the psychotic transference that the analyst's personal and professional needs evoke is equally as important. With careful planning in anticipation of contact and loss traumas, the needs of both parties can generally be acknowledged and attended to. But when a delicate holding on to the analyst is operative, more accommodation and/or consideration by the analyst is generally required. That is, needs are met or responded to insofar as that is possible given the personality of the analyst and the limits of the professional relationship. But inevitably these needs will enter into the formation of the organizing transference and the analyst will be accused of various failings. The organizing transference will be ultimately secured within the frame of these unmet needs.

"DON'T EXPECT ME TO HAVE MORE EGO SKILLS THAN I DO"

At the organizing level there are some conditions that are not present when analyzing inhibiting and constricting structures at the symbiotic, selfother, or neurotic levels. In organizing states there are only rudimentary ego functions operating, so the analytic or therapeutic environment is necessarily going to include providing more than usual holding capacities. There is a variety of ways in which the external world holds the infant when the infant's ego cannot hold him- or herself, and the implications of such early models for holding in analytic work are many. At higher levels of development, there are various kinds of ego structures to keep the person coming to the analysis, relating to the therapist, and maintaining his or her situation in the world so that the therapy can be maintained financially and in other practical ways. At this lower level of psychic functioning, the analyst often has to focus on how the person is simply going to maintain support systems and daily functioning, which makes therapeutic contact a possibility.

"SHOW ME IN PRACTICAL, CONCRETE WAYS HOW I CAN HOLD ON TO YOU LONG ENOUGH TO ORGANIZE MYSELF"

When it comes to the practicalities of maintaining long-term treatment with people who live in pervasive organizing states, it is important to maintain focus on daily mechanical factors that serve to maintain the therapy on an indefinite basis. If we fail in this regard, it will only be a matter of time before some practical situation asserts itself, making it impossible for the therapy to continue. Focusing on such practical matters is not supportive but rather empathic to the levels of ego relatedness possible in the organizing experience. This means we have to think months and sometimes years ahead.

When people living organizing experiences enter a family situation, a marriage, or a work environment, they are likely to be targeted for scapegoating. They may be subjected to prejudice and persecution, sometimes so subtly that they are unaware of it. Or they may have paranoid ideation and claim they are being persecuted when in fact they are not. People living organizing experiences may sense that they are somehow different and may worry about how the world responds to them, but they do not necessarily perceive the forces that are operating against them accurately, nor are they skilled in taking care of themselves.

Therapists working with these clients in long-term, transformative therapy have concerns such as "How is this person going to maintain a marriage that's supporting her until she can begin supporting herself?" "How is he going to maintain a job when he is compelled to be so provocative?" Even if the client appears to be doing well and getting good reviews, that does not mean that the prejudicial and destructive social forces around him or her are not operating in such a way that somewhere down the line they are going to be singled out, blamed, or dumped on.

Sometimes other factors are operating such as the mental health network. But whether the person is with some form of managed health care or is under the care of a private psychiatrist, when he or she goes into a tailspin, who is going to put him on disability so that he does not have to be responsible for maintaining his job? Even if his doctor is willing to medicate him, hospitalize him, or in other ways respond psychiatrically, there may still be mixed results if the care is not administered in conjunction with psychotherapy.

Therapists may need to coach these clients through day-to-day activities such as making a grocery list, balancing a checkbook, cooking dinner, or making love so the partner will stay—all of this so that their situation can remain stable and not disrupt treatment. The support motive here is not to help the person live life better per se, but to be alert to, and to intervene in issues likely to threaten therapy. Even negative influences of the present may provide a better environment than being on his or her own at present. The primary concern is to determine how therapy can continue on an open-ended basis. No matter what other factors the person wants to talk about, therapists who work with organizing experiences redirect the conversation explicitly toward subjects that serve to maintain the therapy if there are threatening issues. Otherwide, simple practical consideration may interrupt therapy, either being used as a contact-rupturing device or accidentally arising as a result of the person's not being able to attend fully to the realistic demands of the world.

"PLEASE DON'T KILL THE BABY"

In attending to the needs of an infant, there are many times when the mother cannot be present and optimally responsive. The mother may have preoccupations, there may be other children making demands, or she may have fallen ill or had an accident and been hospitalized. Or the child may have been hospitalized for some disease or medical emergency, thus preventing the infant's needs from being responded to in a timely manner. Even though caregivers may do their best to be responsive to infantile needs, it is simply not possible and perhaps not even desirable for an infant's demands always to be fully responded to.

Sometimes the infant may have an illness, such as a painful ear infection, that goes on for a considerable period of time, leaving the infant inconsolable and the mother exhausted and at her wit's end. Such mothers appear in consulting rooms, horrified that they have fantasies of wanting to kill or to abandon their babies. Clinicians often attempt to normalize such fantasies in terms of the enormous demand on the mother's psyche and the psychic need to escape the over-whelming demands.

When the infant experiences such intense maternal exaspera-tion, the experiences may well come up again in therapeutic study as transference. Extensive infantile demands that carry the sense of urgency of an infant will be transferred to the therapist. The question is, How is the therapist going to be prepared to respond to such agonizing demands when the person is in a frightened, confused state in which the concreteness of the demand is all that can be attended to at the moment? Transference interpretation is not possible until later. At this point even the therapist's best efforts may be understood by the client as "kill the baby!"

In working with symbiotic experiences, some British psychoan-alysts have advocated ways of working with countertransference and of disclosing it. Following these studies, I (Hedges 1992) have further elaborated a technique for interpreting the countertransference, so as to speak for the infant side of the bonding experience in the symbiosis.

However, when unorganized states are active in the analytic situation, whether in the analysis of someone who is seen as pervasively organizing or with a better-developed person in contact with an organizing experience, countertransference interpretation of this sort may well miss the mark. The reason for this is that an organizing experience is one in which the stillness and receptivity of the maternal partner are central to being able to coalesce one's own private experience and to make it real. When the mother shifts at the wrong moment in feeding, the rhythm of safety becomes disrupted. If the mother answers the telephone or moves about the room, or if the therapist becomes engaged in thinking about or offering interpretations linking the present to previous work done, or discussing transference themes, the mothering partner may be experienced as clumsy or unavailable. The person may feel "dropped."

"PLEASE DON'T AGREE TO HOLD ME IF YOU INTEND TO DROP ME"

I believe there is a serious ethical question regarding whether a therapist should attempt this kind of work. All clinicians agree on the absolute necessity of aggressive intervention when a client is actively contemplating suicide. Other instances of possible danger to the client or to others require the therapist to take action. When working with organizing experiences, there may be days, weeks, or even longer periods of time in which the person's full ego functioning is not available, and the analyst has a responsibility to have the speaker's and others' safety in mind at all times, such as not letting a speaker who has just been in a deep trance leave the office too soon, so as to avoid the possibility of an automobile accident. Little (1981) reports a case in which she even took the car keys away from a client.

In an organizing regression sensory/perceptual/motor functioning may not be adequate to deal safely with external realities, and there may be some concerns regarding safety. There are subtle ways in which a person's body may not be functioning very well. For example, in depression the reflexes may not be functioning right. The analyst has an ethical obligation to consider the client's functioning and, if necessary, to arrange for rides to sessions, medications, hospitalization, and whatever other temporary auxiliary supports may be necessary to assure the client's safety and the safety of those around him or her. The client's family ideally makes these arrangements. These obligations of the therapist are not part of traditional technique because they are not appropriate to the treatment of neurosis. But in the analysis of organizing experiences these situations may arise, and the therapist must be prepared to handle them with dispatch.

With individuals whose overall personality functioning is fairly evolved, but who are currently working on organizing pockets, it is easy for a therapist to make the assumption that the person can quickly transition out of an unorganized state in the consulting room into a safely organized state outside. This assumption many times will be incorrect. The overall good ego functioning, which we know this person generally to possess, may be momentarily out of commission and may remain so for a period of time. This puts the person in a dangerous position during the course of treatment. Speakers should be informed and periodically reminded of such dangers. When a person is functioning in an organizing state, the therapist must be mindful of the potential danger of the person not being able to organize resources that would prevent accidents or harm of any type, including social harms such as saying the wrong thing to the wrong person at the wrong time. Speakers may be advised to alert friends, family members, or employees that they are going through an intense period in therapy and may not quite be themselves for a while. Then others can be involved in helping the person get through a rough period. Repeated reminders and warnings are never out of place.

For example, one woman was working on a great deal of early rage that had been transferred to her husband. When she would get in touch with various angry feelings being directed toward him she would need to be explicitly reminded that she was not at present in condition to present these feelings to her husband in a way that would be helpful in her relationship with him. Further, if she were to say some of these things that she was working on in therapy to him now in a realistic way, it would be cruel to him. It would hurt him deeply and might endanger the relationship. She might say hurtful things he could never forget she had said. So until these feelings are processed and she has a way of saying them responsibly within the context of a realistic relationship, she was told to wait and to continue considering them with the therapist.

"DON'T ASSUME I'M CONNECTED WHEN I'M NOT"

The assumption shared by many therapists is that when two people are in a room conversing, or having a telephone conversation, they somehow are emotionally, meaningfully connected to each other, or at least know how to facilitate meaningful interpersonal contact. This assumption is not valid for much psychotherapy work with organizing states.

In the classical study of neurosis, it is generally assumed that both parties are meaningfully connected most of the time, although when symbolic transferences are operating, resistance to their emergence is manifest until the resistance is analyzed. These times are often called "transference distortions." At preoedipal levels of psychic functioning, the assumption of meaningful connectedness is even more questionable. In Kohut's work with narcissistic personality organization, he even goes so far as to say that the interaction between two people may go on for several weeks without either party perceiving quite how an empathic breach has affected or limited their emotional connectedness. At some later point the analyst may be able to interpret where and how the empathy failure occurred, and to restore the mutual, emotional, interpersonal empathic bond between the two people.

At the symbiotic or borderline level of interpersonal relations, whenever transference scenarios are being lived out or replicated in a relationship, the assumption of meaningful emotional connectedness is temporarily involved. However, because of false self formations, the missing contact may not be readily detectable. Winnicott has pointed out that early in infancy a child learns to conform emotionally to what mother wants, and to leave his or her own true self needs and experiences to the side. Winnicott has labeled ego formations that result from this conforming process "false self," in contrast to more true self experiences in which the child's full nature is known to the mother and received by her.

At the organizing level, even false self formations are rudimentary or not present at all. Mimical self formations serve as an imitation of appropriate affectively connected behavior, but are only an imitation, and not even an adaptation to the emotional responses of the other. Perhaps the most common error in this work is therapists' believing there is a sense of connection between themselves and the client, only to realize retrospectively that they were deluding themselves. Since the therapist's own more differentiated personality includes not only a sense of separateness and constancy, but also a general sense of being emotionally connected or bonded with the other one, the therapist may be deluded by these adaptive or imitative selves that the client puts forward. Better communication skills than are present at the moment are assumed by the therapist, based upon a usually operative set of communication skills, sound intelligence, and the person's living in the world. A person appears to be functioning on a much higher developmental level than he or she actually is when emotional connectedness and the relatedness dimension are being considered in analysis.

"PLEASE SEARCH FOR MY SENSE OF LIFE; SHOW ME HOW TO CONNECT TO YOU WITH IT"

In psychotherapy consultations, it is not unusual for a therapist to begin describing work with a client, thinking or feeling that the client is quite well adapted. The therapist believes that the stories the client tells, and the interpretations that the therapist provides, in some way or another are representative of an emotional bond or connection that is growing between the two. However, the therapist is often able to say that he or she does not feel a gut-level connection to the client, even though the therapy appears to be going well and many important issues and problems are being discussed. The therapist finally sees that what he or she has been experiencing as connection is not emotional engagement at all.

Upon questioning, a psychotherapy consultant may be able to discover that there are a few moments in which the therapist knows that there is more life, animation, and spontaneity flickering between the members of the analytic couple. By focusing on these moments (no matter the content), the therapist can begin watching, focusing, tracking, and even stimulating more emotional liveliness, exchange, and contact. Sometimes when therapists are asked when the client is more alive, the answer may be, "When she tells me about the movies she's seen this week," "When he tells me about the Dungeons and Dragons parties that he and his friends have on Friday night, and how clever he is in these games." Some contacts occur in doing jigsaw puzzles, in card playing, art, or in talking about football games. Often it is in these areas, far removed from more direct human interaction, where there is increased vitality. But it is in these very areas of liveliness that the client may be able to begin with the therapist, for the first time ever, experiencing some life, some exchange, some pleasure, some enjoyment, some true self-functioning and relationship building.

The content areas may strike the therapist as mundane, meaningless, tangential, or irrelevant. Such an attitude reflects on the part of the therapist a lack of understanding about what therapeutic needs are at the organizing level. The need is to form contact between two living beings that is safe and reliable, in any way that two can form it within the bounds of a professional relationship. No subject is too elementary. No way of interaction that provides a sense of life, liveliness, vitality, exchange, communication is to be set aside as worthless. Every opportunity for spontaneous gesture and spontaneous living within the atmosphere of the relationship must be seized upon by the therapist in an effort to stimulate and to sustain moments of contact.

In the interaction between infant and mother, mother's responses—the oohs, the ahhs, the giggles, and forms of prelanguage that are being used for communication—might seem meaningless and lacking appropriate development or depth. But when one understands that it is the affective exchange or contact between the two, the mutual responsiveness, and not the language symbols, that is impor-tant for securing the analytic frame, then a study of the symbols and content is ignored in favor of perceiving the contact that is creating the enlivenment, the structure, and the organization in the infant.

Winnicott (1971) was clear about the importance of play in psychotherapy, citing as his precedent some important comments by Freud. Sanville (1992) reviews the work of Winnicott, Freud, and many other psychoanalysts as well as sociologists, anthropologists, philosophers, and educators on the subject of spontaneous play and interplay and their importance in human development. Sanville takes the position that all worthwhile development begins with play. Rich with ideas, understandings, and vivid pictures about the subject of play and playfulness and the nature of meaningful personal exchange, Sanville's book provides case studies of work with children and adults in which the therapeutic progression and transformation can be seen to occur within an overall context and atmosphere in which play is not only permissible, but understood as crucial and critical to the task. For a child, playing is a great deal of work. Sanville portrays the essential nature of human development within an atmosphere of waiting, of respectful attention, of quiet and silence, of joy and laughter, and sadness, tears, and anger. It is during these interpersonal moments of contact that the human soul rises to its full potential. Sanville also makes clear that the kind of emotional growth that we see in psychoanalytic psychotherapy simply cannot be achieved in rushed short-term therapy, which the industry of managed health is attempting to force upon our profession today. Nor can it be achieved in an atmosphere in which the analyst fails to understand the impor-tance of play and spontaneous gesture.

Empathy with subjective organizing states takes different forms than it does with more highly differentiated psychic states. Likewise the analytic frame, the formal aspects of the analytic relationship, looks very different when working with organizing states. Flexibility on the part of the analyst is required to be able to adapt successfully to the altered forms of empathy and the more basic aspects of the analytic frame.

17

Case Management Issues

DEVELOPMENTAL CONSIDERATIONS

The standard advice to mothers of infants in the first three or four months is not to leave their babies for more than a few hours at a time and in subsequent months not for more than a day, because of the tentative and fragile nature of the child's growing connectedness. Even then it is generally recommended that someone the infant knows in the family, like a grandmother or an aunt, be the caregiver, or someone who is a familiar babysitter if a day's vacation is needed.

When early traumas of loss and separation are being relived in analysis for study, similar considerations hold. However, the problems that may arise are even more complex than those in infancy because there is not a tabula rasa in an adult like there is in a baby. The client has a history of being traumatized by being pushed away and wished gone or dead. The traumas are internalized and reappear as transference. That story must be retold in the way it once occurred for the person to develop an awareness, *complete with a loss of higher ego functions*, of the nature of the original traumas.

LENGTHY ABSENCES

At various times in working with organizing experience the process of trusting delicate links and connections is in formation. When a weekend or the therapist's vacation comes, if the client has only pockets of organizing experience, usually ego strengths can be mobilized to get through these periods of absence. But with a pervasive organizing person or a person in the midst of living an organizing experience, it may not only be terrifying but very destructive to the therapeutic process for the therapist to take lengthy vacations or to stay out of contact for long periods of time. A therapist who wishes to work with pervasively organizing people may need to arrange vacations so that there is never more than a week or ten days without some form of personal contact. Even then telephone contact may be needed in between. In these delicate moments, some people's work cannot be properly sustained and may be altogether lost if the therapist who has become their significant other cannot be reached or if an acceptable substitute cannot be found. Work with organizing experiences is simply different from other forms of psychotherapy and special provisions need to be considered.

THE IMPORTANCE OF A CASE MONITOR

I have addressed some of the inevitable failures that happen in childhood as well as in psychotherapy. I have attempted to imagine how we might best prepare ourselves for the replication of deep-seated failures in psychotherapy. But the longer organizing experiences are studied, the more important it seems that *as a standard aspect of setting up the treatment situation, a third party case monitor be involved from the outset as a part of the "treatment team,"* much as a mother needs to have a father or someone else help her with many of the demands of early mothering. A third party is helpful for these reasons: (1) There may be periods in which the demands are so great that the therapist simply cannot respond to them. (2) The therapist inevitably is unavailable for periods of time, whether weekends, vacations, medical care, or personal emergencies. The case monitor can spell the therapist on such occasions. (3) The content of the organizing experience may turn out to be extensively persecutory, so that when a full-blown psychotic transference is established the therapist becomes a paranoid object, an abusive object, or a seductively enticing object who must (in transference) be attacked or turned away from.

If the organizing experience is pervasive, what can be expected is a transference psychosis in which the full madness of infantile experience is attached to the person of the analyst. Ego functioning can be expected to be temporarily marginal and concrete under these circumstances. Reality testing may be severely impaired so that the person in analysis cannot fully separate the analyst from the internal psychotic mother. Treatment may be abruptly terminated in a negative therapeutic reaction before interpretation is possible. Malpractice suits and ethical complaints frequently arise in such situations with the client acting out in the social justice system the lack of justice that he or she experienced in infancy. See Hedges 1994a for a series of considerations in which therapists are "at risk."

I strongly advocate, as a part of regular treatment technique with any person who seems likely to develop a significant organizing transference, that a third party be involved from the beginning. Long before trouble is in sight, an introduction of a third party may be experienced as the therapist's distancing, and thus needs to be explained to the client carefully. The third party might be a psychiatrist or an attending physician who can be involved from the very beginning, forming a bit of a relationship, the purpose being mainly to spell the therapist when necessary. But there are good reasons to consider having a close professional colleague, optimally in the same office as the therapist but not a close personal friend, who is known to the client and who will be on call at various times. Any anxieties that the client may have about the therapist "passing me on," "rejecting me," "not wanting to work with me," should be addressed firmly: "No, this is not the case. I am worried that there may be times you need to reach me that I won't be available. You may need to talk to someone or to be comforted and I may not be available. I want to know that there is a 'Plan B.' I want to know that, should I be called away for an emergency situation, that you will be cared for by someone that you already know. Furthermore, you have experienced many damaging relationships in your life and you may come to study how that damage has affected you by experiencing me and the way I do therapy as damaging. If so, you may need someone to talk to about me and about our relationship."

In the client's reaching out to find, there will be times in which the therapist is not there to respond. How do we assure that adequate and appropriate response will be provided the client when we set up our plans regarding telephoning, weekends, vacations, and emergencies? This is not only a practical consideration, but an ethical consideration on the part of a therapist who wishes to work with organizing experiences, which demand special consideration.

In better states of ego intactness, a client may well recognize that the therapist needs vacations, rest, and relaxation in order to be a good therapist. But when in the throes of an organizing experience, such recognition is impossible and all manner of transference expectations will be projected onto the therapist's need for time off, including such things as, "you (as my mother) are disgusted by me. You hate me. You want to be away from me. You want me dead." The therapist, in talking about times during which he or she may not be available to respond, must be sensitive to the potential transference manifestations of legitimate therapist needs. With good intentions, therapists try to be present and to do the best thing possible for the client, so as to avoid their own sense of guilt. And in trying to avoid feeling guilty, they may miss the possibility of analyzing the transference rage around the therapist doing the things that he or she needs to do. Merely feeling that one's needs as a mother or therapist are legitimate does not help the baby or the client work through his or her reactions to those needs. Most people with pervasive organizing experiences have suffered neglect and/or abuse as infants. This abuse will be experienced as transference at some point. Will the therapist be ready to be seen as the perpetrator? Is there a third party to help mitigate against an abrupt termination or a serious accusation?

We live in a litigious society in which it is culturally popular to see oneself as a victim. People with significant organizing experiences have indeed been victims to some infantile trauma. The purpose of analytic therapy is to bring that sense of trauma alive in here-and-now transference experiencing. The presence of a third party case monitor further ensures against the high risk of a negative therapeutic reaction in which the analytic speaker feels victim to the therapist in the psychotic transference. Further, a professional colleague actually seeing the speaker, keeping notes, and conferring with the primary therapist (at intervals from weekly to quarterly) reduces the danger of the psychotic transference being acted out in a public area of accusations (a courtroom, an ethics committee, a licensing board). No therapeutic interpretations or working through gets done in a courtroom!

THE ROLE OF THE DESIGNATED
CASE MONITOR

One suggestion for negotiating long weekends, vacations, and difficult periods of transference experiencing is to personally introduce the client, months ahead of time, to someone in your office who will be on call for you. That person then becomes part of the therapeutic experience. It is helpful to have someone within your office so that, should the client call upon that person while you're away, the client returns to familiar surroundings. If this is not possible, then the person should make a visit or two to the case monitor's office ahead of time to become comfortable with him or her. One client referred to her case monitor as a "babysitter," only half jokingly! In addition, it is important that whoever is on call have a definite sense of serving as a "surrogate mother." He or she need not try to do therapeutic work other than to help the client have a sense that the case monitor is the connector between you and the client. One choice for case monitor might be the medical person who has evaluated and perhaps pre-scribed medications. But again, this person must be thoroughly briefed on his or her role while you are gone and be comfortable and familiar with it. He or she must be thoroughly briefed in advance of the potential role of hearing out psychotic transferences should a difficult period arise. The monitor should be asked to keep careful notes on all contacts with the speaker and to provide occasional written comments or summaries. Both analytic listener and monitor need to have signed consent to talk with each other as long as the treatment continues. A "team" notion and its purpose need to be clear to all involved.

In working with organizing experiences that to a fairly significant degree influence people's lives, during times of therapist absence – and perhaps also during times of working through deep abusive transfer-ence manifestations – it is important to have a third party whom the client knows and with whom he or she has developed some sense of continuity over time. This colleague can help in the management of the case through rocky periods and perhaps at times around practical living, supportive matters. An excellent choice for case monitor would be a therapist trained and prepared to do some body work in collab-oration with the transference and resistance work. Consider the client whose early organizing experience was marked with highly intrusive or destructive experiences of molest or physical abuse as the form of loss of contact with mother. When those earlier abuses begin to be remembered through the analytic interaction, the reality testing experience of the client may make it such that it is the therapist who is felt to be the abandoning, abusing, molesting person. It may be important that a third party, who has been following the work, who knows both the therapist and the client, can intervene with some reality testing possibilities to protect the therapeutic alliance from overwhelming transference fears. This consideration becomes all the more important in the current malpractice suit atmosphere, when the psychotic transference may be otherwise unmanageable, and some outside influence causes the person to confuse transference reality with actual reality, and to experience the therapist as the abuser or molester.

It cannot be emphasized too much that early in treatment, optimally during the diagnostic phase, these emergency procedures be put into place, long before vacations or the appearance of psychotic transference. Therapists tend to forget that they too are subject to emergencies that can necessitate their being away unexpectedly. Provisions need to be made as prophylaxis against endangering the therapeutic process. Early in a treatment process I have heard therapists say to consultants who ask about the legal risks of the eventual transference psychoses, "Oh, this person would never sue me." In my view this belief is a dual relationship in which the therapist expects the good will of the client in an intact state to protect the therapist from psychotic rage states resulting from early abuse. Such "trust" to me says that the therapist does not take the person seriously, does not believe in the power of transference to elicit destructive rage, does not understand how likely psychotic rage is to be acted out in the real world in devastatingly dangerous and costly ways to the therapist.

18

Concluding
Thoughts

The theory of the organizing experience and how to work with it is now available, but is still in its nascent stages of development. This book has sought to provide an overview of the central features of the earliest psychological experiences as they influence relationships in later life, especially the psychoanalytic relationship. At each of the four watersheds of self and other experiencing that have thus far been defined as listening perspectives, we see that there are distinctly different ways of constructing an analytic frame for bringing transference and resistance memories into focus. Techniques and modes of interacting that detract from transference and resistance development when working with later phases of self and other experiencing appear essential when listening and responding to fundamental patterns of experiencing that have been retained from the organizing period of psychic development.

I cannot emphasize enough that the treatment and management techniques suggested in this book are not offered in the spirit of supportive, rehabilitative, or reparenting work, which I feel may be appropriate at times, but relatively superficial in its focus and effects. Rather, the ways of thinking and working advocated in this book are offered in the spirit of traditional psychoanalysis at its best.

Psychoanalysis has always advocated a working technique aimed at framing for analysis (understanding, breakdown) those enduring attitudes and patterned personality habits that are operating in a person's life to limit his or her creative and productive potentials. While classical psychoanalytic technique carefully frames advanced (oedipal level) neurotic issues for analysis, Kohut's (1971) self-psychological technique frames narcissistic issues for analysis. A third technique (see Hedges 1992) frames the self and other scenarios from the symbiotic developmental period for analysis. The technique advocated in the present book seeks to frame the enduring effects of the earliest psychological (organizing) movements of the infant toward and away from the surrounding human milieu so that they can come under direct scrutiny and become subject to transformation in the psychoanalytic relationship.

Psychoanalysts since Freud have viewed the case study as the indispensable mode of research into psychological phenomena. In this book it has been possible to give numerous glimpses into features of the organizing experience as it has appeared in case work with a number of different analytic speakers and listeners. It has also been possible to provide a few more lengthy vignettes that illustrate various aspects of transference and resistance analysis with organizing structures. But extended examples of the analytic process and the working through process have not been possible within the framework of the present book. In a companion volume, *Remembering, Repeating, and Working Through Childhood Trauma* (Hedges 1994a), I review the literature on transference psychosis, specify further aspects of the organizing experience with case examples, and provide an extended case illustration of the working-through process with an organizing transference. *Remembering, Repeating, and Working Through Childhood Trauma* also contextualizes different kinds of memories recovered in the psychotherapeutic situation as different kinds of transference and resistance memories peculiar to each of the four phases of self and other development studied by the four listening perspectives. Clinical dilemmas presented by recovered memories, multiple personality, dissociative experiences, reports of satanic ritual abuse, and abduction by aliens are all considered within the framework of the organizing experience. Further, the book discusses the developmental foundations involved in eating disorders, addictions, perversions, and other character orientations, contextualizing them as manifestations of organizing level transferences and resistances.

In 1991, Joyce Hulgus and I conducted a day-long conference on "Working the Organizing Experience." On that day, Dr. Hulgus provided numerous examples from her practice of the organizing experience including an in-depth case study spanning more than ten years. A very engaging and highly instructive video recording of that conference and the case work presented there is available (Hedges and Hulgus 1991).

Soon to be published is a casebook, *In Search of the Lost Mother of Infancy* (Hedges 1994b), which summarizes the theory and research of the organizing experience to date. In that book I present an extended case study of the working-through process of a pocket of organizing experience in an otherwise well-developed person. In contrast, I also present a series of extended case studies of more pervasive organizing experiences of various clinical types, which the treating therapists have followed over a period of many years. There is also a detailed view of the way the organizing transference looks when it is in the process of forming a transference psychosis, along with the intense and dangerous transference and countertransference manifestations that inevitably characterize this kind of depth work. The ways in which therapists who choose to do this kind of work are at risk— personally, legally, and ethically—are considered at length in this companion volume.

Throughout these studies on the organizing experience, several crucial social implications continue to emerge with clarity. First, there are significantly more people in our society suffering from various forms of childhood trauma than has ever been imagined before. These people are now clamoring to be heard, insisting that they be taken seriously as human beings, and demanding that their needs have an opportunity to be addressed therapeutically. These people are women, men, and children who have suffered untold trauma. They are from many minorities who have been oppressed because of race, nationality, socioeconomic status, or sociocultural orientation. What appear to be routine problems of adult social adjustment often turn out to be severe underlying problems of trauma, abuse, and neglect in infancy and early childhood—not simply problems of social discrimination.

Second, it is clear that problems originating from early childhood trauma cannot be treated easily or quickly. The treatment provisions offered these people by emerging managed health care plans are more than absurd, they are bizarre. It takes considerable time for a severely traumatized person to even begin to feel safe in a room with a therapist. It takes considerable time for the invisible power of preverbal abusive transference and resistance memories to begin to appear in the psychotherapeutic relationship. It takes time and skill for the therapist to learn to listen and to respond appropriately to the psychological trauma that continues to operate silently in the analytic speaker's life. And it takes much time, motivation, and hard work for two people to confront the living transference and resistance manifestations in a way that offers the possibility of personality transformation. I feel optimistic that our developing psychotherapy tools will make our work more effective and cut down significantly on the time involved. But human development is always a slow process so that long-term provisions for therapeutic involvement must be made for people to escape the crippling effects of childhood trauma.

Third, the important thought tools required to do this work are only now emerging with any degree of clarity. The average grass roots therapist is still floundering in this bewildering domain of early childhood trauma, still struggling with how to discern the effects it leaves on personality, and not yet knowing how transference and resistance memories from earliest development can best be studied to good effect in the psychotherapeutic situation. Continuing education and ongoing consultation for therapists who wish to engage in this challenging work are required and must be built into the treatment situation.

Fourth, average expectable parents still have little or no idea of the profound impact of their empathic presence and absence in the emerging psychological life of their infants. Working mothers rush back to work leaving their tender and needy newborns in the arms of total strangers. Parents hasten to take extended vacations to refresh themselves, not knowing how to consider the devastating effects that will inevitably be left in the personality structures of their young children. Hospitalizations and other absences are not carefully arranged so as to ensure continuity with the parents during the traumatic time for the child. Divorces seldom include considerations that are in the best emotional interest of the child. Unknowingly, parents are so preoccupied with the concerns of their own busy lives that they miss completely the many subtle psychological needs of the child during the organizing period. A parent's naive eagerness to begin teaching and raising the child may also serve as an intrusive abuse that goes unnoticed by the average parent. Parents simply cannot be expected to know the needs of the organizing baby unless our society is willing to provide learning opportunities for them. And the longer we put off parent education, the more it costs us as a society in the long run.

And last, other professionals in mental health, education, social services, and the justice system encounter vivid and compelling manifestations of the organizing experience in their daily work. But they have no idea what they are witnessing, much less how they might be able to work creatively with the effects of childhood trauma in adult personalities. I recently addressed a group of some 400 Superior Court family law judges and mediators in an attempt to bring to their consciousness some of the effects of residual trauma from early childhood as it affects people in the judicial system. They were, like many other diverse groups of people whom I have occasion to address, fascinated with what I had to say about infantile trauma and eager to expand their knowledge in this area.

Madness in many forms lives around us as well as in us. For centuries we have been pretending that madness only affects a few, choosing not to acknowledge universal forms of private madness. For millennia we have been in denial of the cruel and abusive conditions of childbearing, of the oppression of women and people who are different from the racial and cultural mainstream. We can no longer fail to see how the abuse, the cruelty, and the oppression that have run throughout human culture since the beginning of time work against us. We are confronted daily with the powerful, devastating effects of violence, crime, racism, and prejudice of all kinds, which have at their roots primitive experiences of infant neglect and abuse. The abusive effect is mimicked and passed on to the next generation. We know that punishment only perpetuates the abusive cycle and escalates its effects. The promotion of consciousness raising is clearly the direction in which we must proceed.

We live in a shrinking world in which we can no longer afford to be penny-wise and dollar-foolish when it comes to attending to the treatment needs of those who might be creative and productive members of our society, but for the disabling effects of trauma left over from childhood. We now possess the working tools to begin addressing the effects of childhood trauma throughout our society. We are now in a position to begin working the organizing experience in psychotherapy and elsewhere.

Appendix

Informed Consent Regarding Limited Physical Contact During Psychotherapy

I, _____ , hereby grant permission to my therapist, _____ to engage in limited forms of physical contact with me as a part of our ongoing psychotherapy process.

I understand that the purpose of therapeutic touching is to actualize for study, in concrete physical forms, certain basic aspects of human contact which I may have been deprived of or which may have been distorted in my personal development.

I understand that the purpose of therapeutic touching is not for gratification of physical longings, nor for providing physical comfort or support. Rather, the specific forms and times of the limited physical therapeutic contact are aimed towards understanding issues around the approach to, the achievement of, the sustaining of, and/or the breaking off of human emotional contact.

I understand that limited forms of physical contact such as handshakes, "A.A. type" hugs, occasional hand holding, and other token physical gestures are not uncommon as a part of the interpersonal process of psychotherapy. However, other forms of touching are more rare and need to be clearly understood by both parties and discussed in terms of their possible meanings.

I understand that many professional psychotherapists believe that physical contact of any sort is inappropriate because it fails to encourage verbalization and symbolization of exactly what meanings might be implicit in the physical touch.

I understand that sexual touching of any type is unethical, illegal, and never a part of professional psychotherapy.

I understand that many aspects of the psychotherapeutic process, including the possible value of limited physical contact, cannot be established as clearly beneficial on a scientific basis. But I also understand that physical contact has many values in human relationships and that to categorically exclude it from the psychotherapeutic relationship may be detrimental to my therapeutic process when the critical focus for study needs to be around concrete and personal experiences of meaningful and sustained interpersonal contact.

I HEREBY AGREE THAT SHOULD I HAVE ANY MISGIVINGS, DOUBTS, OR NEGATIVE REACTIONS to therapeutic physical contact or to the anticipation of such, that I will immediately discuss my concerns with my therapist.

If for any reason I experience concerns which I am reluctant to discuss directly with my therapist, or if I feel unsatisfied with our discussion, I HEREBY AGREE TO SEEK IMMEDIATE THIRD PARTY PROFESSIONAL CONSULTATION FROM A LICENSED PSYCHOTHERAPIST OF MY CHOICE OR ONE WHO IS RECOMMENDED BY MY THERAPIST. This part of the agreement is to ensure that no misunderstandings or uncomfortable feelings arise as a result of physical contact or anticipation of therapeutic physical touching.

I understand that I may at any time choose to discontinue this permission by a mutual exchange of written acknowledgments indicating that permission for therapeutic physical contact is revoked.

I HAVE CAREFULLY READ ALL OF THE ABOVE PROVISIONS AND HAVE DISCUSSED THEM WITH MY THERAPIST. ANY QUESTIONS OR MISGIVINGS I HAVE ARE WRITTEN IN THE SPACE PROVIDED BELOW.

Client or Patient   Date

Therapist or Analyst   Date

ADDITIONAL SPECIFIC REQUESTED PROCEDURES:

Request   Initial   Date

Request   Initial   Date

Request   Initial   Date

SPECIFIC QUESTIONS, MISGIVINGS, AND CONCERNS:

References

Alender, F. (1961). *The Scope of Psychoanalysis.* New York: Basic Books.

Alexander, F., and French, T. M. (1946). *Psychoanalytic Therapy.* New York: Ronald Press.

Balint, A. (1933). Uber eine besondere Form der infantilen Angst [The Fear of Being Dropped]. Trans. B. Yorke. *Zeitschrift fur Psycho-analytische Padagogik* 414–417.

_____ (1943). On identification. *International Journal of Psycho-Analysis* 24:97–107.

Bettelheim, B. (1983). *Freud and Man's Soul.* New York: Knopf.

Bion, W. R. (1962). *Learning from Experience.* New York: Basic Books.

_____ (1963). *Elements of Psycho-Analysis.* New York: Basic Books.

_____ (1977). *Second Thoughts.* New York: Jason Aronson.

Blanck, G., and Blanck, R. (1974). *Ego Psychology: Theory and Practice.* New York: Columbia University Press.

Bollas, C. (1979). The transformational object. *International Journal of Psycho-Analysis* 59:97–107.

_____ (1983). Expressive uses of the countertransference: notes to the patient from oneself. *Contemporary Psychoanalysis* January. Reprinted in Bollas (1987).

_____ (1987). *Shadow of the Object: Psychoanalysis of the Unthought Known.* London: Free Association Press.

Bowlby, J. (1969). *Attachment and Loss: Separation Anxiety and Anger,* vol. 1. New York: Basic Books.

_____ (1973). *Attachment and Loss,* vol. 2. New York: Basic Books.

Brazelton, T. B., and Barnard, K. E. (1990). *Touch: The Foundation of Experience.* Madison, CT: International Universities Press.

Casement, P. (1986). Some pressures on the analyst for physical contact during the reliving of an early trauma. In *The British School of Psychoanalysis: The Independent Tradition,* ed. G. Kohn. New Haven and London: Yale University Press.

Ekstein, R. (1979). A case study. Presented at Tufts University.

Ekstein, R., and Motto, R. (1966). *Children of Time and Space of Action and Impulse.* New York: Appleton Century Crofts.

Erikson, E. H. (1950). *Childhood and Society.* New York: W. W. Norton.

Exner, J. E. Jr., and Weiner, I. B. (1982). Assessment of children in adolescence. In *The Rorschach: A Comprehensive System,* vol. 3. New York: John Wiley.

Ferenczi, S. (1927). Termination of analysis. In *Final Contributions to the Problems and Methods of Psycho-Analysis.* New York: Bruner/Mazel.

Fraiberg, S. (1982). Pathological defenses in infancy. *Psychoanalytic Quarterly* 51:612–635.

Freud, A. (1951). Observations on child development. In *Indications for Child Analysis and Other Papers,* pp. 143–162. New York: International Universities Press, 1968.

_____ (1952). The role of bodily illness in the mental life of children. In *Indications for Child Analysis and Other Papers,* pp. 260–279. New York: International Universities Press, 1968.

_____ (1958). Child observation and prediction of development. In *Research at the Hampstead Child-Therapy Clinic and Other Papers,* pp. 102–135, 1970.

Freud, S. (1895). Project for a scientific psychology. *Standard Edition* 1:283–388.

_____ (1900). The interpretation of dreams. *Standard Edition* 4/5.

_____ (1911). (I) Case history. *Standard Edition* 12:12–34.

_____ (1918). An infantile neurosis. *Standard Edition* 17:1–124.

_____ (1923). The ego and the id. *Standard Edition* 19:3–68.

_____ (1925). Negation. *Standard Edition* 19:235–242.

_____ (1933). New introductory lectures on psycho-analysis. *Standard Edition* 22:1–184.

_____ (1940). Splitting of the ego in the process of defence. *Standard Edition* 23:271–278.

_____ (1954). *The Origins of Psycho-Analysis. Letters to Wilhelm Fliess.* New York: Basic Books.

Furman, R. A., and Katan, A. (1969). *The Therapeutic Nursery School.* New York: International Universities Press.

Giovacchini, P. L. (1975). *Psychoanalysis of Character Disorders.* New York: Jason Aronson.

_____ (1979a). *Tactics and Techniques in Psychoanalytic Therapy.* New York: Jason Aronson.

_____ (1979b). *Treatment of Primitive Mental States.* New York: Jason Aronson.

Green, A. (1986). *On Private Madness.* London: Hogarth Press.

Greenacre, P. (1958). Towards the understanding of the physical nucleus of some defence reactions. *International Journal of Psycho-analysis,* 39:69–76.

_____ (1960). Further notes on fetishism. *Psychoanalytic Study of the Child* 15:191–207. New York: International Universities Press.

Grotstein, J., (1981a). *Dare I Disturb the Universe?* Beverly Hills, CA: Caesura.

_____ (1981b). *Splitting and Projective Identification.* New York: Jason Aronson.

Hare, D. (1983). *Plenty.* New York: Plume.

Hartmann, H. (1950). Comments on the psychoanalytic theory of the ego. *Psychoanalytic Study of the Child* 5:74–96. New York: International Universities Press.

Hedges, L. E. (1983). *Listening Perspectives in Psychotherapy.* New York: Jason Aronson.

_____ (1992). *Interpreting the Countertransference.* Northvale, NJ: Jason Aronson.

_____ (1994a). *Remembering, Repeating, and Working Through Childhood Trauma*. Northvale, NJ: Jason Aronson.

_____ (1994b). *In Search of the Lost Mother of Infancy*. Northvale, NJ: Jason Aronson.

_____ (1994c). *Strategic Emotional Involvement*. Northvale, NJ: Jason Aronson.

Hedges, L. E., and Hulgus, J. (1991). Working the organizing experience. A four-hour videotaped presentation given at Charter Hospital in Mission Viejo, CA, September 1991.

Hood, M. (1984). *Adam: the first self deceiver*. Paper delivered at the 14th Philosophy Symposium at California State University at Fullerton, March 1.

Jacobson, E. (1954). The self and object world: vicissitudes of their infantile cathexis and their influence of ideational and effective development. *Psychoanalytic Study of the Child* 9:75–127. New York: International Universities Press.

_____ (1964). *The Self and Object World*. New York: International Universities Press.

Jorgensen, S. (1993). *Inherent potentials and their relation to psychotic features*. Dissertation presented to California Graduate Institute.

Kafka, F. (1926). *The Castle*. New York: Schocken Books.

_____ (1937). *The Trial*. New York: Vintage Books.

_____ (1979). *The Basic Kafka*. New York: Pocket Books.

Karen, R. (1990). Becoming attached: what children need. *The Atlantic* February: 35.

Keleman, S. (1975). *The Human Ground – Sexuality, Self and Survival*. Berkeley, CA: Center Press.

Khan, M. (1963). The concept of cumulative trauma. *Psychoanalytic Study of the Child* 18:286–306. New York: International Universities Press.

_____ (1974). *The Privacy of the Self*. New York: International Universities Press.

Klein, M. (1957). *Envy and Gratitude*. New York: Basic Books.

_____ (1975). *Love, Guilt and Reparation and Other Works*. New York: Delta Books.

Kohut, H. (1971). *The Analysis of the Self*. New York: International Universities Press.

_____ (1977). *The Restoration of the Self*. New York: International Universities Press.

_____ (1981). Summarizing reflections. UCLA Conference on Self Psychology, October 5, 1981. Audio and videotape available through Continuing Education Seminars, 1023 Westholme, Los Angeles, CA.

_____ (1984). *How Does Analysis Cure?* Chicago: University of Chicago Press.

Kosinski, J. (1970). *Being There*. New York: Harcourt, Brace, Jovanovich.

Kris, E. (1951). Some comments and observations on early autoerotic activities. *Psychoanalytic Study of the Child* 6:95–116. New York: International Universities Press.

_____ (1956a). The personal myth. *Journal of the American Psychoanalytic Association* 4:653–681.

_____ (1956b). The recovery of childhood memories in psychoanalysis. *Psychoanalytic Study of the Child* 11:54–88. New York: International Universities Press.

Kuhn, T. (1962). *The Structure of Scientific Revolutions*. Chicago: University of Chicago Press.

Lacan, J. (1949). The mirror stage as formative of the function of the I as revealed in psychoanalytic experience. In *Ecrits: A Selection*. New York: W. W. Norton.

_____ (1953). The function and field of speech and language in psychoanalysis. In *Ecrits: A Selection*. New York: W. W. Norton.

Lakoff, G., and Johnson, M. (1980). *Metaphors We Live By*. Chicago: University of Chicago Press.

Lipton, S. E. (1977). Clinical observations on resistance to the transference. *International Journal of Psycho-Analysis* 58:463–472.

Little, M. (1981). *Transference Neurosis: Transference Psychosis*. New York: Jason Aronson.

_____ (1990). *Psychotic Anxieties and Containment: A Personal Record of an Analysis with Winnicott*. Northvale, NJ: Jason Aronson.

Lowen, A. (1971). *The Language of the Body*. New York: Collier Books.

_____ (1975). *Bioenergetics*. London: Penguin Books.

_____ (1982). *The Will to Live and the Wish to Die*. New York: International Institute for Bioenergetic Analysis.

_____ (1988). *Love, Sex and Your Heart*. New York: Macmillan.

Luria, A. R. (1973). *The Working Brain: An Introduction to Neuropsychology*. New York: Basic Books.

Mahler, M. (1968). *On Human Symbiosis and the Vicissitudes of Individuation. Vol. I, Infantile Psychosis*. New York: International Universities Press.

Maturana, H. (1970). *Biology of Cognition*, BCL Report No. 9.0, Urbana, IL: Biological Computer Laboratory, Department of Electrical Engineering, University of Illinois.

_____ (1972). *Organization of Living Systems*. Chicago, IL: Biological Computer Laboratory, University of Illinois.

Maturana, H., and Varela, F. (1972). *Autopoesis*. Faculdad de Ciencias, Universidad de Chile, Santiago.

McDougall, J. (1986). *Theatres of the Mind*. London: Free Association Press.

Milner, M. (1952). Aspects of symbolism in comprehension of the not-self. *International Journal of Psycho-Analysis* 33.

Modell, A. (1976). The holding environment and the therapeutic action of psychoanalysis. *Journal of the American Psychoanalytic Association* 24:285–308.

Polonyi, M., and Green, M., eds. (1969). *Knowing and Being*. Chicago: University of Chicago Press.

Rosenfeld, H. (1965). *Psychotic States: A Psychoanalytic Approach*. New York: International Universities Press.

Rosenfeld, H., and David, T., eds. (1987). *Impasse and Interpretation on the Treatment of Psychotic and Neurotic Patients*. New York: Tavistock.

Russell, M. J. (1978). Sartre, therapy, and expanding the concept of responsibility. *American Journal of Psychoanalysis* 38:259–269.

_____ (1981). Reflection and self deception. *Journal for Research in Phenomenology* 11:62–74.

_____ (1992). Perversion, eating disorders and sex roles. *International Forum of Psychoanalysis* 1:98–103.

Ryle, G. (1949). *The Concept of Mind*. New York: Barnes and Noble.

Sanville, J. (1992). *The Playground of Psychoanalytic Psychotherapy*. New Jersey: Analytic.

Sartre, J-P. (1956). *Being and Nothingness*. Trans. H. Barnes. New York: Washington Square Press.

Schafer, R. (1976). *A New Language for Psychoanalysis.* New Haven: Yale University Press.

Schwaber, E. (1979). Narcissism, self psychology and the listening perspective. Pre-presentation reading for lecture given at the University of California, Los Angeles Conference on the Psychology of the Self-Narcissism, October.

Searles, H. (1960). *The Nonhuman Environment.* New York: International Universities Press.

_____ (1979). *Countertransference and Related Subjects: Selected Papers.* New York: International Universities Press.

Sechehaye, M. A. (1951). *Symbolic Realization.* New York: International Universities Press.

Spence, D. (1982). *Historical Truth and Narrative Truth.* New York: W. W. Norton.

Stern, D. N. (1985). *The Interpersonal World of the Infant.* New York: Basic Books.

Stolorow, R., and Atwood, G. (1982). Psychoanalytic phenomenology of the dream. *Annual of Psychoanalysis* 10:205–220.

_____ (1992). Dreams and the subjective world. In *Essential Papers on Dreams,* ed. M. Lancky, pp. 272–294. New York: New York University Press.

Stolorow, R., Brandchaft, B., and Atwood, G. (1987). *Psychoanalytic Treatment: An Intersubjective Approach.* Hillsdale, NJ: Analytic Press.

Stolorow, R., and Lachman, F. J. (1980). *Psychoanalysis of Developmental Arrests.* New York: International Universities Press.

Strachey, J. (1934). The nature of the therapeutic action of psychoanalysis. *International Journal of Psycho-Analysis* 50:275–292.

Suskind, P. (1986). *Perfume.* New York: Washington Square Press.

Tausk, V. (1919). On the origin of the influencing machine in schizophrenia. *Psychoanalytic Quarterly* 2:519–556.

Tronick, E., and Cohn, J. (1988). Infant–mother face-to-face communicative interaction: age and gender differences in coordination and the occurrence of miscoordination. *Child Development* 60:85–92.

Tustin, F. (1972). *Autism and Childhood Psychosis.* London: Hogarth.

_____ (1981). *Autistic States in Children.* Boston and London: Routledge and Kegan Paul.

———— (1984). Autistic shapes. *International Review of Psycho-Analysis* 11:279–290.

———— (1985). *Autistic States and Adult Psychopathology: Introductory Remarks and Case Consultation.* Continuing Education Seminars (video). Los Angeles, CA.

———— (1986). *Autistic Barriers in Neurotic Patients.* New Haven: Yale University Press.

Von Foerster, H. (1984). *Observing Systems.* Seaside, CA: Intersystems Publications.

Winnicott, D. W. (1947). Hate in the countertransference. *Through Paediatrics to Psycho-Analysis: Collected Papers of D. W. Winnicott,* pp. 194–203. New York: Basic Books.

———— (1949). Birth memories, birth trauma and anxiety. *Through Paediatrics to Psycho-Analysis: Collected Papers of D. W Winnicott,* pp. 174–193. New York: Basic Books.

———— (1952). Psychoses and child care. In *Through Paediatrics to Psycho-Analysis: Collected Papers of D. W. Winnicott,* pp. 219–228. New York: Basic Books.

———— (1953). Transitional objects and transitional phenomena: a study of the first not-me possession. *International Journal of Psychoanalysis* 34:89–97.

———— (1958, revised 1975). *Through Paediatrics to Psycho-Analysis: Collected Papers of D. W. Winnicott.* New York: Basic Books.

———— (1960). Ego distortion in terms of true and false self. In *The Maturational Processes and the Facilitating Environment: Studies in the Theory of Emotional Development.* New York: International Universities Press.

———— (1965). *The Maturational Processes and the Facilitating, Environment: Studies in the Theory of Emotional Development.* New York: International Universities Press.

———— (1971). *Playing and Reality.* London: Tavistock.

———— (1974). Fear of breakdown. *International Review of Psycho-Analysis* 1:103.

———— (1975). Reparation in respect of mother's organized defense against depression. In *Through Paediatrics to Psycho-Analysis: Collected Papers of D. W. Winnicott.* New York: Basic Books

Wittgenstein, L. (1953). *Philosophical Investigations.* New York: Macmillan.

Index